ACCOMMODATION MANAGEMENT

a systems approach

ACCOMMODATION MANAGEMENT

a systems approach

Christine Jones
Val Paul

B T Batsford Limited · London

© Christine Jones and Val Paul 1985 and 1993
First published 1985
Reprinted 1990, 1992
New edition 1993
Reprinted 1995

Typeset by J&L Composition Ltd, Filey, North Yorkshire
and printed in Great Britain by
Redwood Books, Trowbridge, Wilts
for the publishers
B T Batsford Limited
4 Fitzhardinge Street
London W1H 0AH

A catalogue record for this book is
available from the British Library

ISBN 0 7134 6937 4

Contents

Appendices

Acknowledgment

Our appreciation and gratitude is expressed to our families and friends for their help, understanding and kindness in compiling this book.

CJ and VP 1993

Introduction

The role of accommodation

This book has been written to develop the concepts of Accommodation Management. The provision of accommodation is first put into the context of its role as an industry within the **Services** sector. It is worth emphasising the extent of the 'accommodation industry' which exceeds the boundaries and context of the 'hotel and catering industry' with which it is most commonly associated.

The provision of accommodation may be for the objective of wealth creation, as with an hotel, or accommodation may be provided as a facility to enable the operation of other industries and activities, for example a retail store. The commonality with these examples is that accommodation is provided, and if the operation is to be a success, the accommodation must be managed and maintained. The inference of which is that the accommodation element *services* the operation and, in either case, the service element of the package is vital to the success of the operation.

Services industries have a number of important characteristics and these are considered early on in this book.

The systems approach

Accommodation Management is a complex social system and, in common with most, if not all, social systems, many phenomena associated with it cannot be explained in terms of a simple cause and effect relationship. Components associated with Accommodation Management – the type of building, the human resources, the organisational structure, the customer, the local environment – all influence and are influenced by one another. Many elements or situations acting together may cause any of a number of effects. Thus, the method of study applied to Accommodation Management, in this book, is described following a systems approach or an holistic approach (looking at all causes and effects).

As defined by BILL MAYON-WHITE and DICK MORRIS[1] a system is:

- an assembly of components connected in an organised way.
- The components are affected by being in the system and the behaviour of the system is changed if they leave it.

- The organised assembly of components does something.
- The assembly has been identified by someone as being of particular interest.

In this case 'the system' is the *System of Accommodation Management*. Accommodation Management must not be considered in isolation. It can be seen as a sub-system of the overall organisation or 'system', eg a hospital, a university, an hotel, and techniques developed in *Systems Thinking* applied in this book will, it is hoped, serve to emphasise the facts that:

- the accommodation sub-system does not work independently and that there is a two-way flow of influences between the accommodation sub-system and its environment
- due to systemic influences, to be effective, Accommodation Management must be dynamic (ie constantly changing and adapting).

Suitability of the book

It is anticipated that future and existing managers within the wide sphere of the Accommodation Industry will find this book of value.

It is intended to help those students with specialist knowledge of the hotel and catering industry to appreciate how sound management theories and techniques must be applied to achieve the best of the resources available to the Accommodation Manager. Students with more generalised business and management knowledge will see how techniques have been used selectively for the particular needs of what is a very wide services industry.

Practising managers, too, may well find the approach of the book, and the theories which have been applied, useful aids in evaluating their own operation.

The text commences with an analysis of 'the product' and following chapters consider the main systems involved in Accommodation Management.

Reference

[1] MAYON-WHITE, B and MORRIS, D, *Systems Behaviour*, Open University Press 1974

The Accommodation Product

Objectives

- To identify and explain the common elements which are required within an 'accommodation package'.
- To demonstrate the diversity of accommodation and show how different customer types affect the needs and requirements of the accommodation package.
- To identify different spheres of Accommodation Management.
- To identify the needs for clear objectives to enable accommodation provisions to be focussed.
- To compare the implications of services industries in general with those of Accommodation Services.
- To identify Accommodation Services as a system interacting with its environment and comprising interacting sub-systems.

The term *accommodation*, for the purposes of this book, has been taken in a wide context to include any premises, temporary or permanent, other than domestic dwellings, where shelter and facilities are provided for use by people. It could range from an international conference complex to a marquee, or from a prison to a large shopping complex.

In Figure 1.1, some of the more common elements associated with accommodation are shown.

1.1 THE CUSTOMER

In Figure 1.1, in most cases, elements are prepositioned by the words 'appropriate' or 'satisfactory'. The actual standards required will depend on the particular cross section of customers or accommodation users and their particular needs and requirements.

The customer is the key to the successful provision of accommodation. The needs and requirements of customers must be anticipated and a considerable amount of planning must be focused on identifying and making provision for these.

The customer must be identified by the Accommodation Manager and, indeed, there may be several categories of customer, eg in a hospital situation the Domestic Services Manager must provide a service for:

Figure 1.1 *Some of the common elements often required to produce, what is perceived as, 'Accommodation'*

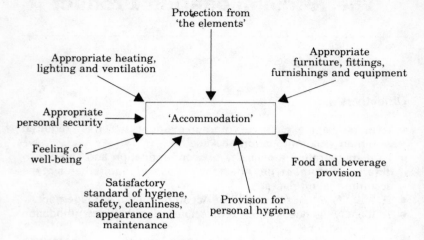

- the patients
- visitors
- medical and nursing staff
- paramedical, auxillary, administrative and other staff
- contract personnel
- advisory and regulatory personnel.

In a commercial situation the question must be asked: 'Which market segment has been targeted?' Specifically, the characteristics of the client with whom the organisation plans to deal must be identified. When the intended client is clearly understood, the elements which will be needed to facilitate his or her activities can be foreseen.

Some facilities, already identified as necessary in Figure 1.1, can then be more exactly specified, eg:

- the **types** and **characteristics** of furniture required by guests at a wedding reception or children in a crêche
- the **actual** temperature requirements for comfort by swimmers in a leisure complex, compared to the squash players' requirements or the office staff's needs.

Other facilities, additional to those shown in Figure 1.1, will also be identified and may include:

- a source of information (eg guests arriving at an hotel)
- privacy (eg students' private study areas in a hall of residence)

- secretarial assistance (eg for the conference organiser)
- hospitality for clients' guests (eg in a business persons' hotel)
- porterage (eg for the family on two weeks holiday)
- car parking facilities (eg for customers to a leisure centre)
- ramp access for wheel chairs
- lift facilities to access upper storey levels (eg in an elderly persons' home)
- personal laundry service (eg for customers on a cruise ship)
- entertainment (eg for children of conference delegates)
- communication facilities (eg visible flashing light fire alarms for the deaf)
- catering facilities, where customers are likely to be using the accommodation for more than an hour or two
- sleeping facilities for customers staying overnight.

Clearly, once the customer is identified, particular needs and requirements can be anticipated.

'Accommodation', therefore, includes a 'package' of facilities and services produced to meet the needs and requirements of particular customers.

The importance of identifying the market segment and the specific needs and requirements of those consumers cannot be over emphasised. Accommodation is expensive to provide. It represents a great capital expense. Return on that expense needs to be maximised. If market segments targeted need to be modified, to increase or otherwise enhance the uptake of the facilities, then accommodation service implications, too, will need to be reassessed.

1.2 THE SPHERE OF ACCOMMODATION MANAGEMENT

The sphere of Accommodation Management varies from one establishment to another. For example, the involvement of the Accommodation staff in a public library will largely be 'behind the scenes', as far as the public is concerned, whereas their role in a hospital will involve daily contact with customers including other staff and patients. In this text examples are given from a cross section of establishments. In Figure 1.1 client requirements are identified. The Accommodation Manager may well have responsibility for all of these areas. However, Food and Beverage Management is seen as a different specialist area, outside the scope of this book.

Management involves identifying and controlling all resources; controlling people, materials, time and money. This is achieved through organisation, co-ordination, and communication. The resources available to the Accommodation Manager are:

- personnel
- equipment and materials

- the building
- energy
- the manager's own experience
- the reputation of the organisation and
- the customer s themselves.

Accommodation Management, like any other sort of management, involves controlling people and other resources to attain objectives. Initially, it involves the determination of these objectives. What is the overall purpose of the organisation? What is its mission? The mission statement could be quite specific, or allow for a considerable amount of flexibility, to meet changing environmental demands and influences.

From this statement, objectives set by managers can become more and more refined and specific as the manager's level in the hierarchy is reduced. Similarly, time spans or planning horizons reduce. For example, in an hotel, at senior management level, decisions will need to be reached as to the market segments to be targeted, and occupancy levels. At departmental level these objectives will be interpreted in terms of the input necessary from that particular department. Detailed planning will be needed to determine how departmental objectives can be met.

1.2.1   Setting objectives

The process of setting objectives can best be shown by example. Such an example might be the Domestic Services Manager in a hospital. If asked to set the objectives of the Domestic Service Department, the most obvious response might be: *'to provide a clinically clean environment'*.

This would allow wounds to heal without risk of infection from the surroundings and also help to ensure that those patients with infectious diseases did not pass the disease on to others.

In setting down this as an objective, however, consideration for the environment in which the system would be operating would be necessary.

- There would be financial restraints
- Possibly, even more importantly, it must be remembered that the process of achieving the objectives will occur in a building occupied by patients, staff, visitors and others.

It is **for the benefit** of these building users that the **service** is being undertaken. To give an extreme example, a clinically clean environment could be better achieved if visitors were not allowed into wards; if patients refrained from drinking sugary drinks which, when spilt, provide a sticky surface to attract dirt; if wards could be closed once a week for thorough cleaning. Whilst enhancing the likelihood of the Domestic Services Department achieving a clean environment, these measures, overall, would probably not benefit patients.

A refinement of the objective, set by the Domestic Services Manager, might, therefore, be something on the lines: *'To provide a clinically clean environment, working in such a manner that will promote the care of patients and the well being of other building users.'*

'Promoting care and wellbeing' is a difficult aspect to define and as such can be the cause of difficulties when drawing up specifications (see Chapter 4) but the main point here is that the provision of accommodation is a service for others. In the case of the hospital example, the clinical standards are aimed for with the wellbeing of the patient in mind, not to achieve cleanliness for its own sake. Accommodation Management falls, therefore, into the category of a Services Industry.

1.3   SERVICES INDUSTRIES

Society, in many developed countries is now described as *Post Industrial*. No longer are manufacturing industries the chief wealth creators in these countries, but rather the services industries. The Accommodation Industry falls into the category of the services sector, along with systems such as health provision, energy provision, education, etc. This does not inevitably mean that the operation is commercially orientated. There are, of course many examples of accommodation being provided for welfare purposes or simply as a facilitator or resource for some other operation.

The product or 'package' produced by services industries comprises three elements:

1   a physical item
2   the environment in which the service contact occurs
3   the nature of the actual service contact.

In an hotel, the *physical item* will include the hotel and its facilities, the *environment* will include the comfort conditions, such as heating, ventilation and aesthetics. Other elements may not be tangible. A receptionist passing the time of day with clients and enquiring as to their satisfaction with their meal, produces nothing tangible but the fact that the enquiry was made, that the receptionist greeted the customers by name and generally projected a feeling of interest in the clients, will have enhanced the 'accommodation package'. This is the intangible 'service' element and is part of the 'nature of the actual service contact'.

1.3.1   A definition of a Service

DAVID COLLIER defines a Service as *'a package of explicit and implicit benefits, performed with a supporting facility and using facilitating goods'*.[1] To apply this to an hotel, for example

- the explicit benefits would include the sleeping accommodation
- the implicit benefits would include privacy, protection from the weather, security, heating, etc, and those intangible elements such as a feeling of well being, of importance, of relaxation, of efficiency, an impression given by staff of a desire to please or to be hospitable
- the supporting facility would be the hotel structure
- the facilitating goods would be the furniture, bed linen, etc.

1.3.2   Characteristics of services industries

Services industries can be identified as having the following characteristics:

- they are labour intensive
- there is a high level of customer participation and the service cannot happen without the customer (eg an hotel bedroom ready for occupation can be produced, but until a customer arrives, no service can take place)
- the service cannot be stored, eg a room not let tonight is a wasted resource
- production and consumption of the service element are simultaneous. A customer is greeted, directed to the room, served early morning tea, etc. In each case the customer is a necessary resource and the intangible service element, eg verbal or non-verbal communication takes place only when the customer is present and at a moment in time
- output of the service element is difficult to measure, eg was the customer greeted with a smile? was information given courteously? did staff give the impression of a desire to please?
- at least part of the service package is intangible, eg the environment in which the service contact is made, such as the ambience of the room, as well as the nature of the service contact.

1.3.2.1 Implications of these characteristics to the Accommodation Manager   These characteristics have important implications as far as the management of the service package is concerned and, taking the characteristics point by point, implications are identified in Figure 1.2.

Figure 1.2 *Characteristics of Services Industries and the implications for the Accommodation Manager*

Characteristic	Implication
Labour intensive	Personnel functions need to be well developed. Recruitment, training, interpersonal skills, safety, motivation, etc, are all important.
Participation of the customer	1 The location of the accommodation must be easily accessible unless: (a) the accommodation is movable, eg marquees, a coach or (b) provision is made to transport customers to the service point, eg hotel taxis 2 Customers must be identified as a resource. They may need 'directing' (training) in the use of the product. Layout may need to take account of customer control and their movement through the facility.
Service cannot be stored	It may be necessary to reduce or increase the capacity* round fluctuations of demand, eg shift work, part-time staff and/or attempt to control demand, eg advertising and marketing.
Simultaneous production and consumption of the service element	Quality is difficult to manage and record. Restricting the numbers of 'contact' staff and concentrating training in customer contact skills so these may be feasible. Automation, too, is a means of effecting control.
Output is difficult to measure	This can be measured by customers and recorded by surveys. By monitoring, 'spot checks' can be made on output and indirect results taken, eg number of return clients.
Intangible element of the package	As has been seen, this causes difficulties in setting, measuring and controlling standards. It also means that services cannot be patented. The market share must be captured quickly. Increasing automation is one effective way of standardising the package. Intensive training and retraining of staff is vital.

* Facilities (including staffing) within an organisation which allow it to achieve a given output.

1.4 THE SYSTEM OF ACCOMMODATION MANAGEMENT

With the characteristics and implications of service industries in mind and with an understanding of the scope of Accommodation Management, taking a Systems Approach, organisational aspects can be evaluated.

In most cases, the System of Accommodation Management can be seen to comprise five sub-systems:

1 **The Building** Some sort of 'supporting facility' is a requisite before a service can be offered and this is, most usually though not always, a building or structure of some kind. This facility usually represents a very high capital investment. Its location and, to a large extent its design and décor, can effectively determine the success or failure of the entire enterprise.

2 **Accommodation Services** In order to maintain the facility and its surfaces in conditions which will enable its continuous and efficient functioning, an appropriate sub-system will need to be devised. Also, depending on the nature of the particular accommodation, other consumer needs may be met through this sub-system.

3 **Human Resources Management** Service industries are characteristically labour intensive and inevitably a good deal of any Accommodation Manager's work will be staff related.

4 **Materials Management** To maintain the building and to ensure that staff have appropriate resources with which to complete their work and fulfil the objectives of their department, certain materials will need to be managed.

5 **The Front Office Dimension** The customer, of course, is the vital ingredient to the operation before any service can be offered. The customer may be identified as a guest, patient, student, visitor or other building user. Although not all staff within the accommodation department may come in direct contact the customer, it must not be forgotten that the customer is the key element, round which other components of the system should evolve.

The Front Office is seen as the major facet of the organisation to interface with the customer and, indeed, to encourage a prospective customer to enter the system, as a customer. Together, the customer and the Front Office function as a discernible sub-system, making certain demands on the rest of the system, and themselves being affected by the rest of the system.

Together, these sub-systems make up the system of Accommodation Management. The system itself operates in an environment and some of the more general features of that environment are shown in Figure 1.3.

Five sub-systems have been identified, and the major relevance of the systems approach is to emphasise that individual elements cannot be considered in isolation from their application. The sub-systems have separate identities, but only to a limited degree. For instance, when looking at Job Descriptions for Housekeeping Staff, at least two sub-systems will be involved, namely Accommodation Services and Human Resources Management. When a company makes a conference booking with specific requirements, such as particular acoustic qualities in the conference hall, timing of room service, conference

Figure 1.3 *The system of Accommodation*

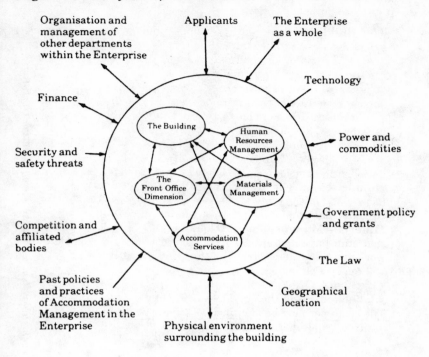

stationary, etc, all sub-systems will be involved. Each sub-system interacts with the others. Another example of the interactions of the sub-systems is shown in Figure 1.4.

Each sub-system also evolves in a particular way, because it is part of that particular system. For instance, Accommodation Services sub-systems in two different hotels will often be very similar in the work they do and the way they do it, but they will not be identical. Certain procedures and characteristics will be determined because of the particular system of which they form part and certain procedures and processes which work well in one situation, may not be appropriate to the other.

1.4.1   The environment

In Figure 1.3 a general environment, within which an Accommodation Management System might be seen to function, is shown. These environmental aspects will now be considered.

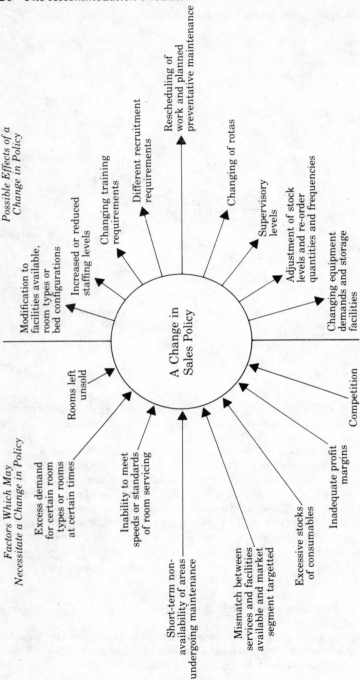

Factors Which May Necessitate a Change in Policy

Excess demand for certain room types or rooms at certain times

Rooms left unsold

Inability to meet speeds or standards of room servicing

Short-term non-availability of areas undergoing maintenance

Mismatch between services and facilities available and market segment targetted

Excessive stocks of consumables

Inadequate profit margins

Competition

Possible Effects of a Change in Policy

Modification to facilities available, room types or bed configurations

Increased or reduced staffing levels

Changing training requirements

Different recruitment requirements

Rescheduling of work and planned preventative maintenance

Changing of rotas

Supervisory levels

Adjustment of stock levels and re-order quantities and frequencies

Changing equipment demands and storage facilities

A Change in Sales Policy

Figure 1.4 *How a change of sales policy would affect each sub-system within the Accommodation Operation*

Figure 1.5 *The interaction between the System of Accommodation and an enterprise as a whole*

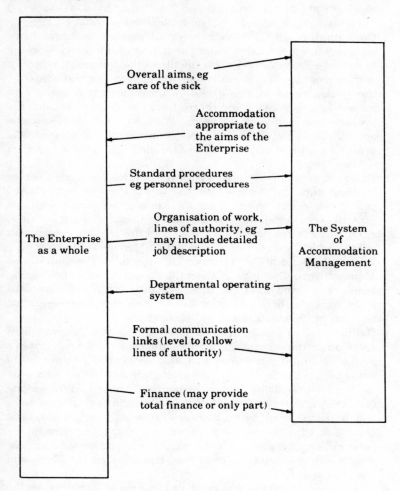

- The **enterprise** as a whole, its purpose, aims, policies and its management will inevitably bear considerable influence on the Accommodation Management system and similarly, the Accommodation Management system will influence the enterprise. An outline of these influences is shown in Figure 1.5. (See also Budgetary aspects, Section 1.5.2.)
- The next environmental component is **technology**. As technological advances are made, so the system of Accommodation Management responds. In some cases major developments can be achieved

rapidly through application of new, fast-moving technology, eg the application of computers. Other technological changes occur more slowly, or at any rate will take much longer to have an impact on the system, eg development of new building materials.

- **Consumables** of the system cover all supplies and provisions, including fuel and energy, water and telecommunications. Working to its best efficiency, the system will utilise these available resources to their greatest effect to achieve its overall aims. For best efficiency, the system needs to identify its own specific requirements with respect to consumables and choose from the options available the product most suited to its needs. Working most effectively the system should be influencing suppliers as to the characteristics of products produced and sold rather than finding a use for a product well marketed.

- Different governments impose **different policies** and are another environmental influence which will affect the system. National policies on privatisation or nationalisation, encouragement and incentives for small businesses, development of tourism, international trade agreements, etc, are just a few possible government policies which will affect Accommodation Management systems.

- **Legal implications** of the various aspects of Accommodation Management will, of course, affect the system. Laws on fire regulations, health and safety aspects, including control of hazardous substances and data protection have all affected Accommodation Systems in Britain in relatively recent years.

- Cultural values and patterns associated with the **geographical location** of the accommodation will influence all the sub-systems of the system of Accommodation Management. The standard of living within the environs of the accommodation will also have its implications. Building styles, materials, furniture, fittings and furnishings, as well as staffing, structures and operating systems will be constrained by such elements as religion, customs and traditions. Similarly the system will affect the environment by creating employment, possibly wealth and other facilities, eg health care or leisure opportunities, depending on the purpose of the enterprise as a whole.

- Characteristics of the **physical environment** surrounding the building influencing the system, together with possible impacts, are shown in Figure 1.6.

- **Past policies** of Accommodation Management will have considerable influence on the current methods. Even when some policies are rescinded, considerable time may need to elapse before effects cease to be seen, eg employment of a particular calibre of staff. Results of other policies may outlast the life of the building, eg selection of certain building materials. Past practices will also affect the current system, and again, some practices are more difficult to end than others, eg working hours of staff in some cases may only be

Figure 1.6 *How the characteristics of the physical environment may influence the system of Accommodation*

Characteristic of physical environment	Influence on the system
Climate	Building design Psychological and physical effect on users Heating and ventilation systems Energy usage Selection and care of surfaces
Atmosphere	Polluted atmosphere may affect selection maintenance and durability of materials May make demands on ventilation system Particularly clean atmosphere will physically and psychologically affect all users and possibly volume of trade
Use of adjoining land	May generate noise or air pollution May create business or competition May improve or detract from visual qualities May affect prestige May affect daylight standards
Access routes	Proximity to main roads or transport terminals may add to or detract from business or affect amenities
Geographical characteristics	Will constrain building structure May affect amenities available

changed when a vacancy occurs. Other past practices may automatically dictate current practice, eg the past use of a certain floor seal may eliminate other possible floor maintenance techniques.

- In profit orientated systems, the role played by **competitors** may be considerable. They may dictate prices charged, facilities offered, images marketed and indeed many practices of the system. Conversely, bodies affiliated to the enterprise, of which the system of Accommodation Management is part, will also create constraints. Operations in other hotels within a group may determine methods and processes adopted. Economic advantages of standardisation can frequently be achieved.
- **Security and safety threats** imposed on the system must be identified and appropriate action taken. Threats of terrorist attack, fire damage, petty theft or infection risks are a few of the possibilities which need to be identified and action taken as appropriate. Security, Health and Safety and Fire Policies, showing possible responses of the system in this area, are considered in Chapter 6.
- The availability of **finance** is another environmental influence which needs consideration. The system of Accommodation Management both uses money and creates it – by the sale of its facilities.

In profit-making enterprises, the profit margin on accommodation sales may be considerable and yet incoming finance may be greatly limited. To make the best use of all monies made available, the system must operate a departmental budget and this is also considered later.

- The system of Accommodation Management in various enterprises will be influenced by different operating departments. In the Health Service, for instance, the Nursing, Medical, Paramedical and Catering systems will impose considerable constraints. In a hall of residence, the teaching system may be the one having most influence and, in an hotel, the accounts system will have an important bearing. Such constraints need to be considered in the development of the system, but similarly, the outgoing influences imposed by the system of Accommodation Management need to be identified before operating methods can be applied.

1.5   CONSTRAINTS ON ACCOMMODATION MANAGEMENT

As can be seen from the systems map (Fig 1.3), Accommodation Management is constrained by its environment in several ways but two aspects in particular need greater emphasis and these are *Health and Safety Issues* and *Budgetary Control*.

1.5.1   Health and safety aspects

Health and safety aspects are of great importance to the Accommodation Manager due to the human element, ie high staff numbers and public access. There are legal requirements which have considerable implications for the Accommodation Manager, including the Occupiers Liability Act 1963, the Fire Precautions Act 1971 and the Health and Safety at Work Act 1974.

Under the Health and Safety at Work Act (1974) the manager has legal responsibilities both as an employer and as an employee. As an employer he/she is required:

- to provide and maintain safe plant and systems
- to ensure, so far as is reasonably practicable, safety and absence of risks to health in connection with the use, handling, storage and transport of articles and substances
- to provide such information, training, instruction and supervision as is necessary to maintain health and safety standards
- to maintain safe places of work, including entrances and exits
- to provide a working environment which is so far as is reasonably practicable, safe and without risks to health and adequate regarding facilities and arrangements for welfare.

To comply with these responsibilities, it is useful to refer to the resources available to the Accommodation Manager. The first resource is *staff*, and here the manager must ensure that their working environment is safe, the materials and equipment they use are safe and that they are trained for their job and appropriately supervised. The next two resources are *equipment* and *materials* and here, to ensure that they are safe in use, they must be selected with due care, stored and maintained as appropriate and staff must be trained and supervised in their use.

Power and *plant* (the *Building*) are the final resources of the Accommodation Manager and to ensure that these are safe for all building users their components must be selected and maintained, hazard notices displayed, where there are unavoidable defects these should receive attention and, again, staff must be trained and supervised in their safe use. Further provisions will often be appropriate for the security of the building and its users.

Major responsibilities under the heading of *Health and Safety* can be identified, and the Accommodation Manager will need to prepare a policy document:

- to identify health and safety hazards specific to the accommodation department/s
- explain how risks will be minimised.

Such a Health and Safety policy would vary from one establishment to another but some of the broader issues are identified in the sample Health and Safety Policy (see Appendix 1). A Fire Policy is also included.

1.5.2   Budgetary aspects

Costs will always be a limiting factor where product design is concerned and, in developing the accommodation services package, cost constraints will need full consideration. The cost constraints will be long term and budgets will be prepared annually. Product development will, therefore, have to be planned. Physical elements must be selected from a terotechnological stance (see chapter 2) and all other on-going costs will need to be appreciated as the product package is devised.

Probably the most important document that the manager produces will be the annual budget. Here, detailed plans are developed for the department and, in this way, the manager aims to influence the allocation of monies within the organisation as a whole.

Budgetary control   The terms *budget* and *estimates* are often used as if synonymous, but here *estimates* are defined as 'plans developed within broad financial targets' whereas 'budgets' will relate to a financial expression of an intention to take a specific course of action. Budgetary control begins with scrutiny of this planned expenditure and, essentially, is a control over the resources devoted to the actions, not just an exercise in the overall control of money.

The Accommodation Manager will need to prepare annual budgets, along with other departmental managers, probably three to six months in advance. When approved and amalgamated these will then constitute the master budget. The cost centres will vary from one establishment to another and from one accounting system to another. They will also vary with the size, scope and organisation of the operation. The Accommodation Department's cost centres will include some of the following:

- **Labour** This will include total costs for each grade of staff employed, also any enhanced rate costs or bonus figures. These can be calculated from the whole-time-equivalent figures, deployment schedules and duty rotas.
- **Supplies** These may include costs for cleaning agents, cleaning equipment (stock and capital items) depreciation of capital equipment or equipment replacement, guest supplies, stationary, crockery, uniforms. These figures may be assessed by considering post budget figures and any changes in supplies systems. Job breakdowns and task frequency figures will also give an indication of costs.
- **Linen and laundry** This may include all types of soft furnishings repairs, cleaning and replacement. It may also include laundry equipment (and maintenance) and product costs where there is an on-premises laundry. Again, to assess these costs, historic data will be valuable.
- **Maintenance** These may include external maintenance, eg grounds, gardens and external fabric and internal costs, eg surfaces, structures, plant and equipment.
- **Contract service**, eg window cleaning, floral arrangements, redecorating.
- **Training** – particularly off the job training programmes.
- **Uniforms**.
- **Furniture and furnishings** This may include all types of furniture, some fittings, carpets, etc.

No item should be included on the Accommodation Manager's budget which is outside the scope of his authority. Where unit costings are to be calculated, the total figure, from the calculations above, can be divided by the number of units (a 'unit' could be a patient's bed or, say, 100 sq m in a hospital, a room or a student in a hall of residence, a bed or bedroom in an hotel (see Chapter 6).

In addition to operational costs, other costs which must be calculated and apportioned for unit costs to be complete are the 'service costs'.

With the standard system of hotel accounts the 'service costs' tend to be classified as 'Service Department Costs' (including administration; sales, advertising and promotion; heat light and power) and General Expenditure (including any item which cannot be allocated to another heading). In this standard system of hotel accounts, repairs and maintenance, plant and machinery and property cost centres are not included in the figures used to calculate the hotel operating profit. This is so that a common classification, up to and including general expenditure, can produce information on income, expenditure and profit which is reasonably uniform and comparable throughout the industry.

Budget preparation In order to prepare a realistic budget, the following comparisons can be made with the budget for the current financial year:

- total costs
- costs per cost centre
- actual expenditure to date.

To facilitate budget preparation and also to enable the ongoing process of budgetary control to operate, *cost statements* or *operating statements* at certain fixed intervals, eg weekly or monthly, can be produced. These reports compare the actual expenditure with the budgetary figure and any variances can be investigated and, hopefully, controlled. In such a way, problems might be identified and rectified at an early stage.

The style of presentation of budgets varies with the operation and its accounting system, but there does need to be a standard format within an organisation.

To operate maximum control over the budget, the Accommodation Manager should be responsible for its preparation, within policies set by higher management. Whilst the manager's budget proposals may not be accepted in their entirety, he/she must be involved in any decision made involving its amendment and given the opportunity to justify the financial plans. Ultimately the manager may have to operate the department under different (probably tighter) financial constraints and to do this, must be aware of all expenses incurred. A regular operating statement will facilitate this, as will any other information appertaining to costs, eg copy invoices of supplies received, information of changing wage rates, bonus payments. Much routine information associated with budgetary control, can be compiled systematically and readily processed by computer for the assistance of the budget holder.

It can be seen, therefore, that the system of Accommodation Management is complex, being influenced by many environmental factors and itself causing continual changes and responses in the environment. These environmental elements are the constraining influences on the development of the system, and the Accommodation

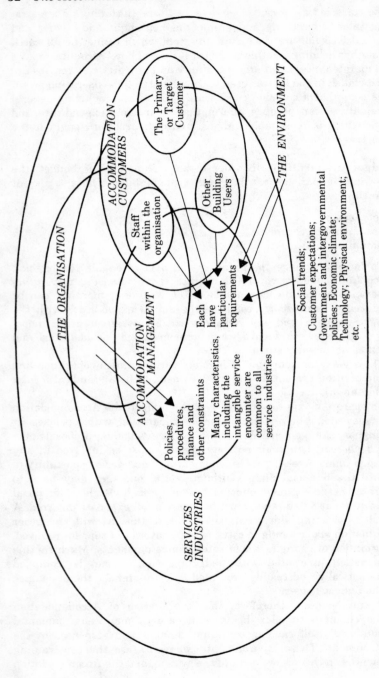

Concept map summarizing the Accommodation Product.

Manager must appreciate that these influences are never static. In response to this the sytem of Accommodation Management must itself be 'organic', ie ever changing in response to various stimulii.

Reference

[1] COLLIER, D, *Services Management*, Prentice Hall 1987

Assignment tasks

1 Identify a particular consumer group, eg family on holiday, shoppers in a department store, and list their specific needs and requirements with respect to accommodation facilities and services.
2 Review trade press and find examples of how particular customer requirements have been identified and specifically catered for by certain establishments.
3 Research two similar establishments, apparently catering for similar customers, and compare and contrast the accommodation facilities and services they offer. Consider how their provision affects the organisation.
4 Research two different establishments which aim to satisfy the needs of different consumer groups and contrast their organisation of accommodation facilities and services.
5 Using David Collier's definition of a Service, identify the different elements with respect to an accommodation provision, other than an hotel.
6 Choose a particular accommodation operation of interest to yourself and draw a systems map of it. Use Figure 1.3 as a starting point but make the diagram specific to your chosen example.

2

The Building

Objectives

- To analyse the design phase of a building and, in particular, identify the roles of the architect and the Accommodation Manager.
- To demonstrate the need for analysis of user requirements early in the design phase of a building.
- To outline the construction phase of a building, commissioning a building and the role of the planning team.
- To analyse the environmental services within a building and show how these can be selected to match user requirements, at the same time emphasising energy conservation.
- To establish the major characteristics of materials and show how analysis of requirements can achieve an effective selection process.
- To show how the Accommodation Manager can and must take a positive approach to security.

It is easy to appreciate that many new managers, within the Accommodation Industry, when faced with such complexities of customer care and staff management, will not place much emphasis on the building resource itself. However, it must be appreciated that the building is a costly resource. The cost of NHS property, for example, is estimated, would represent 20% of the total revenue cost, were capital charging to be implemented. Retention, reduction or expansion of building stock and the revenue consequences of such decisions will ultimately affect resources available.

Looking at the accommodation system of a given establishment, it could be argued that, of all the major subsystems, the building is the one which might exist independently. It could not, however, function as a hospital, hotel or sports complex, without the other subsystems. The building is the least dynamic of all the systems. It is relatively stable and is, therefore, an appropriate place to start an investigation into an accommodation system.

2.1 THE ELEMENTS OF A BUILDING

It is useful, first, to determine what the building is composed of and the effect these elements have on the total system. The elements can be identified as:

- the site
- the structure
- the fittings.

The Site

The site might be the precise size of the building structure itself or it might comprise acres of land. The site has both physical and environmental characteristics which will influence the structure and the operating of the establishment (see Figure 2.1). It can also have a significant effect on energy efficiency.

The structure

The structure of a conventional building consists of:

- foundations, eg footings, pile (the type being dependant on geo-physical aspects and building shape)
- walls, either framed (eg timber, steel, concrete with infill panels of glass reinforced concrete, glass reinforced plastic, brick, etc, and an external cladding of brickwork, ceramic, cement rendering, etc) or load bearing (eg concrete, masonry)
- roof, either flat or ridged.

Figure 2.1 *Site characteristics and their influence on the establishment*

Site characteristics	Influences on the hotel
Geographical location	Proximity to consumers Access Climate Availability of labour and supplies Local planning regulations
Aspect (and other structures in the vicinity)	Amount of sun, shade, wind
Geophysical	Bearing capacity of land Suitability for building Type of structure and foundation Drainage Access
Dimensions	Shape and size of building
Pollutants, eg noise, vibration, carbon, sulphur	Aesthetic desirability of site Building foundations, structure and materials
Other structures	Aesthetic qualities Business

Prefabricated sections or 'pods' may be used in some cases. For example, in the case of hotels, complete guest rooms or offices may be incorporated into the building structure. The benefits of prefabricated units are mainly with respect to the speed of construction.

The structure imparts various physical and psychological qualities on the building. Physically, the structure must be firm to resist forces of compression and tension on the building, eg gravity, water, wind and loads. Physical qualities will be achieved by a combination of the characteristics of the materials used and the configuration of these materials, ie the design and shape of the building. The loads on the building may be 'live', eg furniture, water pressure, snow loading, people, or 'dead', eg gravity and the weight of the building. Most elements of the building are designed to transfer these loads through the walls to the ground (hence the importance of the site and the bearing pressure of the sub-soil).

Psychological qualities of the building will be achieved by a combination of design and shape and of the materials used. Frequently buildings are designed to be a symbolic shape, ie designed to meet peoples' (users' and observers') expectations of what a hospital, a restaurant, or a church, looks like. In addition to these, the client (that is, in this case, the person or enterprise who requires a building to be constructed) and designer will usually desire to achieve further qualities, eg an impression of luxury for a top grade hotel or an impression of relaxation for a leisure centre.

A constraining influence on the client and designer will inevitably be finance. The functional characteristics normally have priority; the building must 'work'. It must also be remembered that clients' priorities vary. One client's first priority might not, in fact, be functionability. Buildings may be primarily for investment.

The fittings
The fittings of a building include:

- partitions
- window frames
- doors
- gutters

- sanitary fitting
- heating and electrical items
- finishing items, eg architraves, skirtings, etc.

They represent the more flexible items of the building and they may be removed without affecting the integrity of the building itself. Nevertheless, they are vital to the function of the building as an accommodation system. As with the structure, fittings impart physical and psychological characteristics.

2.2 PLANNING AND CONSTRUCTION

Now that an analysis has been made of what the building comprises, both physically and psychologically, it will be valuable to consider how a building comes into existence and how it fits into the accommodation system.

Design systems In the planning and constructing of large public buildings, it is common, for designs to be somewhat stereotyped. These buildings are designed for a wide market and they must satisfy many diverse groups now, and in years to come when expectations and requirements may have changed. Building designs unlike cars, furniture or clothes, may need to be archetypal, ie stand the test of time, be as useable and satisfactory in 60 years time as they are today. There are various design systems which can be identified, whether it is a teaspoon which is being developed, or a multi-storey office block.

First is the **Vernacular design**. This is one individual who identifies a need, designs a solution, constructs the solution, then uses it. As the plans and designs are developed, further possibilities are identified and the original need itself develops; as the solution is built and practicalities emerge, plans and designs are further amended. The finished product, depending on the individual's abilities, can be exactly what is required and meet precise requirements. It may be of no use at all to anyone else; the idea may, alternatively, be used by someone else and probably modified and developed.

The second design system is the **Empirical Exchange**. The client analyses their own needs, and commissions another to design and construct a solution. There can be a high degree of individual interpretation on the part of the designer/builder. Designs can be amended during construction. Also, communications between the client and the designer/builder can be informal. Again custom-built items can be constructed to meet the needs of an individual.

Another design system is **Direct Patronage**, where the client is also going to be the user of an object. Individual, custom-built designs are again required but, in this case, the designer passes the design plans to another for construction. As the network becomes more complex, original requirements and requests become more difficult to modify, as the communication process becomes more sophisticated and formal (see Figure 2.2).

Figure 2.2 *Direct patronage design network*

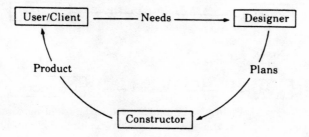

The final design system is the **Rational Network** (see Figure 2.3). The user may not even exist when the product is first considered. The client and the designer must endeavour to predict the user requirements. They must try to satisfy the needs of the maximum number of future users and, inevitably, individualities must be sacrificed and compromises made. It is this design process which is the norm when considering large public buildings. The client may be a health authority; the designer, an architect and the architect's team; the constructor usually consists of a number of contractors. Inevitably, by the time a building is constructed, the users are rarely all satisfied with the overall building but it is stereotyped and aims to satisfy most people most of the time.

As can be seen, design and construction of a building emerge in three separate phases. These are:

1 the problem identification and briefing stage
2 the design phase
3 the construction phase.

2.2.1   Problem identification and briefing

Building design and briefing of a designer must be initiated in some way. The conception of a building first emerges when a problem is identified. Planning predictions in a health authority might foresee too many patients for existing resources; business opportunities for a new hotel are identified; capital is held which a client wishes to invest in a building.

In one way or another the client reaches a decision that there is a need to build. This problem realisation stage leads the client to consult an architect when needs will be explained. Such a consultation would constitute the commencement of briefing the architect. At the first consultation, the architect would not wish the client to outline any definite plans. In the first instance, the architect needs to be briefed on 'the problem', and will need to discuss the client's

Figure 2.3 *Rational design network*

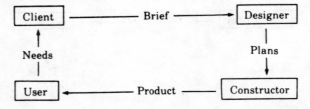

general ideas. A site may or may not have been found at this phase, but detailed planning cannot occur until this element has been acquired.

As has been shown in the Rational Design Network (Figure 2.3), users are not able to represent themselves, nor brief the architect. In order to foresee accurately future users' needs the client will usually organise a planning team. This team will comprise representatives of different disciplines of future users. Frequently these representatives are practising specialists. In a very large concern with different users having separate requirements, some members would be co-opted onto the team as and when required. In the planning of an hotel, a food and beverage manager would be invited to join the team when catering departments were to be discussed. An executive housekeeper might be enlisted to give information regarding requirements of a housekeeping department.

It is worth noting that such practising specialists are not always invited onto planning teams. Accommodation Managers in some situations may indeed have to fight for this right. This being so, when given the opportunity, the Accommodation Manager must capitalise on the situation. The accommodation department within the new building can benefit in many ways if a specialist of that discipline has been involved in the planning process. Some information that a housekeeping representative in an hotel or a domestic services manager in a hospital might contribute includes:

- specific requirements of that department; store rooms, linen rooms, laundry, service rooms, periphery stores, changing facilities, rest rooms. Specifications should include dimensions, services, fittings and surfaces required
- aspects on design which simplify and assist maintenance, servicing and overall standards achieved; siting of power sockets, suitable surfaces and their qualities
- requirements such as access to upper storeys; service lifts, ramps, etc.

All future activities and procedures to take place within a building must be identified at the planning stage. If they are not, the building may well be erected without some seemingly obvious and very basic components. It would not be the first time that an hotel had been constructed without a kitchen, or a hall of residence without a linen room. The needs of different building users must all be considered, including the needs of the disabled as well as those of the able-bodied. A well organised and informed planning team may well not only avoid such omissions, but also could greatly assist to achieve a more satisfied building user. The planning team's objectives, therefore, are to prepare a comprehensive and appropriate brief, and to assist by representing the user in further stages in the development of building plans.

Figure 2.4 *Building feasibility study*

1 The consumer identification	eg Area population, current and predicted population trends, tourism, industry, commerce Population type, eg age, health, wealth Accessibility of the site Communication links of the area Position of the site for accessibility Competition
2 Total capital costs	eg The site Design and construction costs Equipment and furnishings Pre-opening costs, eg stock, salaries, promotion Insurance, rates, rent Debtors
3 Predicted return on capital and running costs	Analysis of expenditure Payback periods Replacement cycles Cash flow

When initial briefing has been completed, early in the design process, a feasibility study, evaluating the potential market, usage of the building, capital costs, profits (where appropriate) and overall assessment of the proposed investment must be completed. The feasibility study may have been completed by the client, or he may commission the architect to make the study. Some of the aspects to be considered in such a feasibility study are outlined in Figure 2.4.

2.2.2   Design phase

The design phase follows problem identification and briefing, though distinction between the two phases is not clear cut and a large degree of back-tracking or reiteration will occur. The design phase emerges following clarification of the needs and requirements of the client and is often considered as having five basic aspects:

1 the brief finalisation
2 analysis of requirements
3 synthesis of plans
4 implementation of plans
5 communication.

Since it is the architect who has prime responsibility for this phase, it will be valuable to consider the architect's role.

An architect must be chosen carefully (though some large organisations employ their own). Commissioning the 'right' architect will inevitably affect the satisfaction of the client, and the Royal Institute of British Architects (RIBA) itself publishes a valuable leaflet on the commissioning of an architect.

Architect is a legal term and, as such, the role carries various legal responsibilities. The architect is responsible for the client's money and is legally responsible for the building. The architect must consider the client, the future building users and those involved in construction, as well as the site, the structures, the methods of construction and the materials used.

2.2.2.1 Briefing The architect may be responsible for the completion of the feasibility study; certainly, the architect must analyse the requirements identified by the client and also the future needs of building users. In the life of the building, a change of function may occur and the needs of users change. Consideration must, be given to these possibilities too, if the building is to be successful.

In some cases the architect will be working on an 80-year life expectancy for the building. In others, the clients' planning horizon and need for a speedy completion, may dictate a much less permanent structure. Flexibility of the building could well be a valuable asset, if not an essential one. For instance, in England, there have been situations in recent years where hospital properties in city centre locations have been sold to businesses moving into the cities, whilst hospitals have been moved out to green field sites.

2.2.2.2 Analysis In the planning and construction of large public buildings, the design network involves the client, the designer, the constructor and the user. Since the users, as individuals, may not yet have been identified, the client and the architect must, together, predict their needs.

The architect will need to consider the building at a macro level (with respect to location) and at a micro level (eg will the hotel guest be able to access the wardrobe effectively?).

In some instances the Rational Design Network may become further sophisticated. Standard packages have been developed in the interests of speed and economy. The Health Service has, for example, developed over the years, standard hospital plans, eg *Best Buy*, *Harness* and *Nucleus*.

The Nucleus set of plans was for a small intensive, first phase hospital, which could stand on its own and be capable of expansion. The theory is that, wherever the unit is required in Britain, the requirements of the users will be the same. From such a standardised process, an enormous amount of time, duplicated effort and money will be saved.

User requirements The users of a building are not just the sports people in a leisure complex or the customers in a restaurant. The building user includes staff, spectators, tradespeople, firefighters and contractors.

User requirements can be considered under two headings:

1   Individual needs

Physical needs, eg shelter, heat, light, food, sanitation, sleeping facilities, ventilation, security and safety.

Functional needs to enable proposed activities to be carried out, eg furniture, equipment

Psychological needs, eg privacy, efficiency, companionship, status.

2   Group needs

These include social interaction requirements, space for business transactions, social functions, etc.

In assessing both group and individual needs, changes in fashion and attitude and the standards of requirements must be considered. All the identified needs must be analysed and their implications interpreted by the architect in the form of plans for the new building.

In developing plans, the architect must aim to allow individual and group activities to be carried out *economically*, *conveniently*, *efficiently* and *comfortably*.

To achieve this, ergonomic theory is applied (see Section 2.2.2.3(2)). This will indicate, among other things, how much space is required by one person, using a bed, storing day clothes, using sanitary facilities, etc.

Before any plans can be drawn up, much analysis must be undertaken to prepare data and evaluate and coordinate ideas. At the analysis stage, the architect must consider which specialists will need to be involved in further development of the building design (for example, the type of linen system proposed will have considerable space implications, hence the value of a domestic services specialist).

2.2.2.3   Synthesis   From the data collected at the synthesis stage, the architect will start drawing conclusions and developing plans. At this stage, it is the architect's aim to offer a variety of possibilities to the client. Testing, checking and redesigning work will occur, as the client and architect meet to discuss the plans. The plans now developed are only at the sketch plan stage.

By this stage, the architect is likely to have involved others in the team, such as engineers and a quantity surveyor to advise on practicalities and economic matters, respectively. Plans proposed must meet legal requirements, and provisional planning permission may be applied for.

2.2.2.3(1)   Principles of planning and room layout

To recap, the architect now has information with respect to building users and their activities. Legal, safety and cost constraints must be considered at the synthesis stage as designs for a building, where all the required activities can take place efficiently and comfortably, are developed. To achieve this, the architect considers data on:

- numbers of people
- types of individual activity
- types of group activity
- timing and places of activities.

For example, in a student hall of residence, the architect might consider:

Students	— arriving and leaving as individuals and sub groups
	— grouping together to eat
	— separating out to sleep
	— grouping together to watch television
	— sub-grouping for cooking
	— individual needs for personal hygiene
	— individual needs for quiet study
Visitors	— arriving and leaving individually
Domestic	— arriving and leaving individually and in groups
staff	— grouping together for instruction
	— separating out for work
	— grouping together for eating
	— individual needs for personal hygiene
Maintenance	— arriving and leaving individually and in groups
staff	— working individually
	— grouping for eating
	— individual needs for personal hygiene
Catering	
staff	
Residential	
staff/Bursar	
etc.	

The architect must consider the implications of different activities, eg noise created or quiet needed; how activities coincide (which will involve consideration of the pattern of movement within the building); and the effect that social and economic trends may have on activities in the future.

Gradually room configurations will be developed which meet individual, group and operational needs.

The detailed planning of room layout can now be considered. The usefulness of a room is affected by the shape and siting of the door and windows which limit the size and arrangement of furniture and, therefore, the activities which can operate within it. Space represents money and must not be wasted, but adequate space must be available to achieve comfort.

2.2.2.3(2)   Ergonomic aspects

To achieve user comfort within a building at the synthesis stage, ergonomic theory is applied. *Ergonomics* is defined as: '*the study of the relationship between man and his environment*' and '*the study of characteristics of people in order to develop equipment and procedures that are properly suited to these characteristics.*'

Ergonomics involves an examination of the capabilities and limitations of people, with respect to gathering and processing information and taking action on that information. Ergonomics involves the study of how well people see; how much light they need; what colours they discriminate; how much information they can handle at once; how quickly they can deal with it; how people take action; how strong they are; how far they can reach; etc. Such information is gathered and then used to design equipment, space, procedures, etc, which are matched to the needs of the users.

Broadly, there are four aspects involved in ergonomics:

1 *Anthropometrics* This involves measurement of the average human dimensions for certain groups, eg soldiers, car drivers, hospital domestic staff, the adult population as a whole.

   Dimensions available are virtually unlimited, eg heights, arm lengths, eye levels, finger lengths. Such information is used by many sectors, eg furniture manufacturers, industrial workplace designers and architects. The information allows the architect to specify dimensions of doors, windows, work surfaces, steps and any other building element to achieve functional, comfortable, convenient, efficient and economic design.

2 *Kinetics* This is a study of the muscles of the human body and their use. Architects need to consider how the user's body will be positioned and the muscles used when undertaking any activity for which the building is being designed. Dimensions need to be such that when, for example, a user is moving a heavy object, space available allows, if not positively encourages, larger muscles in the arms and legs to be used in preference to smaller back muscles.

   In a domestic assistant's cleaning cupboard, for example, a domestic assistant is probably going to need to lift heavy buckets. There needs to be, therefore, space to bend knees when lifting the bucket to enable thigh muscles to take the weight.

3 *Applied physiology* Human physiological data also needs to be applied to building design. The architect needs an understanding of the physical requirements of man, eg fresh air or oxygen requirements; temperature, humidity and lighting requirements; the effect of noise; odour, mechanical vibration and visual effects (including colour, pattern, shape and light intensities); needs for sustenance and sanitary facilities; and the effects of air movements and tactile qualities.

   Responses need to be made by the architect to facilitate needs with respect to all such data.

4 *Applied psychology* This is concerned with man's mental state and needs (again, dependant on the activities carried out and on the specific user groups). Aspects to consider here include; how much mental stimulation to create in an area or, conversely, how to achieve a restful and relaxing environment; how to create an impression of informality, efficiency, opulence, tradition, intimacy, discipline, etc. The mood created may need to be flexible, as indeed, the whole building interior may, but it must be in response to perceived needs. Different groups have different psychological needs and abilities and vary in their motivation, concentration, learning patterns, interactive behaviour, etc.

Applying ergonomic theory can, therefore, assist the architect in designing a practical and economic environment in which users will feel comfortable.

2.2.2.3(3) Room sizes and shapes
As the synthesis stage progresses, and the architect develops room plans and layouts, a recommended schedule of furniture will also be prepared. This will be needed to assist assessment of the plans by the client. Here again, the needs of particular user groups will need to be considered, eg wheelchair users will require lateral transfer space beside beds and baths. In the Health Service, where standardisation for economy is a major objective, a standard Activity Database has been developed, ie given the type of activity within a room, a standard recommended schedule of furniture has been developed. Further than this, given the activity and component (eg activity: emptying or filling a damp mopping bucket; component: a slop sink), Component Database information provides standard specifications for components.

As a logical extension of this, and through developments in building technology, 'components' could now refer to composite units such as a toilet or bathroom module, consisting of a pre-specified package of toilet, cistern, washbasin, tiles and taps, etc, or even a complete bedroom package. Such prefabricated 'pods' can be connected to the mains and fitted with relative speed and ease.

Actual room sizes and shapes will not only be dependent on the fittings, their dimensions and layout, but also on the shape and site of the building and the environment (eg sea view), on the activities planned in that room and the ergonomic needs which have been identified. The needs of the disabled, for instance, as well as the able-bodied should be considered. In the interest of economy, the architect will consider very carefully the use of space. Due to the multiplying effects of costs, even slight increases in room sizes are expensive. There is a definite trend for rooms in newer buildings to be smaller than previously. By careful planning it may be possible to reduce room sizes, but not reduce space availability. Two single rooms may take up 50% more space than one twin room, yet the useable space may only be in the region of 20% greater in the single room.

Space allocations must reflect market demand. Generally, more luxurious hotels have, overall, more space allocated to each customer than the lower grade hotels. Within an hotel, the ratio of single, twin, double or studio rooms must be based on data collected in the feasibility study (see also *Yield management* Section 6.8.3). The architect will also need to consider standardisation of room sizes within an hotel group. Significant economies can be made through standardisation and simplification of 'the product', eg through standardisation of purchases, bulk purchasing, etc, as well as the simplification of the building process, which may well involve the use of certain prefabricated sections or units.

Finally, the architect will be constrained in the design of the building by legal aspects, local bye-laws and fire regulations. Building regulations, for example cover:

- access and egress
- sanitary conveniences
- audience or spectator seating.

These aspects, whilst applied throughout the design process, are crucial at the synthesis stage if abortive work is to be avoided. As options are eliminated, a general agreement is made as to the route to follow, and the architect's brief should not alter after this stage.

2.2.2.4 Implementation The presentation of final designs and plans (in some case alternative proposals may be submitted) by the architect to the client can be considered at the implementation stage. Data has been interpreted in plans, and a definite proposal has been developed. If the client now chooses to alter the brief, work will have been wasted and, ultimately, the client will bear the cost. Working drawings are developed, so that, following acceptance of the plans, tenders can be invited, contracts made and building can commence.

In evaluating plans submitted by the architect, the client must be satisfied with respect to the following:

- overall shape and appearance of the building
- convenience of entering and leaving (various entrances may be needed, eg customers, staff, deliveries)
- external facilities for visitors and other building users
- relation to the external environment
- efficiency of circulation system
- convenience of activity areas in relation to one another
- privacy, quiet and other psychological needs
- detailed provision of heating, lighting and ventilation
- facilities for changing demands, eg weekends/weekdays.

2.2.2.5 Communication Throughout the design process, communication is vital. It has been shown, in the *Rational Design*

Figure 2.5 *Summary of design phase*

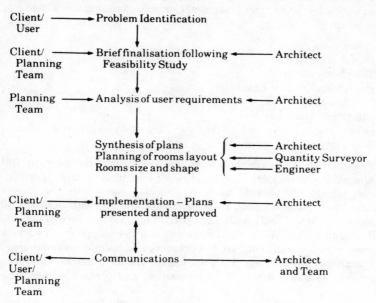

Network, section 2.2.2.2, that the future users' needs must be predicted. The preparation of the architect's brief is vitally important, but up to the implementation stage, modification or further clarification of that brief can be made. Even after this stage, as implications become clearer, as forecasted needs are seen to alter, or omissions or mistakes realised, it is preferable for corrections to be made, at a cost, than for known faults to be ignored.

Communication between architect and client must be free flowing. Communication between the architect and constructor will become more formalised. The client's requirements having been assessed, there is less leeway for negotiations between designer and builder.

A summary of the design phase is given in Figure 2.5.

2.2.3 Construction phase

By the completion of the design phase, detailed design of every part and component of the building has been presented to and passed by the client. Complete cost checkings of all designs will have been carried out and approved, and the architect's team will now comprise quantity surveyors and engineers. Planning permission will have been applied for. Approval of the building plans from a practical point of view, as well as a legal necessity, must not only be granted by the local authority (under the Town and Country Planning Act 1954), but also by the:

- Police
- Fire Authority
- Telephone company
- Health and Safety Executive
- Gas company
- Electricity company
- Other specialised authorities, eg Education Authority, Health Authority as appropriate

The quantity surveyor must now prepare for the architect the Bill of Quantities (a complete list of all requirements and their specifications), which will provide basic information needed in the tender documents. Firms can then be invited to tender. Tendering might be 'selective' or 'open' and contractors will fill in their labour costs on the Bill of Quantities. When the contractor has been appointed, various degrees of sub-contracting are likely before site operations commence. The architect will also appoint the Clerk of Works, a resident building specialist who is responsible for inspecting and controlling work on site.

A conventional construction process will broadly follow the schedule outlined below, depending specifically on the type of construction and use made of prefabricated sections. To a lesser extent the availability of labour and equipment may also affect the order of work.

2.2.3.1   Construction process

- the building is set out, that is the shape is measured out and defined (the building line, ie nearness to the road, is set by the local authority). Hoardings are erected and site access and services established
- excavation and service connections
- foundations
- erection of walls to the damp proof course. Provision of the damp proof course (dpc) or membrane
- hard core and return fill (ie excavated material returned to trenches to provide the sub-base for concrete floors)
- floor level, eg timber, concrete
- basic shell (wood window frames inserted now, steel ones left until later)
- timber joists
- complete walls to roof
- roof carcass
- topping out (ie finishing the wall to the roof)
- plumbing, eg rainwater guttering and other plumbing to roof
- roof covering (approximate half way stage)

- 'first fix' of furnishings and surfaces eg glazing; plumbing; joining; electric; gas (the fixing of these is incomplete, as yet, to enable trades to work around one another)
- plasterboard, ceilings
- partition walls (ie non-load-bearing)
- plastering of ceilings and walls
- second fix (as first fix)
- sanitary appliances, wall fittings and other fittings
- painting
- floor finishes, eg vinyl tiles
- site works, eg drains layed and connected to main services
- clearing of site, laying of paths, erecting fences, landscaping.

Such a process, of course, will not always follow an exact pattern. Since there is not one central firm responsible for construction, each must be managed separately.

The Clerk of Works aims to ensure that the work is completed in a logical order, eg walls plastered before floor coverings are laid, to prevent waste, reduce time and to promote co-operation and job satisfaction of different trades.

When tenders are invited, specifications (from the Bill of Quantities) are given to contractors detailing the workmanship which must take place, and where appropriate, detailed sectional drawings are given to show components (eg guttering). Assembly drawings are also prepared to show how components fit together (eg wall joints and ceilings). Specification must be tight to ensure that standards are reached, eg the paintwork specification might detail not just British Standards colour code, and paint type, but the number of undercoats and topcoats to be applied.

2.2.3.2 Performance specification To prepare valid specifications, performance details or performance specifications must first be prepared. These give details of the required characteristics of an item. For example, with respect to a floor surface the performance specification might detail the following:

- surface suitable for the students' utility room in a hall of residence
- resistance to greasy and wet soilage
- slip resistance, even when wet
- resistance to heat, eg boiling water or fat
- noise absorbency with respect to impact sound
- good heat insulation properties
- comfort to stand on but non-resilience
- resistance to cutting and indentation by falling objects
- washable surface
- attractive appearance, colour, variety, etc.

With these criteria in mind, the architect may specify:

- a particular grade, quality and colour of flooring which most nearly meets all the needs, eg sheet vinyl
- adhesive quality, eg waterproof
- installation details, eg hermetically sealed joints
- finishing details, eg two coats of waterbased seal.

2.2.3.3 Quality management   To ensure that standards are being achieved, the specification is vitally important. In addition, the Clerk of Works will regularly be checking work. Materials used, methods used and workmanship, will be compared with the Bill of Quantities, to ensure that specifications are being met. It is estimated that about 25% of the architect's fees are apportioned to plan supervision. The architect may also visit the site to check on quality.

2.2.3.4 Completion   When a building is said to be 'practically complete', this is a legal term meaning that it is fit for its intended purpose. The last responsibility of the building contractors is frequently the 'builder's clean'. Once in use, a period of defects liability will operate (eg 6 months for any defect, 12 months for engineering defects). During this period a portion of the funds is retained and the architect is responsible for checking the building for any defects and seeing that such work is made good before 'final completion' of the building.

2.2.4   Commissioning of the building

Once the brief has been finalised and plans accepted at the implementation phase, the client passes responsibility for the building to the architect. The client may accompany the architect on site visits, but mostly further involvement awaits the completion stage and the 'handover'. The building does not belong to the client until the handover, and the client may not enter the building without the architect's authority.

During the construction of the building, the client can plan its functioning and, as building completion nears, orders for inventory may be placed, and some staff recruitment, selection and preparatory training can occur.

At the date of the handover, insurance liability for the building passes from the architect to the client. Following the handover of the building, as has been stated, there is a period of defects liability. During this time, the architect should be informed of any defects and should ensure that those occurring as a result of a deviation from the specification are made good.

Frequently, in large buildings, commissioning teams are set up; these usually comprise future users (often departmental heads). Their responsibilities can be divided into four areas:

1 checking acceptability of the building structure
2 identifying equipment needs and ordering appropriately
3 preparing schedules for staffing needs and dealing with recruitment, selection and training of staff
4 preparing schedules of organisation and operational procedures.

Most of the main work of the commissioning team will occur prior to handover and it is probable that they will liaise with the Clerk of Works with respect to building structure matters.

Such is the process of design and construction of the building envelope. In an attempt to ensure the building users are satisfied with the building, their requirements must be accurately predicted, appropriate specifications prepared and controls applied. In Chapter 5 the preparation of specifications is considered further, with respect to supplies.

2.3 THE FITTINGS

The many components within a building will have different life expectancies relative to that of the building itself. Wall coverings, for example, may have comparatively short lives; water and drainage systems may be expected to function throughout the life of the building. In this next section, consideration will be given to elements with which the users will interface most directly; those items in fact, for which the Accommodation Manager will be most likely to carry responsibilities, with respect to maintenance, modification or replacement. In each case, possible performance attributes will be considered and specific types identified. The different characteristics are analysed in three areas:

1 *Environmental services*, ie heating, lighting, ventilation
2 *Surface fittings*, ie wall, floor and ceiling coverings, windows, sanitary fittings, furniture and furnishings
3 *Interior design*

2.3.1 Environmental services

Environmental services are necessary (though not in any specific style) to provide:

- water
- oxygen and carbon dioxide exchanges
- variable lighting
- variable heating.

Another necessity for people is food. Though provision for this may not always form part of a building specification, it often does. Details of necessary building provision for food storage, preparation, service and consumption, represent specialist catering expertise and are covered in detail in many other texts. They have not, therefore, been covered here.

2.3.1.1   Water   Water may be required for any of a number of uses within an establishment eg:

- personal hygiene and sanitation
- culinary uses
- cleaning processes – laundry, environmental cleaning
- manufacturing processes
- heating systems
- fire fighting
- leisure and health pursuits.

For each of these uses, the performance specification might vary, eg depending on the degree of hygiene required. Generally, regardless of the use, the source is the same, namely the water mains which enter the building below ground at a depth adequate to give protection from most frosts and under sufficient pressure to meet fire fighting requirements (though this pressure may be supplemented by a pump in high-rise buildings). Much of British water is classed as hard. Depending on the degree of hardness and subsequent uses from leaving the mains, the water may pass through a softening plant. Softening plants are costly to install but may be necessary where very large quantities of water are used (as in laundries), or where a build-up of calcium and magnesium deposits in pipework would occur relatively quickly, so reducing efficiencies.

It is probable that some water will feed a storage tank, eg for hot water installations. Such tanks can constitute a serious health risk if they are not correctly covered, cleaned and maintained. Water temperatures in such tanks and any dirt introduced to them will support the growth of microbes and some such tanks have been found to contain the bacteria associated with Legionnaires' disease. Bacteria which cause Legionnaires' disease favour temperatures between 20° and 45°C and slow moving or stagnant water. Tanks should therefore not be maintained between these temperatures. Algae contamination, rust or scaling will also encourage bacterial growth.

Water supplying taps for drinking or cooking purposes come from a direct supply.

2.3.1.2   Hot water supply   Ample hot water is not just a convenience in buildings, but also, under the Offices, Shops and Railway Premises Act (1963), it became a requirement. The temperature of the water needs to be such that it is safe to use, economic to produce and maintain, and sufficiently hot to be effective in use. It is estimated that the hot water requirements are:

hotels – approximately 115–135 litres/person/day
hospitals – approximately 130–225 litres/person/day.
An average temperature for hot water is 55°C.
There are four main methods of producing hot water:

1 central storage plant and distributive pipework, servicing the whole building
2 remote storage plant, heated from a common heat source, with zone distribution pipework (pipework feeding separate zones of the building)
3 local storage vessels, heated by independent sources
4 local instantaneous water heaters.

Due to the quantities used and the peak demands, adequate storage is essential for the first three of these.

Factors to consider when selecting a hot water system are:

- economy with respect to
  — fuel, fuel storage, heating apparatus installation
  — distributive system, minimum 'deadlegs', installation costs
  — maintenance costs
  — storage of hot water
- capacity, ie amount of hot water which can be produced in a given period
- temperature requirements
- aesthetics of visible elements and acoustics (eg reverberating pipes)
- ease of cleaning and maintenance of storage tanks to control the risk of infection such as Legionnaires' disease.

2.3.1.3 Heating   Heat within a building is derived from:

- the building occupants (the amount depends on their number, age, sex, activity, period of occupation)
- solar gain (depending on orientation, shape and construction, time of day or year, site of building)
- lighting (dependent on wattage and use)
- electrical and mechanical apparatus (depending on wattage and use)
- the heating system.

Conversely, heat losses are through:

- building materials and contents ('U' values of building materials give the rate of thermal transmittance)
- ventilation (depending on rate of air change, outside and inside temperatures)
- building construction (depending on external radiant temperature and air temperature, wind, moisture in construction)
- refrigeration plant.

Requirements of heating systems vary. Recommendations are made for temperatures within different room types, given a relative humidity of 30-60%; the temperatures are not indisputably suitable in all circumstances, and, in any case, to achieve such average temperatures, heating systems must be flexible and adapt to different conditions. In most situations a 'comfort zone' is aimed for, that is a temperature at which 85% of users feel comfortable.

The performance attributes of the heating system, in general terms, will be to provide optimum room temperatures for given activities, economically and efficiently. More detailed performance attributes will vary with the user, the room use and the building type. Patients in hospital wards, recovering from operations, will usually require higher and more constant temperature than guests in an hotel bedroom. Some attributes which will need to be considered when selecting a heating system include:

- maximum, minimum and average temperature requirements
- temperature variances required, during a day, a week and a year
- speed with which temperatures must be reached
- aesthetics of heat emitters
- control requirements at point of use
- safety aspects
- security
- economy
- maintenance
- space requirements.

These attributes will need to be considered, in their turn, with respect to the following:

- the users: their age, activities, sex, temperature to which they are accustomed
- humidity levels and ventilation system
- hours of use for given activities, days of use (eg exclusive of weekends) and weeks of use
- general décor of an establishment
- degree of flexibility desired in order to meet any one individual's requirements
- cost constancy and reliability of supply of selected fuel
- installation costs
- accommodation and opportunity costs (eg space for boiler room)
- running costs (eg fuel and its efficiency, maintenance, insurance)
- legislation
- any policies with respect to global environmental issues.

Heating systems   Heating systems can broadly be categorised into five types:

1 **warm air** – air is centally warmed and fed into the room via ducts. It is filtered before discharge, and cooler air is returned by separate ducts. (Warm air curtains may also be a feature of this type)

2 **under floor** – heating grids are fitted in the floor screed, and are operated using off peak electricity

3 **ceiling** – low temperature radiant elements are fitted between the ceiling joists and the final finish

4 **localised heaters** – small moveable or fixed units, eg gas, electric or paraffin heaters

5 **radiator system** – comprising a central boiler, distributing pipework and emitters.

The last of these, namely the radiator system, is by far the most commonly used in large buildings, for reasons of economy, efficiency and safety, and there are many variations of this system. Variables include:

- the heat transfer medium, eg pressurised water, steam, air
- distribution system, eg gravity, pumps, single or two pipe system
- boiler fuel, eg gas, oil, various solid fuels
- boiler type, eg new high efficiency boilers
- heat emitter, eg pipes, radiators, convectors, skirting heaters, panels.

2.3.1.4 Energy conservation Whichever heating system is used, to be successful it must fulfil various requirements, one of these

Figure 2.6 *An analysis of heating aspects*

Is heating necessary?	What activities occur in each area and for how long? What are the heat losses? How is heat insulation achieved in the area?
What temperature is required in specific areas?	Avoid overheating. Comfort is also related to humidity (which affects heat exchange) and velocity of air movement (draughts). Ventilation too, must therefore be controlled
For which hours in the day is heating required?	Office areas may only be used for 8 hours per day, 5 days per week. Are unoccupied areas being overheated? Time clocks and thermostats, possibly computer controlled, help efficiency. Zoning of areas for heating may be appropriate
How is the hot water system designed?	'Dead legs' cause heat losses. Pipes should be lagged
What is the operating efficiency of the boiler?	Is regular maintenance carried out?

being economy. With estimates in the UK of 30% of total energy produced being used to heat buildings, an idea is given for the scope available for energy conservation. This issue is further developed in Appendix 2, but here heating implications will specifically be considered.

An analysis of heating aspects is shown in Figure 2.6

A major force in achieving energy conservation is seen as that of increasing staff awareness. Providing unwanted heat obviously causes wastage and it has been estimated that a rise of 1°C above the desired level can result in a 10% increase in energy consumption for the period that the temperature is maintained.

Another aspect is that of heat recovery. With respect to the Accommodation Manager's work, an important application here is within the laundry. Heat must be generated to complete many of the laundry processes, but much of that can be recovered and reused, for example with the use of heat exchangers.

2.3.1.5 Ventilation The purpose of ventilation is to provide a constant oxygen supply and to remove carbon dioxide and exhaled air, smells and gases. The ventilation system within a building will be deemed to be satisfactory or not, depending on:

- the volume of fresh air provided
- the distribution of air and speed of air movement
- the air temperature
- the relative humidity
- the purity of the 'fresh' air.

The volume of air required depends on the number of people in a given area and their activities, legislation, use of the room, odours and condensation. Fresh air needs to be evenly diffused and should not strike directly on occupiers. There needs to be a feeling of air movement, but not a draught (ie air speed greater than 0.5 m/sec), and the temperature of fresh air should not vary greatly from that of the room, or mixing will not occur. In cold weather, fresh air may need humidification or conversely in warm weather drying of air may be desirable.

There are three methods of ventilation:

1 **natural**, ie windows and doors, etc, allow air movement which is induced by temperature effects or wind
2 **mechanical** – air movement is controlled by power driven fans
3 **mixed**, ie either the incoming or outgoing air is induced by power driven fans.

Air cleaning Air within rooms may be cleaned by various apparatus available today. Some clean by filtration, some by ultra-violet radiation. The principle is that air is sucked into the unit, cleaned and returned. Such units may be used to deal with nicotine pollution, odours and other pollution.

Psychrometry This science is involved with the behaviour of air and water vapour. When the highest amount of water vapour, appropriate to the temperature is present, the air is said to be saturated. At lower pressures, this air would be unsaturated, ie could theoretically hold more water. The ratio of the two pressures is the relative humidity, and it is, therefore, the relative humidity which determines the rate of evaporation from, for example, the human skin, and affects comfort.

To create comfort, therefore, air must not only provide oxygen but also a regulated humidity which is important.

Humidifiers Like air cleaners, humidifiers are designed to draw in air from a room, treat it (in this case correct the moisture content) and return the air to the room.

Ionisers Ioniser units may be fitted in certain areas to control the positive/negative ion balance of the atmosphere. High concentrations of negative ions are claimed to affect both mental and physical health.

Air conditioning Air conditioning goes further than ventilation. It also aims to control the humidity factor as well as the air temperature, its purity and gas content. Air conditioning, therefore, provides a system of control for the total atmosphere of a building, ie heating, oxygen replenishment, carbon dioxide removal, odour removal, cleaning of air, humidity controls. It may also have an ioniser fitted. It is expensive to install, involving plant at considerable capital cost, and distributive apparatus, but it is a system which is becoming more popular both from a comfort point of view and from an economic stance, since heat production is carefully controlled and recycling can occur.

2.3.1.6 Lighting The lighting system must meet a variety of needs, which will depend on particular users and their activities, eg in a reception area, staff carrying out office work, guests awaiting a lift, housekeeping staff suction cleaning a carpet, will all have different lighting needs.

Other requirements of the lighting system, include economy and energy efficiency, visual attractiveness and safety. Flexibility is needed to allow intensity control, to create the right atmosphere, maximise the use of space or help to conceal areas.

There are two types of light within a building:

1 *natural light*
2 *artificial light*.

In the interests of energy conservation, use may be made of available natural light, though the amount and quality of this will depend on orientation, cloud cover, time of day, environment and windows. Wall and ceiling windows may save on artificial lighting costs, but privacy, security and heating aspects need also to be balanced against this. Heat losses and excessive solar heat gain in sunny weather are associated problems. Consideration must also be given to glare and adaptation demands (the effect of changing light intensities on the eye), particularly where windows are on one wall only.

With respect to artificial light in building interiors, there are three main types:

1 **tungsten** – fittings are cheap but inefficient in energy use and have relatively short lives
2 **fluorescent** – fittings are more expensive, more efficient and last longer
3 **new generation discharge** – more expensive, more efficient and last longer.

Exterior lighting by artificial means is usually achieved by sodium discharge lamps, mercury halogen or tungsten halogen.

Other elements to be considered, within the lighting system, are the light fitting, light shade, wiring and control switches, and the user.

When planning a lighting installation, the following points must be considered:

- uses of area, light intensities and qualities required, period of use
- lighting control and access of switches for different building users
- safety, eg of wiring, a night circuit, stairs
- structure, shape, aspects of windows, view
- window furnishings
- reflectiveness of interior surfaces
- uniformity of lighting (generally variable levels required)
- energy conservation
- running costs, replacement costs and replacement cycle
- heat generation
- visual appearance of fittings and effect on light distribution
- colour rendering of light source
- siting of fittings, eg wall or ceiling mounted, free standing, concealed
- siting of controls.

Recommended lighting levels for given activities are available (see *Further reading*).

2.3.2   Surface fittings

Characteristics and suitability of surface fittings, eg floors and walls are determined by:

- the characteristics of the materials used
- the manner in which the materials are fitted together, installed and maintained.

It is useful to look first at the characteristics of different materials. With an understanding of the basic properties, this information can be applied to different types of surfaces.

2.3.2.1 Properties of materials There are three basic criteria involved in the selection of materials: aesthetics; prestige; and cost efficiency.

The fundamental properties of materials are related to three areas inherent within their specific structures. These are:

1 **stiffness** – that is the opposite of elastic, ie the ability to recover and this depends on stress
2 **strength** – the force needed to break it
3 **toughness** – the resistance to cracks.

These basic properties vary in any material depending on its condition, eg whether under compression or tension, temperature, eg steel is usually strong, but, at low temperatures, it is brittle. The properties are determined by the:

– macrostructure   – molecular structure
– microstructure   – atomic structure of the material.

The main adjectives used to describe materials are listed below:

- acoustic properties
- aesthetic value
- colour and pattern
- corrosion resistance (ie degradation as a result of chemical action)
- cost
- durability
- electrical resistance
- elasticity/flexibility
- function
- light reflectance/absorption
- porosity
- prestige value
- resilience
- slipperiness
- strength
- temperature resistance
- transparency
- toughness.

2.3.2.2 Floor coverings About three-quarters of all cleaning costs will, during the life of a building, be spent on floor maintenance.

Figure 2.7 *Performance specification of floor coverings*

Material property	Possible application to floor covering
1 Acoustic properties	May need to be sound reflecting or absorbing
2 Aesthetic value	More important in prestige areas. Also consider appearance retention
3 Colour and pattern	Variety may be important, also retention of this and effect on apparent soilage
4 Corrosion resistance	Consider spillages, sunlight degradation
5 Cost	Dependent on replacement cycle
6 Durability	Dependent on user density and activity
7 Electrical resistance	Important, eg in operating theatres where static electricity may develop
8 Elasticity	Consider quality of sub-floor
9 Function	Consider maintenance
10 Light reflection	Important in relation to maintenance
11 Porosity	Consider spillages and ease of maintenance
12 Prestige	Consider in relation to aesthetics
13 Resilience	Affects comfort of users
14 Slipperiness	Very important, particularly when wet
15 Strength	Consider impacts (compression), underlying sub-floors could necessitate tensile strength
16 Temperature resistance	Consider spillages, cigarette ends, insulation
17 Transparency	Usually opaque required
18 Toughness	Abrasion resistance, resistance to cutting, etc, from falling objects

If terotechnology is applied (ie looking at total costs during the life of the surface) and initial selection is good, savings will be made in the long term and, possibly, common accidents, such as slipping, minimised. Statistics show that out of every 100 workers hurt, 16 are injured by falls on the level.

In preparing a performance specification for a floor covering, criteria to be considered include those shown in Figure 2.7. In addition to these, installation, replacement and repair also need consideration, as does the compatibility of the floor surface with the type and condition of the sub-floor.

Floor types, characteristics and selection

Depending on their macro- and microstructure (ie a structure seen by the naked eye, or only by means of a microscope, respectively), floor coverings have been classified as:

- *porous*, eg wood, cork and concrete
- *semi porous*, eg vinyl, vinyl asbestos, PVC, thermoplastic
- *non porous*, eg epoxy resin, quarry tiles and marble
- *soft floor coverings*.

The porosity of the floor will greatly influence its resistance to soilage and, therefore, the required maintenance. Depending on the maintenance programme, inherent properties, eg attractive appearance, durability, chemical resistance, water resistance, slip resistance may be enhanced. Other characteristics, eg acoustic properties and insulation properties will remain unchanged.

2.3.2.3 Wall and ceiling coverings

Wall coverings are much less vulnerable than floor coverings to the effects of abrasion, spillages and impacts. Wall coverings do need to withstand certain elements, however, eg water in the form of steam; they may be selected for their protective abilities, hygiene qualities, or heat or sound insulation characteristics. Appearance characteristics may prevail also amongst the selection criteria. Some of the performance characteristics which might be applied to wall coverings are shown in Figure 2.8.

As with floor coverings, terotechnology must be applied. Installation, maintenance, replacement and repair all need consideration. Replacement cycles of wall and ceiling coverings are, generally, more frequent than that of floor coverings (particularly hard floors), but convenience of replacement might be critical, eg speed of redecorating a room in an hotel to minimise the loss of revenue. Coverings must be compatible with the type and condition of the base wall or ceiling, eg vinyl paints should not be applied to new plaster without the appropriate drying out period.

Figure 2.8 *Performance specification of wall coverings*

Material property	Possible application to wall/ceiling covering
1 Acoustic properties	May need to absorb radiating noise, eg restaurant
2 Aesthetic value	Appearance can dramatically change a room
3 Colour and pattern	Variety may be important, hide imperfections
4 Corrosion resistance	Eg grease and condensation in kitchens Nicotine stains
5 Cost	Dependent on replacement cycle
6 Durability	Consider resistance to rubbing
7 Electrical resistance	Will contribute to overall static levels in room
8 Elasticity	May need to cover cracks and surface defects
9 Function	Consider usage of area
10 Light reflection	Dependent on colour, texture, degree of gloss
11 Porosity	Acoustic and soilage resistance properties could conflict. Tactile properties could be important
12 Prestige	Consider visual impact, eg in entrance area
13 Resilience	Impacts in busy corridors, eg from trolleys
14 Slipperiness	Less relevence
15 Strength	Consider impacts. Also consider resistance to insects and pests
16 Temperature resistance	Flammability could be crucial
17 Transparency	Usually opaque required
18 Toughness	Consider abrasion resistance

Wall and ceiling coverings; types, characteristics and selection

Paints   There are many types; on some occasions they may be applied directly to the plaster or wall itself, on others, primers and sealers are required. Paints are composed of:

- pigment (insoluble particles)
- vehicle (comprising binder for gloss, toughness, etc, and solvent)
- additives, eg to assist drying or application.

Some paints dry by evaporation of the solvent, though most require an additional chemical reaction, either resulting from air contact or within the paint itself. Some of the varying qualities of paints include:

- ease of application
- adhesion
- strength
- degree of gloss
- durability
- odour
- toxicity
- drying speed.

Some of the different types include water paints, emulsions, alkyd resins, cellulose, etc.

Wall and ceiling papers   For contract use, wallpapers are subject to British Standards tests for bursting strength, tearing strength, tensile strength and light fastness. Commonly, 'duplex' papers are used, consisting of a base paper and a top paper. 'Simplex' papers are rarely as durable. Some types include embossed, flock, metallic and relief papers.

Plastic wall and ceiling coverings   There are two types of plastic, namely, thermosetting and thermoplastic. An example of thermoplastic wall and ceiling coverings is laminated plastics; thermoplastics include PVC, bonded paper, and expanded polystyrene.

Fabric wall coverings   These become more diverse and imaginative as time goes on, ranging from hessian types, through wool, and wool strands to silk.

Other wall and ceiling coverings   The range is diverse, and includes wood, cork, ceramic tiles, terrazzo, stone, metal eg copper, brick and glass.

2.3.2.4   Glazing   Glazing is taken to include external and internal windows and partitions, glass coverings and mirrors. As with any surface, the specific use will determine the criteria for selection.

Safety and durability will be aspects which will need to be considered and here the selection of the glazing frames and installation will be important.

The performance attributes of glass and glazing are given in Figure 2.9.

Figure 2.9 *Performance specification of glass and glazing*

Material property	Possible application to glass and glazing
1 Acoustic properties	May be required to minimise noise transfer
2 Aesthetic value	Mirrors or windows used as decoration
3 Colour and pattern	Stained or textured glass is decorative. Tinted glass used to minimise solar heat transfer or vision
4 Corrosion resistance	External windows subjected to air pollutants, eg sulphur, carbon
5 Cost	Probably related to aesthetics
6 Durability	Impact resistance, also compression from window frames and tension on table tops
7 Electrical resistance	Consider light fittings
8 Elasticity	Required when used as coating material
9 Function	Eg allow maximum vision. Sound insulation
10 Light reflection	Windows usually do allow maximum light transfer
11 Porosity	Minimal for glazing
12 Prestige	To be in keeping with general design
13 Resiliance	Impact resistance
14 Slipperiness	To aid cleaning and soilage resistance
15 Strength	Security could be important feature
16 Temperature resistance	To prevent fire spread. Heat insulation
17 Transparency	May need to be transparent or translucent for privacy
18 Toughness	Shatter-proof materials may be required

External windows will be installed relatively early on in the construction of a building, other items of glazing, eg mirrors will be fitted during commissioning. Replacement cycles will be similarly variable. Glass, the traditional material used for glazing, is characteristically brittle and facilities to ease replacement must be considered.

Glass and glazing types, characteristics and selection

Glass The basic constituents for manufacture are silica, soda and lime. The main types are:

- soda lime glass
- lead crystal
- borosilicate

Soda lime glass is the basis of most flat glass used in windows and doors, specialised types include:

- toughened and laminated – for safety and security applications
- tinted – to provide colour and protection from solar radiation
- patterned – for privacy and decoration
- wired – for fire resistance
- organic coated – for safety and security.

Not only the ingredients for manufacture but the manufacturing process itself will determine the quality and characteristics of the finished product.

Plastics

Several types of plastic are used in glazing. The most common are:

- *polymethyl-methacrylate (acrylic)* which has good impact properties, used for security and for shower and bath enclosures.
- *polycarbonate* – virtually unbreakable when glazed
- *polyvinylchloride (rigid PVC)* – high resistance to breakage, good clarity and chemical resistance.

Plastics are available in flat sheet, patterned sheet or thermoformed shaped panels in a wide range of thicknesses and sizes, clear or tinted.

Comparing glass with plastics for glazing, in general terms, plastics have a higher resistance to impact and are less heavy; glass has better clarity, fire resistance and chemical resistance.

2.3.2.5 Sanitary fittings Sanitary fittings can be defined as *'appliances fitted to a drainage system for the collection and discharge of foul or waste matter.'* They are classified into two types:

- Soil appliances, used for the collection and discharge of excretory matter, eg wcs, urinals and slop sinks.
- Waste appliances for the collection and discharge of water after use, for ablutionary, culinary or other domestic purposes, eg baths, bidets, lavatory basins, sinks, showers and jacuzzis.

The relationship between sanitary fittings and the water supply has been covered in the *Environmental services* Section 2.3.1. Here the types and characteristics of the fittings themselves will be considered (see Figure 2.10). Not only the characteristics of the material, but also the shape and design of the sanitary fitting, will affect selection. To maximise hygiene standards and ease maintenance, sanitary fittings need to be streamlined without corners or crevices where soilage can collect. Also, the internal surface needs to be shaped to drain water, (here installation is important also), and the shape of the fitting should be such as to minimise soiling of surrounding surfaces during use.

Materials used for sanitary fittings, characteristics and selection

Ceramic

- *Fireclay* – strong but semi-porous thus glazing is important
- *Vitreous china* – non-porous with fused ceramic glaze

Cast Iron Mainly used for baths and coated with porcelain enamel.

Figure 2.10 Performance specification of sanitary fittings

Material properties	Possible application to sanitary fittings
1 Acoustic properties	Electrical apparatus eg dishwashers can be source of nuisance
2 Aesthetic value	Appearance may need to be in keeping with décor
3 Colour and pattern	Colour variety may be required. Smooth surfaces required for hygiene
4 Corrosion resistance	Besides water, uric acid, hypochloride and detergents are common contaminants
5 Cost	Dependant on replacement cycle
6 Durability	Resistance to impacts, particularly service sinks
7 Electrical resistance	Rarely a consideration
8 Elasticity	Rigidity usually required
9 Function	Must hold water and drain
10 Light reflection	Consider in relation to appearance
11 Porosity	Impervious surface required
12 Prestige	Shape and fittings affect overall appearance
13 Resiliance	Impact resistance
14 Slipperiness	To aid soilage resistance, but consider safety in baths and showers
15 Strength	To hold volume of water and user
16 Temperature resistance	Boiling water may be in contact
17 Transparency	Opaque usually required
18 Toughness	Chip resistance

Vitreous enamel steel   Steel is very strong but the enamel may chip, these appliances are noisy.
Stainless steel   May be mirror or satin finish, the satin having better resistance to scratching; good corrosion resistance; impact resistance is found a useful quality in areas where fittings are subject to very heavy use, or misuse.
Plastics   Acrylic or glass fibre reinforced acrylic plastic mouldings are very light weight (assisting installation), slip resistant, with good heat insulation properties, but abrasives, flames (eg cigarettes) and some chemicals, eg solvents may cause damage.

In selecting sanitary appliances, the appropriate auxiliary fittings such as taps and plugs must be considered.
Taps   Types include the conventional pillar type, spray taps, push-down, elbow action, supataps and electronically operated types.

Selection criteria will include:

• requirements of main users, eg nurses for hand washing, kitchen staff for vegetable preparation
• hygiene standards required
• hot water conservation
• type of drainage outlet and plug
• materials required, eg chromed brass, ceramic topped.

Plugs   Types of plugs include: conventional plugs on chains, captive plugs (which may be raised or lowered), standing wastes (hollow pipe waste fittings). Some installations, eg those fitted with spray taps, may not be designed to take plugs. (Hand washing under running water is more hygienic than filling a sink for washing.)

Cisterns   Types include bell type and plunger type. Materials include thermoplastics and vitreous china. Cisterns may be close coupled low level or high level and may be fitted with dual flush siphons (to reduce water consumption), or automatic flushers, eg urinals. Flushing troughs may be used which service several WCs or urinals.

In selecting suitable sanitary fittings, criteria for consideration include:

- material of the fitting and colour
- type of fitting
- shape and dimensions of fitting
- type, style and material of accessories.

With respect to numbers of fittings, there are specified legal requirements, dependant on the use of an establishment and the number of users.

Following selection, careful installation is necessary to ensure that the fittings work efficiently and without leakage and have an acceptable lifespan. The degree of slope to allow drainage, suitable jointing materials to provide hygienic and leak free finishes, careful attachment to plumbing system, and walls and floor anchorages and buffering are important.

2.3.2.6   Furniture   Furniture may be purchased for many reasons. A certain item may be acquired as a focal point in a room; other items might be bought in order to develop a theme, others for prestige. The majority of furniture is, however, bought primarily for functional reasons. It is needed to enable an activity to occur, or to occur with greater comfort.

To be functional, some basic criteria are necessary:

- it must meet customer requirements (the 'customer' being the main user of the furniture). These requirements can be identified by first analysing the activity or activities for which the user requires the furniture and then applying ergonomic theory (see Section 2.2.2.3(2)).

    For example, for a chair required by a secretary, the aspects of ergonomics are applied below:
- *anthropometric data*, eg the height, width and depth of seat, degree of slope
- *kinetics*, eg siting of back rest, knobs for adjusting heights, varying tilt, etc
- *applied physiology*, eg absorbtion quality of the material and heat transfer characteristics

- *applied psychology*, eg does it look like a secretary's chair, is there any prestige associated with its style?

The relationship of one piece of furniture with another is also important. In the example above, the chair and desk must be considered together.

- It must meet maintenance requirements (the 'maintainer' could be a domestic assistant in the case of table, chairs etc, or include an electrician in the case of a television). Again, ergonomic theory can be applied. As the activity changes, eg cleaning a chair, rather than sitting on it, so the requirements change.
- Furniture needs to be strong, if it is to be functional in public buildings. Furniture purchased for use by the public should be contract furniture and typical areas of weakness, such as joints, should be checked for durability.
- Stability is another requirement of contract furniture. It is an ergonomic requirement of users, but furniture should also be stable when not in use, eg empty wardrobes.
- Durability too is necessary. Replacement cycles of different establishments will vary. In some, the theme will be changed as frequently as biannually, but even so, contract furniture will be subject to heavy wear. In assessing durability, design, construction, finishing materials and finishes need consideration. The ability to make unit replacements, or component replacements must also be considered.
- Other characteristics required, might include:

  — stackability
  — manoeuvrability
  — fitted or free standing
  — adaptability
  — modular co-ordination, ie different units which all have a similar style.

As well as being functional, furniture needs to be aesthetically pleasing and suit the required décor of an area.

Finally, selection will be influenced by price in relation to the perceived standard of quality.

Furniture elements   When considering the qualities of any item of furniture, the individual elements of the item must be considered, namely:

- the basic structure material/materials, eg wood in many forms and composition, wicker, cane, plastic, metals, etc
- the finish/finishes, eg wax, french polish, nitrocellular, polyester, electroplating, lacquers, etc
- the upholstery materials – comprising filling or base and finish.

Bases   include foam, resilient webbing, tension springs, and *finishes* include vinyl, wool, fabrics and hide.

Figure 2.11 *Performance specification of furniture*

Material property	Revelance to structure	Relevance to finish	Revelance to upholstery material
Acoustic property	•	•	• (particularly bases)
Aesthetic value	• (shape)	• (appearance)	•
Colour and pattern	•	•	•
Corrosion resistance		Most relevance here	Relevance to finish
Cost	Each element affects overall cost		
Durability	• (joints)	• (corrosion and impact)	•
Electrical resistance			• (finish)
Elasticity			• (finish)
Function	•	•	•
Light reflection		•	• (finish)
Porosity		•	•
Prestige	•	•	•
Resilience		•	•
Slipperiness		•	• (finish)
Strength	•		
Temperature resistance		•	• (particularly base material fire resistance)
Transparancy		•	
Toughness		•	

In developing performance specifications for furniture, it is necessary to consider the requirements for each of the elements listed above as well as the requirements of the item as a whole (see Figure 2.11)

When furniture is successfully chosen it will be fit for its intended purpose, and its appearance will be pleasing. In these circumstances, together with consideration for its appropriate layout, users will be comfortable using the item, and are less likely to misuse it, such as swinging on chair legs, sitting on tables. Furniture is, therefore, more likely to be durable and its 'live costs' will be minimised.

2.3.2.7 Textiles Of the surface fittings so far considered, textiles are likely to have relatively short lives. By implementing a fairly short replacement cycle on furnishing, the décor of the establishment can be kept reasonably up to date without being unduly costly. Textiles include:

- carpets
- upholstery
- cushions
- pillows
- napiery
- towels

Figure 2.12 *Textiles: process and influence chart*

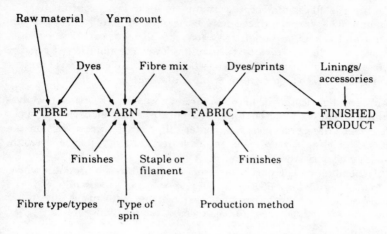

- uniforms
- bed linen and bedding
- curtains

Obviously, with such diverse uses as floor covering to napkins the performance criteria will vary considerably. Nevertheless, it will be useful to consider the basic material characteristics and to identify some applications. It must be remembered that, when dealing with textiles, many components combine to give the overall characteristics of a finished product as can be seen in the process and influence chart (Figure 2.12).

At each stage in the production ie yarn, fabric, finishing, the product's characteristics are augmented by various other factors.

Fibre   Fibres are classified as:
natural eg wool, cotton, silk flax
manufactured — regenerated eg rayon acetate
— synthetic, eg polyamides, polyesters, acrylics.

The fibre type influences the following characteristics of the finished product: micro- and macro-structures, appearance, tensile strength, elongation, elasticity, specific gravity, effect of moisture, thermal properties, effect of sunlight, chemical properties, effect of acid, alkali and organic substance, resistance to insects and micro-organisms and the electrical properties.

Yarn   Yarn is conventionally manufactured by the spinning process of drawing and twisting the fibres in a process of wet spinning, dry spinning or melt spinning. The fibres used may be staple (short), mono-filament (one continuous filament), multi-filament (several continuous filaments) or tow (many thousands of continuous filaments). The yarn produced may be simple, ie usually fibres of one kind and colour, although they may be blended; complex, eg slub, knot, loop, flock to give texture, and allow a combination of colours, fibres and thicknesses; textured (where synthetic continuous filament yarns are treated, eg to form crimp, bulk, loops).

Fabric   Fabric may be manufactured by weaving, knitting, a weave-knit process, felting or bonding. (A separate section on carpeting types follows.) These processes, too, confer different characteristics on the product such as texture, pattern, longevity, elasticity, tensile strength, specific gravity, thermal properties.

Depending on the particular process applied to the fibre and yarns already, eg dying, bleaching, fire resistance processing, etc, the finished fabric may be treated, eg by dying or printing, and other finishes applied, eg grease resistance, water repellance, etc.

Finished product   Other factors affecting quality include, eg quality of braiding round blankets, whether curtaining has bonded

Figure 2.13 *Performance specification for bed sheets*

Possible specification	Relevant fibre/fabric characteristics
1 Comfort	Absorbency, eg cotton, linen, silk Smooth soft texture, eg simple yarn, plain yarn or knit Low static, eg cotton, linen, silk Cool, eg cotton plain weave or warm, eg cotton flannelette
2 Durability — resistance to rubbing — resistance to snagging	 eg nylon, silk, eg plain weave or knit eg simple yarn, plain weave, cotton, linen, silk
3 Withstand high temperatures for laundering	eg cotton, linen
4 Alkali resistance for laundering agents	eg cotton, linen
5 Crease resistance – necessity for ironing	eg polyester, nylon
6 Suitable for storage – resistant to yeasts, fungi and moths	eg linen (kept dry), polyester
7 Good retention of shape and dimension	Low elastic properties, eg cotton, nylon, linen, polyester, close weaves, bonded fabrics
8 Light weight for ease of bed making	eg silk, polyester, plain knit or weave
9 Low cost	eg rayon, nylon
10 Appearance, eg colour variety	eg polyester, cotton, silk

lining or requires loose lining, quality of buttons, zips, etc, on uniforms, quality of stitching on hems.

It can be seen, therefore, that when selecting textiles, many factors influence the characteristics of the finished product, and a careful product specification must be proposed. As an example of how the theory works in practice, selection of bed sheets will be considered (see Figure 2.13).

Once a choice has been made with respect to fibre and fabric, another factor, influencing comfort, shape retention, cost and appearance is the process of manufacturing and finishing. Depths of hems, whether double hems are used, stitching, application of logos, etc, all must be considerd before a product is finally selected.

Thus, depending on the specific application, the financial constraints,customer comfort ratio, and the linen system operational, a selection could be made. It must be remembered that this approach is simplistic; there are many different types and grade of cotton for instance; a popular choice is a cotton/polyester mix; processes applied to the fibre will affect its overall attributes, eg polyester for sheeting may be subjected to singeing, desizeing, scouring and setting before a print, eg transfer print, is applied.

Carpets Much of the above information relating to other textiles is directly relevant to carpeting, eg fibre characteristics and yarn. The carpet manufacturing processes are easily comparable, but, nevertheless, worthy of identification and some comment:

Woven Woven carpets have the pile and backing woven simultaneously and tend to be the most expensive, combining resilience and appearance qualities with durability. There are three main types:

1 **Wilton** Due to the thickness of the backing (produced by carrying yarn under the carpet when it is not required in the pile pattern) and the usual density of the pile, these tend to represent good quality carpeting.
2 **Axminster** Backings are not always as thick as in Wilton carpeting, as colours are inserted only as required in the pattern. Qualities vary enormously depending on fibres, pile tufts per cm and rows per cm. Patterns in Axminsters can incorporate an infinite number of colours, unlike Wilton carpets where the maximum number of colours for practical reasons is five.
3 **Oriental** These are hand woven, if genuine, and are very hard wearing. Their high market values are due, not only to their practical qualities, but also to their aesthetic and ethnic values.

Tufted Tufted carpets are extemely popular, offering the appearance and resilience of a woven carpet at a lower cost. With good pile density and suitable fibre choice, they can compete well with woven types. Their lower cost is a consequence of the cheaper manufacturing process, whereby pile, primary backing and secondary backing/underlay are produced separately, then bonded together. The primary backing is merely a polypropylene or hessian material used, together with latex, to anchor the pile tufts.

Needlepunch   These are less resiliant, generally with lower appearance retention, but can represent very hard wearing floor coverings produced comparatively cheaply. A yarn is not required. Staple fibres are bonded together by the needlepunch process, in a comparable manner to the production of felted fabrics.

Adhesively bonded   Again, these carpets have relatively low resilience, though in appearance they may resemble a Wilton cord carpet. Spun or unspun fibres (depending on the particular process) are again bonded together, and the result is a low cost carpet, frequently with patterns limited to flecked shades.

Electrostatically bonded   These were initially used for car interiors and had rather low durability. Considerable advances have now been made with respect to durability. The carpet is very low pile with low resilience, but one option is for a non-porous floor covering which can withstand high temperatures, frequent cleaning, many chemicals and heavy wear.

Knitted   Knitted carpets are not common; drawbacks being, snagging pile and low dimensional stability. Technological development in knitting processes are, however, advancing rapidly, and new techniques may be applied to carpet manufacturing.

A few of the performance criteria to be considered when selecting carpeting have been considered. Figure 2.14 gives a more comprehensive list of these, together with the carpet characteristics most likely to affect them. As can be seen from this chart, the durability of the carpet is not only affected by the characteristics of the carpet itself, but also by the underlay used and the expertise applied to the fixing process. Some carpets need to be adhesively fixed to the floor, others perform better with perimeter fixing. In any case the floor surface to which they are applied needs to be clean, dry and even. The standard of cleaning and maintenance will also have considerable influence on a carpet's life.

2.3.3   Interior design

With respect to the interior of the building, an analysis has now been made of the environmental services and of the surface fittings. It will be useful to consider, briefly, how these two elements, together with the building envelope, and other design elements, may be integrated to produce functional and pleasing surroundings with the right mood, ambience and atmosphere. Comfortable users will be more likely to use the building carefully, and higher standards of cleaning and maintenance will be encouraged. The overall appearance of an establishment is an essential part of merchandising, and of the

Figure 2.14 *Performance criteria of carpets and the carpet characteristics most likely to affect these*

	Pile fibre	Pile density	Pile height	Loop or cut pile	Colour/ pattern	Manu- facturing process	Backing	Underlay	Fixing	Special treat- ment	Comments
Acoustic properties	•	•	•	•			•	•			Depending on specific qualities required
Appearance retention	•	•	•	•		•	•	•	•	•	
Colour fastness	•				•					•	
Compression and resiliance	•	•	•	•		•	•	•			May be short or long term loading
Dimensional stability	•					•	•	•	•		
Fire resistance	•						•	•		•	
Soiling resistance	•	•	•	•	•			•		•	May be real or apparent soilage
Static properties	•						•	•		•	Associated with low humidity
Thermal insulation	•	•	•	•				•			With underfloor heating low insulation required
Thickness retention	•	•	•	•		•	•	•	•	•	
Wear	•	•	•	•		•	•	•	•		

Figure 2.15 *Integrated design*

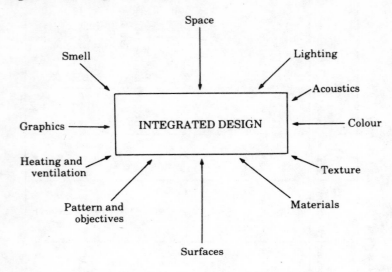

product image and internal comfort. The appropriateness of the décor and furnishings, and the efficiency of the environmental services are all part of sales promotion and user satisfaction.

The main design elements are shown in Figure 2.15. Many of these elements have been discussed earlier, but mainly in a practical vein. It will be useful now to consider psychological aspects as well. Consideration of each element as it integrates with other elements and its effect on the total décor are given below:

Space   One objective of interior design will be to maximise the use of space. Space represents capital outlay and other fixed and variable costs. Furniture layout, colour and pattern will encourage the use of space and, as well as being concerned with the efficiency of activities and the practicalities, the apparent shape and the mood or atmosphere can also be affected. Formality or informality within a room can largely be achieved by furniture layout.

Light   Once again the practical functions of lighting have already been considered, but this element, too, can go a long way to dictating atmosphere, eg efficiency, intimacy and entertainment. Lighting must be closely integrated with furniture layout and with colour, and it can be used to emphasise features, reveal or conceal, heighten or diminish spaces, create pattern, texture and colour contrast.

Acoustics   Practical aspects to consider, with respect to sound, include the reduction of 'noise', ie unwanted sound, and the reflection of other sounds. Machine noises, process noises, traffic noises, etc, need to be minimised (though, in the interests of safety, this is not invariably so – noise can act as a warning). Other sounds, eg a lecturer's voice, musical instruments, television, may need to be reflected within an area but not transmitted outside. Some sounds are more irritating than others; high frequencies cause more annoyance than low frequencies; intermittent noises more than constant. People can become accustomed to a certain type of noise. Noise may be airborne, eg external traffic, or resonating, eg door slamming, and different techniques can be applied to reduce each. Some methods of noise reduction are as follows:

- isolation of the noise source from other areas
- in planning interiors, activities identified as being noise sensitive, can be protected from noisy areas by placing intermediate rooms between them to baffle the noise, eg offices, sanitary areas, circulation areas, will be less noise sensitive than sleeping areas and lounges. Hotel bathrooms, grouped back-to-back, baffle the noise between one bedroom and another
- noisy rooms may be located near noisy exterior areas
- machinery radiating sound may be located in basement areas where the general building structure is likely to be heavier and more sound insulating and vibrations can be absorbed into the earth
- the selection of heavier construction materials will enable more noise to be absorbed, eg thick doors
- airborne exterior noise may be reduced by fitting airtight windows
- structural discontinuity reduces resonance, eg cavity walls and suspended ceilings
- noise may be reduced at source by insulating machines or rooms, eg use of soft furnishings and carpets, double-doors.

Colour Colour is said to induce a sense of comfort, discomfort, activity or calmness. Other psychological effects of colour are to enlarge or reduce apparent space, and to accentuate or disguise certain facets, eg sharp contrasts or bright colours. Whilst colour is a personal matter, good colour schemes can be admired by all and there are various classic schemes:

- *complementary* – using colours on opposite sides of the colour wheel
- *analogous* – adjoining colours on the colour wheel are used
- *monochromatic* – one colour is used with various tints and shades
- *triad* – contrasting colours are used against a neutral background.

Besides psychological effects, colour selection must be made with practical considerations in mind as well. Apparent soilage will depend on the colours of the soilage matter as well as the colours of the surfaces. Black is rarely the best colour to disguise soilage. With respect to carpets, research has shown that medium range colours, eg gold, generally give best results. Another practical consideration is the lighting type which will affect the perceived colour. It is essential that colours are chosen under the lighting conditions in the area in which it is to be used (this may well mean natural and artifical lighting conditions). Colour used well can have the maximum effect on the ambience level within a room for the minimum capital cost.

Texture   All materials have textural qualities and are perceived as having certain associated tactile qualities. Textural qualities will also affect acoustic properties. Variations in textures are required to give balance to a room, but too much variation in texture can be as disturbing and inappropriate as too little. Textural contrasts include warm and cold, soft and hard, shiny and dull, rough and smooth, antique and modern. Natural surfaces tend to have associated textures. Synthetic materials, although of similar types to each other, may have different textural qualities applied. To be used to the best advantage, textural qualities must be complemented by the lighting design. Practically, rougher, or varied textures, may show less soilage than smooth or plain textures, eg carpets compared with hard floor surfaces. They may also tend to trap soilage and be more difficult to clean. Compare, for instance, a textured wall plaster with a plastic laminate wall covering. In clinical areas, smooth surfaces are chosen for their low soilage holding capacity.

Materials   The practical considerations of material selection have been discussed earlier; the psychological aspects must be considered in relation to the other design elements in order to create balance and variety. Shapes, forms and dimensions of furniture need to be appropriate to those elements within the space, eg an antique theme would determine furniture styles and influence materials selection.

Pattern   Pattern may be achieved through colours, material variations, textures, lighting, fixtures, pictures, ornaments, etc. Psychological effects of pattern can be similar to the effects of colour, eg enlarging or diminishing space, creating atmosphere. Practical effects of pattern can be to disguise soilage and wear or, in clinical conditions, to reveal soilage.

Heating and ventilation   Many of the practical implications have already been explored. With respect to the psychological effects, again, the systems chosen need to be in keeping with the overall plan. Despite all their practical drawbacks, open fires are still used as focal points or to develop an atmosphere (though, frequently, the heat generated is supplementary to a central heating system, and the ventilation currents created may not always be desirable). In other situations, heating systems may be selected because they are barely visible and do not detract from the décor.

Graphics   In public buildings, signs, room numbers, directions and printed stationery are normal practice. The form of these graphics, as well as the location of signs, etc, must be considered from both a practical and psychological viewpoint. Practically, they must communicate effectively. Users may be of various nationalities, some may be disabled in some way. To communicate effectively then, the specific needs of different users must be considered. For example, the use of internationally recognised signs or multilingual signs, the use of Braille room numbers, the height at which signs should be placed in order for users in wheel chairs to be able to see them, may all be pertinent considerations. Other practicalities may include the need to meet legal obligations, eg for fire safety. From an aesthetic point of view, graphics must be considered with the general décor, design and possibly corporate image of the organisation in mind. Printed notepaper or names on buildings may be the first impression customers have of an establishment.

2.3.3.1 Principles of design From the above, a constant interlinking and cross referencing of design elements can be seen; none of the elements can be considered independently. Lighting installations affect colour perception, accentuate pattern and texture and can enlarge or diminish apparent space.

Colours must be balanced with pattern and texture and selections made in the lighting conditions of that space. Acoustic properties are affected by texture, material selection, dimensions of space and situation. In this manner, elements intermingle and, to achieve good integration, four overall principles have been identified:

- unity, variety and balance should be achieved, eg in line, form, texture and colour. If several colours are used, texture and pattern variations should balance this. A sense of order is required, without becoming monotonous
- one centre of interest or one dominant idea should be identified
- the design should incorporate rhythm, which is a means of leading the eye to the centre of interest
- there should be good proportions and scale, eg of patterns, furniture and dimensions

Integrated design must create environments which are, above all, safe to use. They must be practical and they must achieve the right atmosphere for the planned activities.

2.4 SECURITY

In the design of a building, great care and consideration must be given to the aspects of security. Whilst systems may be developed by management to improve security by such measures of staff awareness, controlling building access, etc, security cannot be considered as an 'add on extra' when the building is completed. Public buildings are inevitably security risks, by the very fact that so many people have access to them. They must, therefore, be designed and constructed for security, without this conflicting too blatantly with appearing welcoming to the bona fide customer.

The siting of entrances and the internal layout can greatly assist in the monitoring of those entering and leaving the building. Lobbies and entrances/waiting areas are particularly vulnerable, as they are public places.

Security provision must be made for the protection of all building users, buildings, interior plant, equipment, furniture and furnishings and for property owned by staff and customers. Security threats include: intrusions, attack, vandalism, dishonesty and fire.

It is necessary, in the first place, to identify the risks in order to produce a policy statement indicating the security measures to be taken to minimise these risks. This will include a building survey to determine the vulnerability of the premises and structural alterations which are necessary.

The following checklist is based on a series of questions on security issued by the Metropolitan Police Hotel Collation and Intelligence Unit.

2.4.1   Security of premises

Grounds

- Do you control entrances/exits to the grounds of your property?
- Is lighting on drives, pathways and in car parks adequate at night?
- Is surveillance equipment in the grounds required for the well being of building users?
- Do you need security patrol services particularly in the evening/ during the night?

Buildings

- Do you control entrances/exits to buildings?
- Do you need surveillance equipment particularly at certain/ unattended entrances/exits?
- Do you lock entrances/exits at night?
- Do you restrict entry to certain areas and need ID/authorisation?
- Do you need anti-intrusion devices, eg security lights, alarms, barred windows, non-drying paints, wedges on windows?
- Do you train personnel to report suspicious people?
- Do you regularly check fire exits to ensure they are secured from the inside?
- Are cash/wages offices easily accessible to the public and/or personnel?
- Do you have a laid down procedure for personnel in the event of armed robbery, terrorist attack and bomb scares and are they regularly reviewed?
- Do you regularly check doors and locks to ensure they are in good working order?
- Do you know how many grand master/master and sub-master keys there are, who the holders are and if they still have them? Do they

have to sign them in and out and hand them in before leaving the premises?
- Do you maintain a register of lost keys?

Hotel property

- Do you take up references for all personnel before engaging them?
- Do you include a 'right of search' of staff in their contract of employment?
- Do you have a 'pass out' system for staff taking property out of the premises?
- Do you have a clear company policy for the prosecution of persons committing offences?
- Do you thoroughly check all deliveries of stock?
- Do you make checks on property leaving the premises such as waste or laundry?
- Do you have master keys for staff lockers?
- Do you spot check staff cash/stock balances?
- Do you avoid banking cash on a regular basis?
- Do you accept 'chance' reservations without pre-payment?
- Do you institute an efficient credit check of customer accounts?
- Do you take reasonable precautions to prevent/reduce crime on the premises?
- Are all serial numbers of major pieces of equipment recorded?

Customers

- Do you properly register customers (as required by law)?
- Do you display the notice setting out liabilities of the hotel under the Hotels Proprietors Act 1956 (or equivalent elsewhere)?
- Do you issue all customers with key identification cards?
- Are blank key cards kept out of reach of the general public?
- Do you supply safety deposit facilities for customers?
- Do you keep duplicate keys for the above elsewhere than on the premises?
- Do you encourage customers to use safety deposit facilities, by publicising them?
- Do you provide room safes free of charge (with a disclaimer on the safe to overcome the operation's liability)?
- Are key boards visible (accessible by the general public)?
- Do you ensure room keys are not left on the reception desk and provide a 'deep' key deposit box?
- If a customer's room key is lost, is the room lock changed?
- Do you reserve a series of rooms for single women guests which are 'secure'/nearer reception/not on the ground floor?
- Do you avoid allocating a room to a single woman amidst rooms allocated to men?
- Do you avoid announcing loudly the room number allocated to a single woman on registration?
- Are bedroom doors secure with chains and spy holes?

Concept Map summarizing the building.

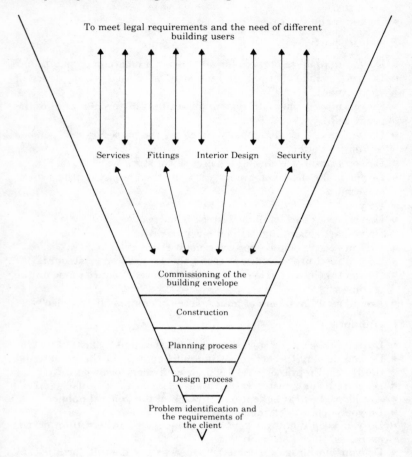

To meet legal requirements and the need of different
building users

Services   Fittings   Interior Design   Security

Commissioning of the
building envelope

Construction

Planning process

Design process

Problem identification and
the requirements of
the client

Many large operations have their own Security Manager and teams of professional security personnel; in many other cases security is an important role of the portering department. Really everyone within the operation has a responsibility for security and as such the biggest single security measure is training personnel to be ever-watchful, know what to look for and what action to take. Attempts should also be made to make customers more security conscious.

The whole or part of the security system may be contracted out. For instance, in very large hotels/condominiums or college/university campuses, grounds and/or night security may well be contracted out to a security firm. The cost and sophistication of any measures implemented will depend on the perceived risk.

Further reading

Architects' and Specifiers' Guide to: Doors and Windows; Fabrics, Wallcoverings and Furniture

BENNETT, H, *Who Needs Architecture?* Health Services Management, October 1991

BILLINGHAM, N and ROBERTS, B, *Building Services Engineering*, Pergamon 1982

BORSENIK, FRANK, D, *The Management of Maintenance and Engineering Systems in Hospitality Industries*, Wiley Management Services 1979

BRE Digest: *Services and Environmental Engineering*

BRE Digest: *Energy Heating and Thermal Comfort* Constructional Press 1978

Croner's Record Keeping Book for COSHH, 1989, Croner Publications Ltd

DARTFORD, JAMES, *Architects' Data Sheets: Dining Spaces*, Architecture Design and Technology Press 1990

EDWARDS, J K P. *Floors and their Maintenance*, Butterworth 1969

Energy Manager's Workbook, Energy Publications BIM and Dept Energy 1985

GORDON, J E, *The New Science of Strong Materials*, Pelican 1968

Health and Safety Executive, *Health and Safety (First Aid) Regulations*, 1981

Health and Safety Executive, *Reporting of Injuries, Diseases and Dangerous Occurrences Regulations* (1985)

Hotel Catering and Institutional Management Association Technical Briefs No 1 *Precautions Against Legionnaires Disease*

No 2 *Precautions Against Aids*

No 4 *Keeping Pests out by Design*

No 7 *Guide to Electric Lighting*

No 16 *Choosing Your Gas Boiler*

No 19 *Providing Accessible Accommodation*

HOPE, PETER, S, editor, *Handbook of Building Security and Design* 1979

JONES, DR W T, *The Health and Safety at Work Act: A Practical Point of View*, Graham and Trothers

LAWSON, F R, *Hotels, Motels and Condominiums*, Architectural Press 1976

LAWSON, F R, *Restaurants Clubs and Bars*, Archictectural Press 1987

LEE, R, *Building Maintenance Management*, Crosby, Lockwood and Staples 3rd edition 1987

McLAUGHLIN, T P, *The Cleaning Hygiene and Maintenance Handbook*, Business Books 1969

PITA, EDWARD G, *Air Conditioning Principles and Systems: An Energy Approach* 2nd edition, Prentice-Hall 1989

RIBA, *Commissioning an Architect*

STONE, PETER, editor, *British Hospital and Health Care Buildings*. Architectural Press 1980

TUCKER and SCHNEIDER, *Professional Housekeeper*, Cahners 1975

WISE, ALAN F, *Water, Sanitary and Waste Services for Buildings*, Mitchell's Professional Library 1986

Assignment tasks

1 Describe the Rational Design Network and explain why this is the most likely process to be applied when public buildings are designed.
2 Discuss the role of the Executive Housekeeper as a member of the planning team for a new hotel.
3 Prepare an evaluation sheet which could be used to carry out the first stage of an energy audit in a public building of your choice
4 Compare the environmental service requirements of hotel guests with those of shoppers in a department store, making recommendations.
5 Explain the principles of design and evaluate the integration of design in a reception area of a named public building.
6 Design a lighting system for a student's study bedroom justifying your reasons for choice.

Accommodation Services

Objectives

- To consider the aims, scope, characteristics and management of the maintenance, housekeeping and linen and laundry services.
- To discuss infection control and the implementation of a hygiene policy.
- To highlight issues relating to waste disposal.
- To consider the provision of floral and pest control services.

3.1 HOUSEKEEPING AND MAINTENANCE SERVICES

3.1.1 Scope and characteristics

Housekeeping is defined here as the cleaning and maintenance of the interior of a building and the provision of tangible client-care services such as beverage, laundry and dry cleaning services.

Maintenance refers to the upkeep of the fabric of the building, including its exterior, the plant, eg mechanical ventilation systems and lifts, and services such as gas and electricity. Maintenance normally encompasses care of the grounds of the property.

Both housekeeping and maintenance may involve customer contact (ie the intangible element). The extent and scope of the contact will be variable, ranging from a floor housekeeper negotiating a request with an individual customer, to a maintenance engineer encountering the general public whilst servicing a lift. A contract cleaning operative, however, will have no contact with customers when cleaning offices or departments at night. Indeed, customer interface may well be an important aspect of an operative's job such as a domestic assistant on a hospital ward.

The scope of housekeeping and maintenance services is variable, with housekeeping varying from purely a cleaning service in one operation to cleaning, maintenance and extensive client-care services in another, such as a five star hotel or private hospital. The scope of maintenance varies from a part-time odd job person in a very small operation, eg private hotel to a full complement of maintenance personnel in a large hotel or district hospital.

Although cleaning may be perceived as an integral part of the total maintenance system, contributing to the overall aim of the maintenance plan (which is to extend the physical life of the building) in reality these two services are usually separate ventures, each service having its own organisational structure and managed by its own departmental head. The Head of Maintenance is often a professional engineer or surveyor.

The success of any housekeeping and maintenance service is influenced by company policy and the attitude of higher management to the value of these services within the total operation and, hence, whether or not the necessary finance is made available.

The only feasible housekeeping or maintenance system to adopt is one which is planned. This involves analysing the building users' requirements and the physical needs of the building, and then programming the appropriate activities to be undertaken at optimum frequencies.

The alternative, which unfortunately often exists in practice, is a haphazard system where, as R. LEE (1987)[1] suggests, 'over a period of time a number of unrelated compromises between the physical needs of the building and the available finance occur', usually as a result of crises management where little attention is paid to the inevitable consequences of such ad hoc arrangements.

It is vital to consider the benefits of cleaning and maintenance, and their cost, in the context of the whole enterprise and the total building needs, bearing in mind that there may be several properties involved over a wide radius.

3.1.2   Benefits of a planned system

The benefits to be gained from adopting a planned housekeeping and maintenance system can be considered in financial, functional, aesthetic and human terms.

- **Financial benefits**
  Over a period of time, it should prove more cost effective to provide cleaning and maintenance services on a regular planned basis, so extending the life span of equipment, plant, surfaces, furniture, fittings and furnishings, and deferring the heavy expenditure of frequent replacements or renovations.

  A haphazard system does tend to result in more frequent replacement costs and/or high renovation costs.

  A planned system involves levelling out costs over the cycle, rather than incurring extreme fluctuations from year to year. The property value might be reduced if little attention has been paid to cleaning and maintenance over a period of time and deterioration has occurred.

A building maintained in a good state of repair and décor is easier to clean and promote. Occupancy levels can be maintained, if not improved, and sales and productivity increased.

- **Functional benefits**
Effective cleaning and maintenance should preserve the physical characteristics of the building and its surfaces and services, ensuring that everything functions satisfactorily, thus preventing rapid deterioration and breakdown. Inconvenience, down-time of equipment and plant and the probability of accidents and emergency repairs are reduced, and future cleaning and maintenance costs lowered.
- **Aesthetic benefits**
Cleaning is not only essential to retain the appearance of surfaces and total areas, both inside and outside the building, but in some cases actually improves appearance. For instance, by using initial treatments, such as a pigmented seal, the appearance of a concrete floor can be improved. This action also prevents the dust worn off bare concrete from being trodden elsewhere. Appearance and apparent cleanliness do have a psychological effect on the building users, whether customers or personnel, who may make a value judgement of the total experience based on their perception (often their initial perception) of appearance and standards of cleanliness.

In a profit-making operation particularly, first impressions are important. Surveys undertaken in the past have shown that aesthetic standards do affect reputation and repeat business and, as such, can be regarded as part of the corporate image and marketing strategy.
- **Human benefits**
Clean, attractive, well-maintained surroundings are more pleasant, enjoyable and comfortable for customers to use, increase customer satisfaction, affect repeat business and improve public image. They also encourage good working standards, pride in work, personal appearance and morale of personnel. These not only affect labour turnover and recruitment generally but are also of paramount importance when motivating personnel to maintain quality building standards.

Cleaning and maintenance also contribute to the removal of fire, health, hygiene and safety hazards. Since the implementation of the Health and Safety at Work Act 1974 in Britain, the health, both physical and mental, and the safety of all building users must be maintained.

3.2 THE MAINTENANCE SERVICE

3.2.1 Aims

Maintenance can extend the physical life of a building almost indefinitely, provided the structure of the building is sound initially.

Effective maintenance will delay deterioration and replacement and so defer the expenditure on new construction. If the building has been designed with flexibility in mind and can be modified internally to accommodate changing user requirements, maintenance can be regarded as a substitute for new construction, but only if the building remains functionally satisfactory. A relationship does exist between the adaptability of the original building design, the life of the building, maintenance costs and new construction costs.

The extent to which maintenance is considered at the design stage is likely to depend on whether the client commissioning the construction of the building is likely to be the subsequent proprietor, manager or user. For instance a Property Developer may not be interested in knowing that a white sheet vinyl floor covering in the entrance of a building will be more costly to clean than an alternative floor covering.

Unfortunately, in some cases maintenance (and cleaning) seems to be the last consideration at the design stage (see Chapter 2).

3.2.2   Definitions

There are numerous definitions of maintenance including the British Standard definition (BS 3811: 1964) which defines maintenance as: '*a combination of any actions carried out to retain an item in or restore it to an acceptable condition*'. However, the following definition seems more useful:

> '*Work undertaken in order to keep, restore or improve every facility, ie every part of the building, its services and surrounds, to a currently acceptable standard and to sustain the utility and value of the facility.*' HMSO (1972)[2]

It infers that there are several dimensions of maintenance to consider: *firstly* that maintenance is about preventive action, ie keeping or retaining an acceptable standard where maintenance is carried out in anticipation of failure. *Secondly* that maintenance involves restoring to an acceptable standard, in other words carrying out maintenance activities after failure has occurred, ie a corrective action.

Thirdly that maintenance involves some degree of improvement, for instance replacing or renewing with an improved component, which is endorsed by reference to a *currently* accepted standard, which implies a standard higher than the initial one.

However, the perception of what is an *accepted standard* will vary according to the viewpoint of the client paying for the work, the building user, or an outside authority enforcing minimum standards, such as the Fire Authority or Health and Safety Inspector.

3.2.3 Developing a maintenance policy

BS 3811: 1964 defines a maintenance policy as a *'strategy within which decisions on maintenance are taken'*. Alternatively it can be defined as: *'the ground rules for the allocation of resources (men, materials and money) between alternative types of maintenance action available to management.'* (LEE 1987)[1]

In order to make a rational allocation of resources it is necessary to identify the benefits of maintenance activities to the whole operation and consider the costs involved.

The following questions need to be asked:

- what does maintenance have to achieve, ie the objectives, which must be considered in the context of the organisation's overall building needs?
- what is to be gained, ie the benefits, in the short and long term and in financial, technical, aesthetic and human terms?
- what strategies need to be implemented?

The maintenance policy devised will be influenced by company policy, the attitude of higher management, available finance and the number and locations of the buildings involved. Operational and cost objectives will have to be formulated which will involve analysing the needs and requirements and usage of the building and thus identifying the maintenance activities to be undertaken, the quality standards to be achieved and the financial framework and budget limitations within which to operate. A balance has to be achieved between preventive and corrective maintenance to ensure that preventive measures are not carried out more often than necessary, incurring excessive expenditure. A balance also has to be achieved between maintenance activities which can be programmed, such as repainting, roof tile replacement and window cleaning, and work which is requisitioned by the building user, such as emergency repairs, eg replacing a washer, mending the toilet, or new requirements such as putting up shelves on a small scale, or modification of space for a new use on a larger scale. In most operations a proportion of maintenance work tends to be put out to contract. Company policy will dictate the extent to which maintenance is contracted out and the type of maintenance activities put out to contract but a balance between direct and contract labour should be sought.

The outcome of these considerations will affect the structure and staffing of the maintenance department. Where a number of properties are involved, the extent to which day to day management of the maintenance function is decentralised will have to be decided.

3.2.4 Planned preventative maintenance (PPM)

In the interests of efficiency there is only one maintenance system that can be adopted and that is a planned preventative maintenance system rather than the ad hoc system which was referred to in Section 3.1.1.

A *planned preventative maintenance system* is one which ensures that all the maintenance activities (which must be carried out to ensure that the building structure, surfaces, plant, services, equipment, etc, meet an acceptable condition) are identified and undertaken at prescribed intervals according to a predetermined plan. This system obviously relies on a good recording and retrieval system.

LEE (1987)[1] suggests that a planned preventive maintenance system must possess at least four essential features, namely that:

- failures must be anticipated
- appropriate procedures for prevention and rectification must be devised
- a course of action to deal with the inevitable consequences of deterioration must be planned
- measures for even remote possibilities must be devised.

However, a planned preventive system is only acceptable if it

- is cost effective
- meets statutory and other legal requirements
- reduces the incidence of faults which precipitate user requisitions
- meets operational needs
- ensures a higher percentage of actual work for the skilled maintenance personnel to undertake rather than purely inspection of items
- has the backing and support of senior management
- is an integral part of total company policy.

The concept of PPM is more often applied to plant and equipment which are subject to mechanical wear, but most building elements such as walls, windows and roofs can also justify inclusion in this system.

3.2.4.1 The benefits of planned maintenance systems

When devising a maintenance policy, it is essential to consider the benefits of a planned maintenance programme, the objectives which should be achieved and the costs involved in the context of the whole operation. It is vital to consider both the short-term and the long-term benefits of maintenance, the latter often being swept aside. It is usual, for maintenance purposes, to define the life cycle of a building, which is often a 60 year span, but some buildings or parts of buildings, eg portacabins, will have a much shorter life cycle.

3.2.5 Devising a planned preventative maintenance system

When devising a planned preventative maintenance system, the factors to consider are not unlike those involved in devising the cleaning programme discussed in Section 3.3.

3.2.5.1 Building survey A building survey must be undertaken to evaluate and record the existing and anticipated future state of each building element, service, utility, plant, etc.

This database then forms the basis for forecasting and estimating maintenance operations over a period of time (the maintenance cycle is based on the defined life cycle of the building). The information recorded will include a description of construction materials used, state of repair, problems, and any other information deemed appropriate. Figure 3.1 identifies the scope of the maintenance system.

Figure 3.1 *Scope of maintenance*

	Internal	External
Plant	Heating, lighting, ventilation centralised vacuumation, lifts and escalators, plumbing	Lighting, fuel stores
Services	Electricity, gas, water	Drainage, sewage
Machinery and equipment	Catering, laundry, cleaning, firefighting, access	Transport, fire fighting, access
Specialised areas	Swimming pools, operating theatres, computer rooms	Swimming pools, gazebos, barbecue areas
Building envelope	Doors, windows, walls, ceilings, paintwork, structural repairs, redecoration	Roof, guttering, fire escapes, masonry, chimneys, paintwork, windows, structural repairs, redecoration
Site		Gardens, pathways, fences, gates, boundary walls

3.2.5.2 Maintenance operations The maintenance operations or tasks necessary to combat progressive deterioration and retain or restore the item to an acceptable functional or aesthetic condition must now be defined. LEE (1987)[1] suggests that these generally include:

- patching or more or less regular replacement of small parts or areas
- replacement of whole elements or components which are:
    - not working satisfactorily
    - incurring high running or maintenance costs
    - aesthetically unacceptable
- application of protective coatings to extend life or preserve or improve appearance
- cleaning to arrest deterioration or preserve appearance.

3.2.5.3   Frequencies   The frequencies of maintenance activities are more difficult to predict than cleaning tasks (see Section 3.3.2.3) as it is harder to know with certainty the precise outcome of the effects of wear and tear and deterioration on the properties and life span of building elements, services, plant, etc. LEE (1987)[1] again suggests that it is convenient to group together those elements which are probably likely to fail at a similar rate. Figure 3.2 outlines his suggested grouping.

Figure 3.2 *Groups of elements subject to similar rates of failure (LEE, 1987)[1]*

Group 1	those elements likely to last the lifetime of the building, without requiring attention, if properly designed and constructed, eg foundations
Group 2	those elements whose life can be prolonged by the replacement of small parts at more or less regular intervals, eg rooftiles (although there will be a time when it is more economic to renew the whole)
Group 3	those elements subject to wear by the building user and the activities which they perform, eg floor surfaces subject to heavy traffic
Group 4	those elements prone to obsolescence as a result of technological advances or changing fashion, eg heating and ventilation systems
Group 5	those elements which are exposed to climatic conditions, which in time may fail or disfigure, eg wall claddings
Group 6	those elements with protective finishes for aesthetic or functional purposes, eg metals, timber floors

The frequency of maintenance tasks will also be affected by climatic conditions, the building user, and user activities. The deterioration caused by these maintenance generators may be viewed as 'normal' or 'abnormal' LEE (1987).[1] The extent to which these factors influence the frequency of maintenance tasks will depend on the following:

- the fitness for purpose of the surfaces/materials used
- the suitability of the original design
- the standard of work in the initial construction and subsequent maintenance of the property
- the extent to which future needs and expectations have been anticipated in the initial design
- the extent to which changing tastes and fashions can be accommodated (these may create a demand for maintenance activities rather than cause deterioration of the existing elements)

- the effect of deterioration in one element subsequently causing deterioration in another.

An attempt should be made to reconcile the potential cost of maintenance over a period of time, with the potential cost of failure over the same period. For instance, an item may be purchased and various maintenance actions scheduled over a 10-year period at a particular cost whereas if no maintenance occurred that same item may last eight years before failure and then have to be replaced. The replacement cost may be less than the maintenance cost with the added value of purchasing a new 'state of the art' item.

3.2.5.4 Programming When planning the frequencies of maintenance activities and deciding what tasks have to be undertaken at what period of time, it is useful to anticipate the probable condition of each element or item at regular intervals throughout the defined life cycle of the building, and estimate the cost of remedial work at

Figure 3.3 *Matrix of the anticipated condition of the building elements*

	0	5	10	15	20	25	30	35	40	45	50	55	60 years
Constructional Framework													
Roof construction													
Frame													
Storey floors													
Ground floor													
Foundations													
Decoration													
Ironmongery eg fire escapes													
Steps													
Building exterior													
Roof covering													
External walls – pointing													
Windows													
Doors													
Drainage													
Signs													

Figure 3.3 *Continued*

External works	0	5	10	15	20	25	30	35	40	45	50	55	60 years
Gardens													
Pathways													
Boundary fences													
Gates													
Cattle grids													
Lighting													
Summer houses													
Signs													
Interior													
Stairs													
Wall finishes													
Partitions													
Floor finishes													
Ceiling finish													
Decoration													
Sanitary fittings													
Water													
Heating – boiler pipes and radiators													
Electrical wiring fittings													
Lighting													
Lift and escalators													
Signs													

these times. The data can be collated in matrix form either manually or by computer. See Figure 3.3.

Decisions will have to be made as to when it is most viable to repair, replace partially or totally renew. Replacement and renewal decisions have to be considered when a component or whole element is either functionally or aesthetically unsatisfactory or repairs and running

Figure 3.4 *Impact of increased user requirements versus deterioration over time*

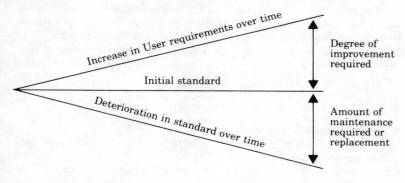

costs are excessive. Thought also has to be given to replacing or renewing with the same or an improved component or whole element. Most maintenance tasks usually involve some degree of improvement, as explained in Figure 3.4.

It is now possible to build up a cost pattern for each building element or item. This indicates the estimated cost of each maintenance activity for that element or item at specified frequencies over the cycle period. This is of value when analysing the maintenance profile of the whole property.

For programming purposes, maintenance activities tend to fall into two types:

1 tasks initiated by the Maintenance Manager
2 tasks requested by the building users.

The former can be easily planned in advance and generally includes the larger, less frequent activities involving high expenditure. These are usually necessary for the long-term preservation of the building. Unfortunately these activities are not always perceived by Senior Management as being urgent or necessary, and the apportioned capital is often subject to cut-backs. Inspections required to predict future requirements and consequently prevent problems occurring also need to be programmed.

On the other hand, user requests are not so easy to programme as the work usually tends to involve a high proportion of small jobs which tend to be urgent, if not emergencies, such as unblocking a toilet or an electrical fault. An allowance must be included to allow the necessary resources to be available for this type of activity. The building user might also request alterations and conversion particularly when the use of an area changes or a new activity is to be performed, eg leisure activities in an hotel. A PPM system should reduce the number of emergencies and user requests.

Generally, maintenance tasks are scheduled on a short-term, even immediate basis, medium-term and long-term basis. Operational management techniques, such as network analysis and other project management techniques, are useful aids for programming long term activities and queueing theory is applicable for short term programming.

3.2.5.5   Control of the maintenance programme

- **Bring forward system**

  It is vital, especially where long-term maintenance activities are concerned, to implement an effective and foolproof bring-forward system to ensure that due tasks are brought to the attention of the Maintenance Manager, so that resources can be allocated. The bring-forward system can be manual or computerised.

- **Monitoring**

  Continual performance monitoring is essential to ensure that:

  - maintenance staff are being used effectively and not under or overloaded
  - maintenance activities are undertaken in accordance with the programme, at the right time and to the defined quality standard
  - costs are commensurate with the benefits of the PPM system
  - there is a reduction in emergency work and user requests.

- **Cost control**

  Maintenance Management tend to use a system of job costing whereby a cost, including materials, parts and labour, is estimated for an activity. This is adjusted in light of experience and becomes a 'standard cost' or yardstick for future activities. It is also useful to analyse the percentage expenditure spent on the various maintenance activities such as painting and decoration, fabric maintenance, grounds maintenance, plant, services, utility maintenance, etc, to see where high and low expenditure exists and investigation is needed. This can be presented in pie chart format and used to analyse trends over a period of time.

  Maintenance cost in some organisations are apportioned – often on a percentage basis to each operating department or they may be written off as an overhead expenditure against the total operation.

  Maintenance costs can be expressed as:

  - a percentage of the initial cost of the building
  - unit cost per $100m^2$ of floor area.

  The pattern of maintenance costs over the life of a building is known as the *maintenance profile* and is often presented as a histogram (see figure 3.5).

  The peaks of expenditure are normally attributed to major

renewals and replacements which could be deferred if necessary but may then incur higher running costs and some loss of amenity. It is useful, where a number of properties are involved, to analyse the maintenance profiles of each property with a view to making adjustments to tasks and frequencies to achieve a more uniform workload and distribution of expenditure over a period of time.

- **Analysis**
  It may be useful to evaluate which activities or costs are regarded as normal in relation to the property design, constructional materials and function of the building; which result from design faults, technical errors re choice of materials, layouts, etc, and which result from demands for better standards or changed uses which could not have been anticipated in the original design.

  The ratio between total costs and administrative costs may also be analysed.

3.2.5.6 Maintenance manual Ideally a maintenance manual should be created for any building, particularly a new one. It should contain:

- the working plans of the building
- dimensions of each area
- specifications of materials used for both exterior and interior surfaces and fittings
- maintenance requirements for each element and each area plus details of finishes and treatments given.

Figure 3.5 *Sample maintenance profile*

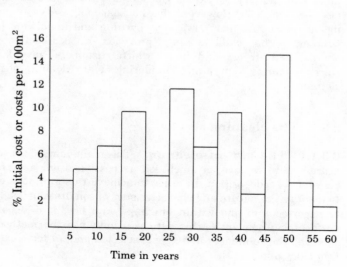

It should, of course, be updated when maintenance has been undertaken or alterations have been made to the building. It should be passed on with the sale of a property to the new owners. This manual will be invaluable to subsequent Maintenance Managers and provide useful information to the Cleaning Manager as well.

Insufficient historical information about a building can lead to expensive mistakes and inefficiencies.

3.2.6   The customer

The design, condition and appearance of a building must have an impact on the building user – both internal and external customers. How many potential customers never even enter a property because they are 'put off' by its external appearance or state of repair? How many customers never return because they are unimpressed by the standards of décor, cleanliness and/or maintenance? It is impossible to equate the quantity of business lost in this way against the cost of maintenance. The customer must therefore be an important resource to be enticed into the building initially and then used as a valuable source of information for quality assurance and product development.

3.3   THE HOUSEKEEPING SERVICE

The main part of the housekeeping service relates to the cleaning of the building interior. This may or may not incorporate the cleaning of 'linens' and soft furnishings. For the purposes of this book the linen and laundry service is considered as a separate sub-system (see Section 3.6). However, the housekeeping service could also include such customer services as packing and unpacking luggage, running baths, child-minding, provision of bed-boards, ironing boards, hair dryers and items which customers have forgotten, shirt laundering service and laundering or dry cleaning of personal clothing.

3.3.1   The cleaning service

3.3.1.1   The aim of cleaning   The main aim of the cleaning process is to remove as much soil as possible from a surface and prevent its redeposition. In order to achieve this aim, it is essential to identify the nature and characteristics of soil, its sources, how it is transported into and within buildings, and how it is deposited on surfaces. Subsequently, this data will influence the method of soil removal, the equipment and agents selected and, to some extent, the frequency of removal.

3.3.1.2 Defining standards of cleanliness The standard of cleanliness required in a particular area will depend on the following factors:

- the user's requirements
- the user's activities
- the type of area
- the infection risk
- the type of establishment
- the available finance.

The standard set for a particular area will define the appearance and the level of hygiene required.
Different standards will of course be required in:

- different areas within the same building, eg operating theatres and offices.
- the same type of area in different types of establishments, eg a hospital dayroom and a students common room.

Generally standards of cleanliness are defined as either *aesthetic* where the objective is to achieve a clean, pleasant and attractive appearance or *clinical* where the objective is also to remove as much soil and therefore micro-organisms as possible, prevent cross infection and achieve as high a degree of hygiene as deemed necessary for that particular area. The infection risk in specified areas can be identified and in high risk areas, such as operating theatres, infectious diseases units and burns units, the emphasis must be on achieving aseptic conditions.

Although not stated as such, two factors are implicit from the above definitions. Firstly there are varying degrees of each type of cleanliness and secondly aseptic conditions can never be totally achieved in environmental cleaning.

Different writers have defined standards of cleanliness in rather different ways. Figure 3.6 attempts to correlate three other authors' definitions.[4,5]

Figure 3.6 *Spectrum of Standards (ALLEN, JONES and PHILLIPS)[4,5]*

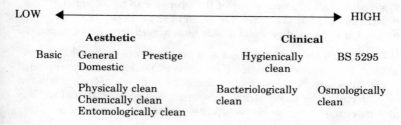

LOW				HIGH
	Aesthetic		**Clinical**	
Basic	General Domestic	Prestige	Hygienically clean	BS 5295
	Physically clean Chemically clean Entomologically clean		Bacteriologically clean	Osmologically clean

The standards of cleanliness actually achieved will depend on:

- the time allowed for the cleaning tasks to be accomplished
- methods of cleaning selected
- adequacy of type, design, condition and quantity of equipment and supplies
- capabilities and motivation of staff
- training
- supervision
- frequency of cleaning
- existing condition of surfaces and items
- the amount of use and/or abuse of the item or area.

Cost, of course, will be a constraint. Frequencies, costs and standards are interlinked. Frequencies and standards in a given situation have to be correlated. Generally speaking the more frequently a task is performed or an area cleaned, the higher the standard of cleanliness achieved and also the cost. However, a too high frequency of some tasks could result in lower standards but even higher costs. For instance, too frequent floor polish application can eventually reduce appearance and result in a higher proportion of time and effort to remove the build-up.

3.3.2   Planning the cleaning service

Planning the cleaning service will involve analysing both the needs of the building and its users (whether personnel, customers or clients) in order to determine what tasks and services have to be undertaken. Once this has been done, the effective methods, equipment and agents required for each task can be assessed and standards of performance specified, including optimum frequencies for performing tasks.

This information forms the basis for estimating human resource levels and subsequently scheduling and rostering of personnel. These aspects will be considered in Chapter 4.

3.3.2.1   Specification of work
Firstly it is essential to produce a specification of the work or tasks to be undertaken. This will basically involve:

- specifying all physical areas of the property to be included
- identifying all tasks, activities or services to be performed
- specifying the quality standards to be achieved. (See also Chapter 7.)

This will ensure that all areas and activities are included and none left out. In a contract situation if an area or task has not been included in the work specification and has therefore not been costed, it will not be undertaken by the contract personnel. The specification of work is also essential in the in-house situation in order to avoid those 'grey areas', which are either not undertaken by anyone or duplicated by different members of staff.

This specification of work lays down the ground rules or terms of reference for the cleaning or housekeeping service and forms the basis for estimating human resource levels and producing staff deployment/ coverage plans and subsequently estimating the cost or budget required. It must be approved by a higher authority. It is of paramount importance in the competitive tendering process which is discussed fully in Section 4.19.

How is the specification produced?
The production of the specification involves a number of stages.

Figure 3.7 A room schedule

Name of Establishment ————	Room Schedule (Code No.) ————
Room No./Name ————	Room Type (Description/Code No.) —
Location ————	Dimensions ————

Items	Quantity/Dimension	Description	Comments

Comments

Area determination

Firstly, as with the maintenance service, a building survey has to be conducted and a database set up. The room or area types, eg bedrooms, corridors, sanitary areas, clinical and public areas which have to be included, are defined and quantified. Their layout, location and relationships to each other are noted. It is useful to have a set of working plans of the building.

A Room Schedule (or Accommodation Schedule) is used for each room or area type to record the information required. If all single rooms for instance are the same, then only one room schedule would be produced but noting the quantity of that room type. It is useful to develop a standard format such as the one suggested in Figure 3.7.

It is then necessary to produce a detailed inventory for each room or area type, identifying the surfaces, furniture and fittings located there and noting their condition, state of repair and any initial or previous treatments.

This survey can be greatly assisted by the use of the working plans of the building. The database can be manual or computerised.

It is also useful to note the following information:

- furniture density – this will influence the amount of time required to clean the area, eg lounge versus a gymnasium
- usage density, ie the quantity of users, peaks and troughs and times of usage. This will influence methods, treatments and access times
- any peculiar problems, eg very old porous linoleum
- general standards required, eg clinical or aesthetic.

Unless this database is developed, it is impossible to determine, in specific terms, what cleaning and maintenance (ie maintenance tasks performed by cleaning personnel such as floor maintenance) tasks have to be performed and, consequently quantify the work to be done.

The concept of a room inventory can be useful when implementing any one of the following:

- a planned preventative maintenance programme
- room control procedure for controlling furniture and furnishing stocks
- a redecoration and interior design scheme appraisal
- an aide-memoire system in conjunction with room photographs for front office personnel responsible for increasing accommodation sales.

Task determination

It is now possible to specify what tasks have to be undertaken in that room or area type. The type of tasks will be influenced by the needs and requirements of the building and the usage of the space, ie number of users, their activities, needs and requirements.

In general terms, these tasks can be identified under the following headings:

- *Cleaning tasks* eg suction cleaning, damp dusting
- *Maintenance tasks* eg polish stripping, sanding, maintenance checks
- *Services to be provided* eg early morning teas, dish-washing
- *Special requirements* eg barrier cleaning, chemical disinfection.

The chart format used for the Room Schedule can be extended to record the specific tasks to be carried out on each surface or item. See Figure 3.8.

Figure 3.8 *Task sheet*

Name of Establishment ——————— Room Schedule (Code No.) ———————

Room No./Name ——————— Room Type (Description/Code No.) —

Location ——————— Dimensions ———————

Items	Quantity/Dimension	Description	Task
Floor	60m^2	80/20 Wilton	Vacuum Spot check Shampoo
Chairs	20	Polyproplene	Damp dust
Wastebins	3	Fibreglass	Empty Damp clean

Frequencies
How often each task is to be performed then needs to be considered. Frequencies, standards and costs are interlinked, as already suggested in 3.3.1.2 The more often a specific task is performed the more work-hours have to be allocated over a period and the higher the cost of cleaning will be. Frequencies and standards in a given situation do have to be correlated to determine the optimum frequency. Some of the following factors will affect the frequency of the tasks to be performed:

- type of area
- type and condition of surfaces
- user density
- functions of the area and activities taking place
- type(s) of soil present
- how much soil is transported to the area and by what means
- how far the soil has been transported/location of area
- the degree of infection risk
- the quality standard required
- the amount of money available.

It is possible to extend the chart further to specify the anticipated frequency for each task/service identified. See Figure 3.9.

Figure 3.9 *Task sheet to show frequencies*

Name of Establishment _____ Room Schedule (Code No.) _____

Room No./Name _____ Room Type (Description/Code No.) __

Location _____ Dimensions _____

Items	Quantity/Dimensions	Description	Tasks	Frequency
Floor	60m²	80/20 Wilton	Vacuum	Daily
			Spot check	Daily
			Shampoo	6 monthly

It is normally convenient to establish the frequency for each task on each surface in each area in terms of daily, weekly and periodic tasks, which range from fortnightly, monthly, quarterly, six monthly, annually and even five yearly in some situations.

For housekeeping purposes an annual cycle is the norm, although redecoration and upgrading schemes may be organised on a two or three year cycle, whereas a maintenance programme may extend over a 60 year cycle.

Standard procedures
It is now possible to build up a series of Standards or Standard Procedures. These are simply a list of all the tasks to be performed and their specified frequencies for each room or area type. See Figure 3.10. These are usually coded and should be recorded within the database.

3.3.3 Method development

Having identified all the tasks to be included in the specification, it is essential now to define each one to avoid ambiguity, misunderstanding and misinterpretation, eg

Mop sweeping – Removal of soil, litter and debris by means of an impregnated or static mop.

Each task can then be examined to:

● define its objective or purpose
● develop the method of performance, which will involve specifying equipment, agents and supplies to be used; examining the stages involved in a logical sequence and highlighting hygiene, safety and fire aspects
● describe the anticipated outcome or end result – which in fact is really specifying the 'acceptable standard' to be achieved.

Figure 3.10 *Example of Standard Procedure with times*

Standard Procedure 0032
2nd Oct 1993

WARD A

Surface/ Item	Type	Action	DAY	WEEK	MONTH	YEAR	TOT /wk
Floor	Carpet	Suction Cl Spot Cl Shampoo	1 1			 6	84 21 1.4
Furniture	Non-medical, includes beds	Damp dust	1				210
Wash hand basins	Basin, taps, fittings, surrounds, dispensers	Damp clean Replenish supplies	2 2				98 4.5
High level surfaces	Walls, ledges, rails	Damp clean			 1	1 1	0 0 0
Low level surfaces	Skirtings Paintwork Doors	Damp clean Spot clean Wash Spot clean Damp clean	 1 1	1 1		 1	16 9 0 2.5 2
Waste	Bins Bags	Empty Damp clean Empty	2 1 1				4 8 6
Glass	Mirrors Windows Partitions	Damp clean Wash/rinse Spot clean Wash/rinse	1 1		 1 1		14 0 2 0
Total minutes per week							482·4

(Timings of 0 indicate task not completed by this department.)

The actual method specified will influence the time element to be allocated to the task. Basically a method study or task analysis has been undertaken, the benefits of which could be described as:

- establishing the method most appropriate for the situation (in terms of the best, most time-saving, most hygienic, safest, simplest)

- setting a specific and defined standard to aid the training and supervisory processes
- standardising the method for a particular task so establishing uniformity and consistency
- standardising on supplies to effect economy of purchase.

This can then be recorded. Various terms are used for this kind of documentation such as *Job Breakdown, Work Procedure, Job Procedure, Task Analysis Sheet*. A standardised method of performance, laying down the quality standard to be achieved has thus been developed (see Chapter 7).

These Job Breakdowns can be collated into one *Standard Operating Manual* or *Standards of Performance Manual*. This is a useful document for use by higher management, regulatory and inspectory bodies such as the Health and Safety Executive or BS 5750 Inspectors.

Job Breakdowns also provide a very useful base for the preparation of practical or on-the-job training sessions. See Figure 3.11 for a sample Job Breakdown.

Figure 3.11 *Job Breakdown*

Task:	Cleaning a toilet
Purpose:	To remove organic matter and bacteria and maintain a clean appearance
Supplies:	Toilet brush and holder Blue bucket of neutral detergent solution + blue cloth toilet cleanser (X brand)*
Special factors:	1 The blue bucket and cloth must be used for toilet cleaning only 2 A toilet brush and holder is supplied in each toilet area or toilet cubicle (public toilets) to prevent spreading infection 3 Wear protective clothing and rubber gloves and wash the gloved hands after completing toilet cleaning 4 NEVER mix toilet cleanser with any other cleaning agent especially bleach as a poisonous chlorine gas will be given off 5 NEVER use toilet cleanser on any other surface as it will cause damage.

Procedure	Key points
1 Collect all supplies	To make sure everything is handy
2 Flush toilet	To remove any matter in the pan
3 Lift the lid and the seat and push water out of the pan	Using the toilet brush in firm downward strokes pump as much water as possible out of the pan This exposes the water line and does not dilute the toilet cleanser as much

4	Apply the toilet cleanser evenly under the rim	To contact all the rim area and allow it to drain down all sides into the pan Allow a few minutes whilst cleaning the rest of the toilet for the chemical to work
5	Damp dust the rest of the toilet	With the neutral detergent solution wash the pedestal, pipes and cistern, including the handle, rinsing the cloth in the solution frequently Wipe the top of the bowl, the hinges, the upper and lower sides of the seat and lid
6	Clean the toilet pan	Using the brush clean under the rim, the sides of the pan, the water line and round the bend Pay particular attention to the rim in a hard water area
7	Flush the toilet	To remove traces of toilet cleanser hold the brush under the flushing water Flush again if necessary Wash the brush and holder thoroughly at least once a week
8	Leave the seat and the lid down	(May have to put a sanitised label over the seat) Replenish the toilet roll if necessary leaving the spare flap of paper in a V, ie by tucking in the sides
9	Clean equipment	Throw the dirty solution down the sluice and clean the bucket and cloth thoroughly and leave to dry.

* Neutral detergent may be used instead for daily cleaning

Thus the *Specification of Work* and *Standard Operating Manual* have been produced. These form the basis for measuring the workload, estimating human resource levels, deploying labour and producing the budget for the service, which are discussed in Chapter 4.

Monitoring and control

This information also provides the basis for developing a monitoring and control system (see Chapter 7). However, it is recommended that the monitoring and control system is devised at the same time as the work specification.

3.4 INFECTION CONTROL AND HYGIENE POLICY

The consideration of infection control and the development of a hygiene policy should be an integral part of the work specification. A contractor may well be asked to provide the Company's Hygiene Policy document as part of the tender submission (see Section 3.4.2).

3.4.1 Devising an infection control plan

The first essential of any infection control plan is to identify areas of potential risk and examine the infection cycle and the degree of danger. Only then can the appropriate control measures be considered.

3.4.1.1 The infection risk

An infection risk may be created within an area:

- by the nature of the activities undertaken, such as in sanitary areas or research and microbiology units or by the characteristics of the users, eg infectious diseases patients
- by the vulnerability of the users to infection, for instance in baby units, operating theatres or burns units.

In the first case, transmission of infection outwards must be prevented and in the second, transmission inwards must be prevented.

3.4.1.2 The infection cycle The infection cycle comprises a source, a link or intermediate and a potential victim.

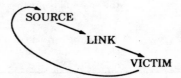

If the potential victim becomes infected, at worst a fatality ensues, at best a new source of infection is created. The aim is to break the link to prevent the occurrence of cross infection, remove the source or prevent a source from occurring.

In the example illustrated below, if the toilet seat and handle are correctly cleaned by the domestic assistant (who must also use appropriate hygiene precautions), the link is broken and neither the domestic assistant nor the next user will become contaminated.

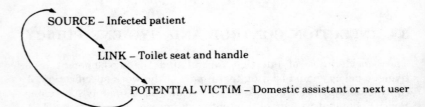

3.4.1.3 Cross infection *Cross infection* or *cross contamination* are terms widely used in a hospital situation and can be defined as *'the transmission of harmful bacteria (pathogens) from one medium to another by means of a carrier'*. Figure 3.12 outlines possible sources and carriers of infection.

Cross infection, in a hospital especially, must be prevented. A healthy person can generally build up a bodily resistance to combat a certain amount of harmful microbes, whereas a hospital patient, generally with reduced resistance, is susceptible to disease and may, therefore, contract a secondary infection.

Figure 3.12 *Sources and carriers of infection*

Sources

Food stuffs infected at source

Vermin, pests and animals

Human beings
— may carry a germ, after being ill and becoming immune
— may carry a germ unknowingly and not even have been ill
— may be suffering from a transmittable disease or infection
— may have an open or infected wound
— AIDS and Hepititis B carriers

Other carriers

Foodstuffs contaminated during preparation
Humans pick up infection on hands or feet
Clothing and bedding
Towels
Soap
Surfaces contaminated by hand, faeces, pus, blood, vomit
Air
Water (showers, eg Legionnaires' disease)

The risk of cross infection must be minimised by breaking the link and reducing the level of microbes present to an 'acceptable' level, recognising that it is impossible to remove all bacteria all of the time, ie achieve totally aseptic conditions.

3.4.1.4 The role of cleaning It is recognised that effective cleaning (ie effective in terms of soil removal and incorporating means of preventing transmission of bacteria), is one way of reducing the level of bacteria present by removing contaminants and so helping to break the infection cycle. On the other hand, infrequent cleaning, use of unhygienic methods, contaminated equipment and cleaning solutions and contaminated staff, can contribute to the infection risk by increasing bacteria levels or becoming the source or the link in the infection cycle. For instance, a domestic assistant cleans the toilets, then prepares to serve beverages to the patient, without washing his/

her hands or the room attendant washes the early morning tea cups in the en-suite bathroom and dries them with a used towel.

3.4.1.5 Spread of infection Infection can be spread through the cleaning process in the following ways:

- use of dirty or contaminated mops, dusters, buckets, floor maintenance machines
- dirty or contaminated water
- inefficient filters on suction cleaners blowing contaminated air back into the atmosphere
- dry cleaning methods, which scatter dust such as sweeping, dry mopping, dry dusting
- dirty or contaminated towels or tea towels
- poor waste disposal methods eg uncovered containers
- emptying suction cleaners, waste bins carelessly so rescattering dust
- transferring equipment from one area to another, eg infectious unit to surgical ward or entrance area to operating theatre.

Domestic or housekeeping personnel may also spread infection:

- through lack of personal hygiene, eg not washing hands after using the toilet
- not washing hands after completing a 'dirty' task
- on personal clothing
- on uniforms and protective clothing
- if suffering from coughs, colds, infections, skin lesions
- washing hands in sink over crockery
- smoking, scratching and other 'bad' habits.

3.4.1.6 Hygiene precautions The following hygiene precautions should be an integral part of the housekeeping provision and be inherent in the cleaning methods developed:

- staff training in personal hygiene, cleaning technology, infection control
- provision of 'personal hygiene' facilities
  - changing areas with locker facilities to prevent contamination of personal clothing or uniforms
  - adequate toilet facilities with facilities for handwashing and drying, bearing in mind that tablet soap, nail brushes and textile hand towels are potential carriers of infection
  - provision of barrier and hand cream to encourage hand and nail care
- supervision to ensure equipment is thoroughly cleaned after use and correctly stored (a time allowance must also be given on the work schedule to encourage this practice)

- an organised system for laundering of dusters, cloths, mop heads, tea towels
- selection of cleaning equipment recognising their ease of cleaning and possible autoclaving
- equipment allocated to high risk areas and only used there, not transported elsewhere, eg floor maintenance machine kept in operating theatre
- provision of protective clothing, overshoes and masks, waterproof aprons, rubber gloves
- colour coded equipment to prevent using the same mop, bucket or cloths in wrong areas for instance in a hospital
  — *blue* for ward cleaning
  — *red* for sanitary areas
  — *yellow* for ward kitchen
- barrier cleaning routines in very high risk areas. This involves washing hands in a specified disinfectant solution prior to entering the cubicle (such as an infectious diseases, individual cubicle ward) donning a gown on entry, cleaning the cubicle with equipment located there, taking off the gown on leaving and washing the hands again. Double barrier cleaning involves washing hands inside and outside the cubicle
- reverse barrier cleaning occurs in certain areas where infection brought in to the area can be critical, such as burns or baby units, therefore, hands are washed and the gown is donned to cover contaminated uniform before entry to the area
- use of disposable items, eg cloths, sheets, gowns to minimise infection risks – although hygienic disposal of these items must also be considered
- Precautions against AIDS (HCIMA 1987)[3] include:
  — disposing of sharp items such as razor blades and hypodermic needles with care into impenetrable containers and being aware of such objects when emptying waste bins in sanitary areas
  — providing customers with disposable razors or at least razors with freshly sterilised heads
  — employing a safe disposal system for sanitary towels and nappies
  — ensuring high quality laundering and safe handling of soiled linen
  — ensuring that towels are not used by more than one person. In public toilets warm air dryers, disposable towels with lidded waste receptacle or automatic roller towel dispensers are required
  — always wearing waterproof gloves and ensuring the gloves have no splits in them when mopping up spillages of blood, vomit or excreta. Disposing of mopping-up materials hygienically, and incinerating if possible. Disinfecting surfaces with hypochlorite disinfectant. Laundering contaminated clothing.

Some of the precautions mentioned are required in Britain by such laws as the Offices, Shops and Railway Premises Act, 1963 but general standards of health and hygiene are encomapssed within the Health and Safety at Work Act, 1974.

3.4.2   Hygiene policy

Thus the basis of a hygiene policy has been formulated. It is easy to perceive that a hygiene policy is essential in a hospital situation, but a hygiene policy should be developed in other types of establishments also, to ensure that bad practices do not occur, that lack of up-to-date knowledge in cleaning technology is overcome; to ensure that hygiene precautions are adopted in identified areas of risk, and protect personnel when in contact with potential sources of infection.

The formulation and control of a hygiene policy is not purely the responsibility of the Domestic Manager or Housekeeper. In a hospital, a corporate policy must be formulated, encompassing medical, nursing, paramedical and catering practices. Often a Control of Infection Officer or Committee is commissioned to consider the total environment and all building users.

Chemical disinfectants still tend to be used indiscriminately in some sectors of the industry. It is, therefore, worth including a statement on the use and control of chemical disinfectants within the hygiene policy.

3.4.3   Chemical disinfectants

In a hospital, chemical disinfectants will be used by several departments and the Control of Infection Officer must evaluate all needs and all chemical disinfectants in use, with a view to rationalising and standardising usage, distribution and purchasing.

No chemical disinfectant is universally effective and there are many problems associated with their use.

The first question is to ask whether a chemical disinfectant is required at all. Before this question can be adequately answered it is necessary to identify the risk areas and analyse the potential sources of infection and the types and levels of microbes likely to be present. Only then can the decision be made either to sterilise (ie destroy all microbes including spores, fungi and viruses, usually by the use of steam under pressure in an autoclave) or to desiccate (ie dry up to kill the bacteria) or to disinfect (ie remove or destroy harmful bacteria but not necessarily spores).

Disinfection may be achieved by the use of heat, which is the most reliable method, or chemical disinfectants. It can be argued that cleaning is a method of disinfection as up to 85% of soil and, therefore, micro-organisms are removed during the cleaning process and disposed of, although not destroyed.

Heat treatment, wet or dry, has limited application in the cleaning process and can only be used in some instances, such as laundering or dish washing processes. It may be decided that effective cleaning will suffice and there is not always reliable scientific evidence to show that the regular use of chemical disinfectants results in a more hygienic result. There is no evidence, for instance, to suggest that regular use of a chemical disinfectant for damp mopping achieves a more hygienic floor, for more than a brief moment, than using an effective damp mopping procedure with a neutral detergent. Dust resettles from the atmosphere or is transported into the area in a matter of minutes.

In this example not only is a chemical disinfectant of little value from an infection control point of view but it also constitutes an extra item to purchase and an extra labour cost to apply it. As many chemical disinfectants are not cleaning agents and, in fact, may be inactivated by dirt, cleaning has to take place prior to disinfection. Hence the floor would have to be cleaned and then chemically disinfected – resulting in two processes, twice as much time and, therefore, additional labour costs. Careful thought therefore must be given to whether a chemical disinfectant is essential and the hygiene benefits must be weighed against the cost and labour implications. It is quite possible in most types of establishments, even hospitals, that a chemical disinfectant for environmental cleaning is not required at all, or only required for use in toilet areas.

If a chemical disinfectant is deemed necessary for specific tasks or areas, then careful selection is important and the following criteria according to COLLINS (1983)[6] must be considered:

- it should be active against a wide range of microbes
- it should be rapid in action, since once the surface to which it has been applied has dried it is no longer active
- it should be bactericidal in nature, ie kills rather than inhibits growth and prevents multiplication
- it should not be neutralised or inactivated by substances likely to be present on the surface such as organic matter, the medium in which it is used such as very hard water, the equipment with which it will be used, eg cellulosic mop head materials or the materials used for the storage containers, eg cork or certain plastics
- it should cause the minimum possible damage to the surface to which it is to be applied or the personnel using it. It should be non-toxic, non-corrosive and non-irritating to skin or eyes
- it should be reasonably priced.

If the chemical disinfectant is to be of value it must be used correctly:

- for the intended purpose. It is dangerous to the user and the surface to use a caustic coal tar disinfectant, purchased for drains, for general floor cleaning

- at the correct dilution rate. Too weak a solution will not be effective, too strong a solution will not necessarily kill more microbes. In either case, money is being wasted. It is a good idea for a micro-biologist to carry out in-use tests to determine the optimum dilution rate in a particular area, according to the number of microbes present
- for the specified length of time. A quick dip or application which immediately dries is not sufficient. The solution is only effective whilst wet
- at the correct temperature. Most chemical disinfectants work more efficiently in hot rather than cold water
- generally **after** cleaning, unless specifically stated. Some chemical disinfectants are inactivated by organic soil, A chemical disinfectant has to penetrate the bacterial cell before it can kill it and substances such as grease may form a waterproof protection around the cell. Hence cleaning first is necessary to remove soil and emulsify and remove the grease
- a fresh solution is more effective than one prepared a few days ago. Prepared solutions deteriorate over a period of time, some very rapidly
- never mix with soaps or detergents as both agents may be neutralised. For instance, if an anionic detergent, which ionises in water to give negative ions, is mixed with a quaternary ammonium compound, based on a cationic detergent which ionises in water to give positive ions, the result is neutralisation. This solution will not only be inactivated but becomes a potential breeding ground for bacteria.

So, it can be seen that the use of chemical disinfectants is rather complex and as management have to rely on personnel for their effective usage, it is essential to introduce a number of control measures. Staff training is essential as most personnel do not realise the latent dangers involved. With the use of chemical disinfectants any measure that can be introduced to simplify diluting the solution to ensure the correct strength is always used, must be worthwhile. Personnel do not necessarily understand ratios (1:100 solution) or percentages (a 10% solution) so 1 cap to a bucketful is more meaningful to them. They must be aware of the significance of the correct dilution rate. Caps, proportioners, measured pumps or pre-packed sachets are available options. If solutions are centrally prepared and distributed, sterile, dry containers must be used, and labelled, with all product details itemised, including the date of issue and the last date of usage. Effective supervision involves regular checks to ensure solutions are not used after deterioration.

It is also necessary, from time to time, to carry out microbial tests to ensure that bacteria levels are being controlled, that specified dilution rates are effective and the correct dilution rate is being maintained.

Generally, the only types of chemical disinfectants which may be seriously considered for environmental disinfection purposes are:

● hypochlorite disinfectants (bleaches) – also recommended for AIDS
● phenolic disinfectants, ie clear soluble synthetic phenols (not coal tar)
● quaternary ammonium compounds in food areas.

COLLINS (1983)[6] suggests the only acceptable ues of chemical disinfectants for environmental purposes in a hospital are:

● for disinfection of known contaminated spillages such as urine, blood, pus, faeces and vomit
● for terminal disinfection of rooms after use by a patient with infectious conditions resulting from organisms not normally present in the environment, gut or on the skin (which may affect the healthy hospital worker or other patients)
● routine cleaning in areas where patients are highly susceptible to infection and are likely to become infected by normal microbial inhabitants of the environment, eg premature baby units, intensive care units
● routine cleaning in units where patients with infectious diseases are treated on a regular basis
● possibly for routine cleaning of operating theatre floors, although the actual value is doubtful.

Aromatic chemical disinfectants, often used indiscriminately, are only active against a very limited range of microbes and their use should be seriously considered against the cost of purchase and application. 'Smell' has absolutely nothing to do with the effectiveness of chemical disinfectants.

It can be seen then that chemical disinfectants should only be used as part of a carefully formulated policy.

3.5 WASTE DISPOSAL

Recent legislation in the UK dictates that under 'the duty of care' all reasonable steps must be taken to look after any waste generated by an organisation and prevent its illegal disposal by others. Unlimited fines could be imposed for breaking the law. Waste disposal is an activity often managed by the Accommodation Manager.

The waste disposal system involves either collecting up the waste, holding it in suitable containers, moving it to a central collection point and finally arranging for its final removal or incineration, or disposing of it at source through disposal units or sanitary appliances. Initially, waste disposal may seem to be a minor activity, but waste products do constitute fire, hygiene and safety hazards. Certainly, in a large operation, where a vast amount of waste has to be disposed of daily, it can be a major problem, especially if an effective disposal system has not been devised, and waste is left lying around. It is unsightly, starts to smell and attracts pests and vermin. The aim therefore, is to dispose of all waste materials in a hygienic, safe and environmentally friendly manner, as economically as possible, preventing an unsightly appearance and a fire and health hazard.

3.5.1 Waste collection

Before a satisfactory collection and disposal system can be devised, it is vital to analyse not only the type of waste within the operation and its characteristics but also its source and the quantity to be dealt with. Each type of waste may well require different collection, storage and disposal arrangements and the quantity may influence the most cost-effective disposal option and the decision to buy certain types of equipment such as shredders and compactors.

Corporate policy on recycling and environmental issues will also influence decisions and the resources, particularly finance made available for this activity.

In the first place, the different types of waste products, such as those identified in Figure 3.13, will need to be segregated into different coloured or types of containers at the point of accumulation. Colour coding will allow identification of a particular type of waste product to ensure the procedures and safety measures for that waste type are followed throughout the whole collection and disposal process. Most

Figure 3.13 *Types of waste materials*

- Kitchen waste – Food
  – Tins, Packaging
- Litter, dirt and waste paper (often referred to as rubbish, garbage or trash)
- Soiled dressings and sanitary towels ⎱
- Operating theatre and pathology waste – solid organic waste ⎰ Clinical
  – human remains and   waste
  organs

- Containers – aerosols, bottles
- Sharps – razor blades, syringes
- * Effluent
- * Factory/Industrial waste – chemicals
  – radioactive
  – nuclear
- * Fuel emission
- * Scrap metal

* Beyond the scope of this section.

organisations have well defined policies and procedures for radio-active and 'clinical' waste, and nowadays the disposal of sharps with regard to AIDS. All waste products to be recycled will also need to be identified. Procedures adopted for handling waste must be clear.

Thought must also be given to the adequate provision of receptacles in sanitary areas to contain used paper towels and prevent littering the floor area, and ashtrays to ensure cigarette ends are segregated from waste paper bins (not only for fire safety reasons but also to try and prevent damage to floor coverings by smouldering cigarette ends being stubbed out under foot).

3.5.2 Suitable containers

Some waste products may be disposed of at source, for instance, food waste by means of waste disposal units and soiled dressings in sanitary areas by incineration.

Many types of waste need to be stored in suitable containers to await collection. Containers may be colour coded for ease of identification as already suggested.

The suitability of the container depends to some degree on whether the waste is wet or dry in nature but should possess most, if not all, of the following characteristics:

- be large enough to hold the amount of waste collected from one pick-up to the next, but not too large for handling and transporting
- have a lid or a tie to prevent dust scattering and waste falling out
- have a foot control for the lid to avoid contaminating hands
- be made of a tough durable material which does not burst or split
- be made from a non-absorbent material which does not disintegrate when holding wet waste
- either be disposable or easy to clean or sterilise
- fit on a stand to aid packing and avoid falling over
- be non-flammable.

Containers may be galvanised iron, rubber, plastic, fibreglass, paper, polythene or polythene lined paper.

3.5.3 Central collection

The waste then has to be transported from the point of accumulation to the central collection point. The following issues need to be considered:

How will it be transported? – porters, trolley, motorised trucks
Who will transport it? – porters, refuse gang, domestic staff

| How often will it be transported? | – at least once a day in a busy area to avoid fire and hygiene problems |

The central collection point itself must also be considered in terms of:

Where is it to be sited?	– is it convenient for transportation from all sources? – is it inside or outside? – is it camouflaged to prevent building users seeing it?
What size must it be?	– is it large enough to hold the quantity of waste to be received?
What features must it possess?	– does it have easy to clean, non absorbent surfaces and a water point and drain outlet?
How will it be cleaned?	– can it be cleaned down regularly, preferably by hosing or high pressure water spraying equipment?
What storage containers are required?	– are large storage containers required, if so what type, what characteristics are required? will contractors' skips be used?

Many types of waste may be easily ignited either directly, for instance by a smouldering cigarette end or by spontaneous combustion. Waste constitutes a fire hazard. It is crucial that staff do not smoke whilst handling waste.

If thought is not given to the suitability of this central site, waste may well accumulate and obstruct fire doors, fire fighting equipment and escape routes, so constituting a safety hazard. Some waste, particularly if it is wet in nature, also constitutes a hygiene hazard, soon starts to smell and attracts pests and vermin. Frequent removal from the central collection point needs to be arranged to shorten the storage period and reduce the risks.

3.5.4   Disposal

The method of disposal will be determined by the type and quantity of waste to be disposed, environmental policies, costs involved and available finance, the market value, if any, of certain types of waste and geographic location. Most organisations used to dispose of waste must be legally authorised to dispose of the types of waste involved. Charities and voluntary organisations may be exempt. The following options can be investigated:

- **Incineration** Theatre waste and soiled dressings must be incinerated to meet ethical standards. Other waste products such as general rubbish, sanitary towels and confidential information such as old records may also be incinerated. Apart from being a hygienic means of disposal, it also reduces the amount of waste to be disposed by other means, and in some cases the heat generated can be recycled. It is dangerous to burn certain items, such as aerosols which explode and must, therefore, be segregated from the general rubbish. Clean Air regulations may influence the use of this option.

- **Local authority refuse collection** This needs to be arranged on a frequent and regular basis and does involve a charge to the operation dependant on local policies.
- **Contract refuse collection** This may be more efficient and cost effective than the local authority option. Contractors often leave their own skips, for collection at prescribed times.

At certain periods in time, certain waste products such as waste paper, fabric or food waste may have a good market value and it may be worth 'selling' them although transport costs have to be deducted. It is essential to check that contracted waste carriers are authorised to deal with the type of waste involved. A written description of the waste and transfer note have to be completed, signed and retained by both parties.

It may be worth investigating the feasibility of purchasing equipment such as shredders, compactors, compressors or baling machines to reduce the volume of the waste, particularly where large amounts of waste paper, some of which contains confidential information, are concerned. Storage space and transport costs may be affected by such a purchase.

- **Chemical disposal** This is a useful means of disposing of sanitary towels. As it is a contract service, it is convenient to operate, hygienic, and reduces unpleasantness for domestic staff. A disposal unit is usually placed in each female public convenience, and replaced at a pre-arranged frequency.
- **Recycling** The use of Bottle Banks may be useful where many non-returnable empty bottles are generated. Paper, fabrics, plastics, cans and even soap, may also be taken to local collection sites for recycling.

If a decision is to be taken to increase the use of disposable items such as crockery, cutlery, napiery and bedding, thought must be given to the method of disposal and the effect of this decision on the existing waste disposal system, and the corporate environmental policy.

3.5.5 Monitoring and control

As with any system, the waste disposal cycle must be regularly monitored to spot potential problems and control costs.

3.6   THE LINEN AND LAUNDRY SERVICES

A comprehensive linen system involves providing sufficient quantities of usable items, replacing the dirty linen with clean at the point of usage, processing the dirty linen, repairing or replacing worn linen, storing and redistributing it, and controlling the whole procedure as cost effectively as possible.

Four linen and laundry options are available for consideration:

- purchasing linen for the operation and laundering on site
- purchasing linen for the operation and laundering off site
- purchasing easy-care linen and laundering on site
- linen hire.

Sometimes a combination of two systems might be more appropriate. An establishment may purchase bed linen and send it to an off-site laundry for processing and hire staff uniforms and banqueting cloths for a seasonal trade. Disposable linen may even be used in certain circumstances where hygiene is required, eg disposable sheets for a treatment couch in a doctor's office or disposable gowns in a theatre suite; to prevent cross-infection, eg where sheets from an infectious diseases unit need to be incinerated; for convenience where inadequate laundry arrangements exist, eg table linen or in case of emergency such as a laundry workers' strike.

The linen and laundry system involves two sub-systems, the *linen control system* and the *processing* (laundering or dry cleaning) *system*. The term *linen* in this context does not necessarily refer to the linen fibre produced from flax, but is a generic term encompassing all launderable items used by any operation. If the linen and laundry system is to be truly comprehensive, it should also encompass all fabric items including those items of bedding and soft furnishings which have to be dry cleaned but excluding carpets. Uniforms and personal clothing may also be included. As dry cleaning is very expensive it is beneficial to purchase as many items as possible which are launderable.

3.6.1   The linen control system

The linen control system involves selecting and purchasing items which are suitable for their purpose, in sufficient quantities to maintain standards and ensure operational ease on an economic basis. Factors to consider when selecting items will be discussed in Chapter 5. A flow chart of the stages involved in the Linen Cycle, (from the collection of clean linen from a secondary or peripheral storage area to the redistribution of clean linen from the central store to top up the items used from this secondary store), facilitates explaining the facets of the *Linen Control System*, see Figure 3.14.

Figure 3.14 *The linen control chart*

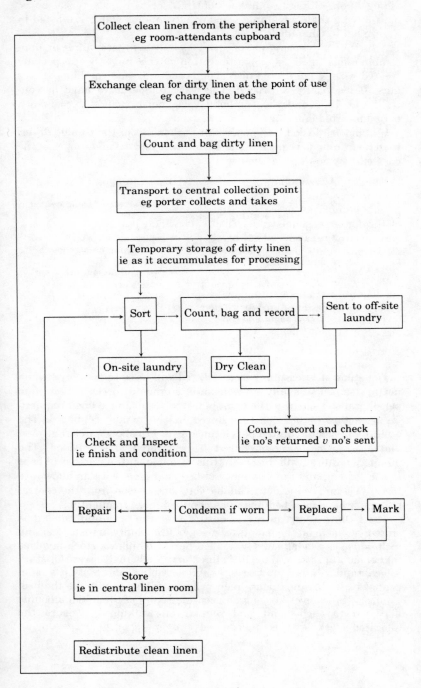

3.6.1.1 Provision of linen
There are alternative ways of providing linen, either to purchase outright or hire on a rental basis, both having their advantages and disadvantages which are listed in Figure 5.9 in Chapter 5.

A further purchasing option involves only synthetic fibres or fibre combinations such as polyester/cotton which have been specially treated with a 'non-iron' finish. The laundering and tumbling stages must be especially controlled. The wash temperature must be controlled at 15°C and the tumbling cycle must include a cool-down period to avoid creasing.

If items are folded well as they are taken out of the tumble dryer, then no ironing is required. The advantages and disadvantages of the easy care or no-iron system are:

	Advantages	Disadvantages
Easy Care	• smaller stocks • speedier processing cycle (2 hrs) • cuts out cost of ironing, labour and equipment • equipment may be hired or bought • small area for equipment • few staff • facilities used for all items and bedding and soft furnishings • capital asset reduced	• initial costs of equipment if not leased • repair costs • replacement costs • overloading creates loss of standard • customer acceptance – not quite as crisp a finish

The stock of linen purchased or hired will have to be stored when not in use. This usually involves bulk storage at a central site and peripheral storage near the point of usage, for instance linen required for a section of bedrooms is stored in the maids' cupboard. The quantity of stock required plus a contingency to allow for change over and a possible emergency must be estimated and provided. The quantity required will depend in this example on the number of beds in the section, and the frequency of bed-changing, with an allowance in case clean linen is not available for some reason from the central storage area, or if a bed has to be changed more frequently.

Strict control is required to ensure that the optimum amount is stored at each of the points of usage. Probability and forecasting techniques can be effectively applied here. Too high a stock involves higher capital costs and too little linen may well create stress for staff, affect standards and productivity, and possibly profitability if a room cannot be let because clean linen is not available to remake the bed. Control also involves keeping an accurate record of the initial amounts allocated to each point and regular stocktaking to ensure the allocated stock level is maintained and losses or pilferage do not occur.

3.6.1.2 Exchange The frequency of replacing dirty linen with clean from the peripheral store will be determined either according to the turnover of customers, for instance the table cloth is changed for every new customer sitting down, or by company policy, eg beds will be changed daily for however long the guest is staying. The exchange creates two problems. Firstly, the dirty linen has to be dealt with and secondly, the stock in the peripheral store has to be replenished. The latter problem will be discussed under redistribution in Section 3.6.15. It is helpful in many cases to provide the employee changing the dirty linen with a trolley to aid productivity and prevent numerous trips backwards and forwards to the storage area. Dirty linen piled high in hotel corridors as rooms are stripped is an eyesore, as well as an obstruction and safety hazard.

Departmental policy may dictate that dirty linen should not be left in the corridor. Sorting of dirty linen into like items or according to its state, for instance, infected or fouled linen in a hospital (in fact, fouled would be segregated straight away), may take place at this point or in the central storage area. The number of items may be recorded here so the amount by which the stock has to be replenished is known.

The dirty linen will have to be bagged in some kind of container to facilitate transport, avoid damage and prevent cross-contamination. The containers may be fabric, usually nylon or a non-absorbent synthetic fibre, plastic or fibre glass. Certainly, in the National Health Service bags are colour coded to denote ordinary soiled linen, fouled linen, infected linen or theatre and renal linen.

The bags containing fouled and infected linen may be sewn with alginate thread which dissolves with the heat at the pre-wash stage of the laundry process. This avoids contamination of the laundry worker who is sorting the dirty linen.

A decision has to be made as to which grade of staff will collect and transport the dirty linen from each peripheral storage area to the central linen area. Room attendants, porters or linen room staff may be involved or a linen chute may be 'in built' to ease transportation.

3.6.1.3 Processing Dirty linen will be transported by whatever means to a central site, which will probably be the laundry area, if an on-site laundry operates, or the central storage area if dirty linen is to be sent to an off-site laundry. A special area should be designated for the accumulation of dirty linen to avoid cross-contaminating clean linen. The accumulated dirty linen will have to be sorted, usually into like items, counted, recorded and bagged for transport to the off-site laundry. The containers used will be similar to those already mentioned but, possibly larger, and vans or some mechanical type of transport may be required. To avoid cross infection, clean linen should not be transported in a van which has been used for dirty linen, and the inside of the van should be cleaned regularly. Processing of dirty linen will take place either on site or off site as already indicated.

If 'traditional' items of linen made from natural and artificial fibres have been purchased then processing may take place on-site in a laundry, requiring the whole range of laundering equipment, or it may take place off-site at a commercial laundry. Where 'easy-care', non-iron items have been purchased and are to be processed on-site, a modified laundry, with no ironing equipment is required. If linen has been hired, then it is returned to the linen hire company (off-site) for processing. The advantage and disadvantage of each laundry option are outlined in Figure 3.15.

Some items may have to be dry cleaned rather than laundered. Control measures must be instituted particularly if processing is off-site. The amounts returned must be counted, recorded and checked against the laundry statement and the amount sent. 'Losses and shorts' must be recorded and the occurrence investigated immediately. The quality of the laundry finish is often checked, although this is time consuming, and inspection for repairs or the need to condemn is undertaken simultaneously.

Items may be rejected and returned to the laundry, sent to the sewing room for repair, or condemned. Condemned items are recorded and replacements are issued from new stock if this exists, or ordered from the supplier when there is sufficient need. Repaired items may

Figure 3.15 *The advantages and disadvantages of laundry options*

Option	Advantages	Disadvantages
On-site	Can specify treatments Can vary treatments Can reduce length of total linen and laundry process No losses/shorts should occur Less stock required as quicker cycle Capital asset Cover emergency requirements Can launder bedding and soft furnishings easily	Capital outlay Higher labour costs Technical expertise or specialised Management Factories Act 1961 Repairs, cleaning and maintenance Replacement of equipment and premises Opportunity costs
Off-site	No capital outlay Less skilled staff on premises Little technical expertise	Limited specification of treatment Extra costs for special treatments and stain removal Losses may occur Delivery and collection delays may occur Higher stocks required Longer time involved in total proces

have to be relaundered or at least reironed. Satisfactory items are then stored.

3.6.1.4 Storage All linen should be stored securely to prevent pilferage or loss, and safely to avoid the risk of fire. Processed linen will wear better and last longer if it is allowed to 'rest' before going back into circulation. Therefore good rotation of stock is essential. A well-designed storage area will facilitate stock rotation.

It is vital that a stock check is undertaken on a regular basis to audit those stocks in central storage and undergoing processing as well as stocks in the peripheral stores. If stocktaking can be undertaken without prior notice, all on the same day, it will be more effective, otherwise items may circulate and be counted more than once.

3.6.1.5 Redistribution The stock in the peripheral stores has to be replaced and this may be undertaken by various means. The distribution options include those discussed in Chapter 5 in the section on stock control, namely, the clean for dirty, counter exchange, topping-up or imprest, requisition, standard pack or complete trolley systems. Again the decision as to which staff – linen maids, porters, or room attendants – are involved in the redistribution system has to be made. Effective control requires a record to be kept of amounts of clean linen distributed to each location (peripheral store) and any variances against amounts of dirty linen sent for processing. The linen cycle then commences again.

3.6.1.6 Bedding and soft furnishings Blankets, soft furnishings, such as bedspreads, valances and curtains, staff uniforms and overalls and personal linen of residents (whether personnel or customers) are not usually included in the general linen cycle discussed, so alternative arrangements have to be made for each of these. Blankets, duvets and soft furnishings are usually laundered or dry cleaned, whichever is applicable, on a less frequent basis. The frequency of cleaning should be specified and a recording and control system devised to ensure that these items are processed at the required frequency. Control and cleaning of staff uniforms can be an enormous problem especially in a large operation (see Section 3.6.5).

The system devised for dealing with residents' personal laundry will depend on the type of establishment and whether personnel or customers are involved. The type of customer, their requirements and their average length of stay, will influence the arrangements made, for instance, businessmen staying a couple of nights may need a speedy shirt service.

Figure 3.16 *The laundry system*

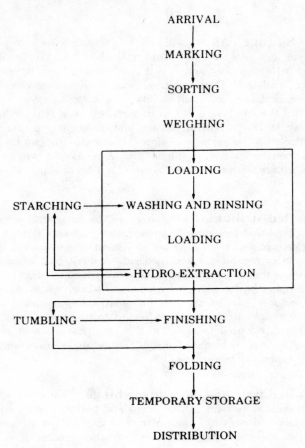

ARRIVAL

MARKING

SORTING

WEIGHING

LOADING

STARCHING ⟶ WASHING AND RINSING

LOADING

HYDRO-EXTRACTION

TUMBLING ⟶ FINISHING

FOLDING

TEMPORARY STORAGE

DISTRIBUTION

3.6.2   The laundry system

The stages involved in the laundry system are as outlined in Figure 3.16. They remain the same except for marking, whether an on-site or an off-site laundry is used, although where easy-care linen is concerned the finishing process is not required.

3.6.2.1   Arrival   When the dirty linen arrives at the laundry it has to be unloaded and stored temporarily until processing commences. The dirty linen should be dealt with quickly to avoid growth of infection, mildew and odour problems occurring. Piles of dirty linen are subject to spontaneous combustion and so constitute a fire hazard.

In a modern hospital operation, infected and fouled linen is physically segregated from the rest of the dirty linen to avoid cross contamination.

3.6.2.2 Marking In a commercial laundry the article being laundered must be marked with some kind of code to identify it with the appropriate establishment or individual owner. This mark helps to ensure that the laundered article is returned to the rightful user. In a large operation with an on-site laundry marking may occur only if items have to be returned to a specific area or department but generally a pool system operates.

Bar coding is now being used in some laundry operations to trace and control specific items.

In some cases linen may have been premarked with, for example, a company logo during the weaving process.

3.6.2.3 Sorting In an on-site laundry, such as in a hospital, sorting or classification of linen may be the first stage in the operation. Where colour-coded bags are used to denote the condition of the dirty linen, eg in a hospital, the dirty linen is sorted according to the colour of the bag, as each type must be processed separately.

The following factors vary according to the type of item being laundered:

- the amount and type of chemicals to use
- the water temperature
- the number and length of wash cycles
- the number of rinses.

Therefore, the batches will have to be sorted according to:

- the type of item
- the fibre type
- the colour and dye fastness
- the degree of soilage
- the risk of infection.

3.6.2.4 Weighing Each bundle of dirty linen has to be weighed to conform to the capacity of the machine which, in an industrial laundry, may be 50 kg, 250 kg, or even 500 kg dry weight of items.

3.6.2.5 Loading The weighed load of items may then be loaded into the washing machine, either manually or by mechanical means. Manual loading and unloading of a large washing machine involves considerable effort, especially unloading, when the work carries with it a great weight of water. Overloading of the machine should be avoided because effective washing may not occur, linen may be damaged and even creasing of crease-resistant items may occur. The weight of loads of bulkier items such as towels or blankets should be reduced to ensure washing takes place effectively. For economic reasons machines should not be underloaded.

3.6.2.6   Washing and rinsing

Washing

The washing process must be designed to perform three basic operations:
1 to remove soil from the fabric
2 to suspend soil
3 to discharge the soil from the machine to the drain.

Laundries at present depend mainly on the rotary washing machine. Larger rotary machines are divided into compartments with internal partitions which enable separate loads to be washed together by the same process without the loads becoming mixed.

The laundry supplies, such as soap, synthetic detergents, alkalis and bleaches, may be added manually or automatically controlled.

● *Devising an effective wash programme*

When devising an effective wash programme the following variables must be borne in mind:

- ● the fibre and fabric
- ● the type the type of item
- ● the dye fastness
- ● the'amount of soilage
- ● the hardness of the water.

These variables will influence:

- ● the number of wash cycles
- ● the number of rinse cycles
- ● the pH value of the wash liquors
- ● the depth of the wash liquors
- ● the temperature
- ● the time needed for soil removal.

Manufacturers in Britain use the labelling scheme devised by the Home Laundering Consultative Council (HLCC), giving different laundering instructions, appropriate to the article to which it is attached. Although designed essentially for home laundering this information can be interpreted to ensure suitable treatments in a commercial laundry.

Rinsing

Once the wash cycles have been completed, then rinsing has to take place. Rinsing should:
- ● remove the laundry supplies once they have served their purpose

● remove the small amount of dirt which has been removed from the fabrics but which remains in the 'carry over' liquor, ie the residue which has not escaped from the last cycle, in the load at the end of the final wash.

These requirements are met by adding water to the machine so as to dilute the 'carry over' liquor.

It is normal practice to use only cold water for rinsing. The load and liquor which is retained carries over heat from the final wash and this warms the rinse water. This procedure is repeated from each rinse to the next, so the temperature falls only gradually, giving conditions which are entirely satisfactory in most circumstances.

If any articles, such as sheets or slips, require to be starched but only to a moderate stiffness then the starch liquor is added to the washing machine after the final rinse and then, after a few minutes, the starch not taken up is discarded.

Rinsing leaves the work saturated with water, which then has to be removed by mechanical means, known as *hydro-extraction*.

3.6.2.7 Hydro-extraction   There are two principal types of hydro-extractors. The most widely used is a centrifugal extractor, which can range in size, with capacities of up to 250 kg dry weight, but most are smaller than this.

Artificial fibres and polycotton retain less water than natural fibres and should only be hydro-ed briefly, otherwise compression of the fabric produces creases which may be impossible to remove.

Certain precautions are necessary when loading a hydro-extractor. The load should be distributed as uniformly as possibly throughout the basket, otherwise the basket is unbalanced, and each article should be bunched up so it is free to move towards the wall of the basket when the hydro runs. If this movement is restricted the article could tear.

A hydraulic extractor removes water merely by subjecting the load to a direct external pressure. The only movement which the articles undergo is a small displacement due to the application of pressure.

Even after hydro-extraction, the laundry is still in a damp state, cotton for instance retains an amount of water, roughly half its own dry weight. When the work is discharged from the hydro-extractor it is tightly squeezed into a fairly solid mass which needs to be loosened and separated into individual items before the items can be handled by the finishing departments.

● *Washer extractors*
   In the absence of mechanical handling aids, such as cranes, a considerable amount of effort is involved in transferring work from a washing machine to a hydro-exractor. Each 50 kg dry weight of fabric holds at least 150 kg of water when saturated.
   This effort can be avoided by using a machine which serves as

both washer and extractor. The load remains in the machine at the end of the washing process to undergo the hydro-extraction procedure. The machine is capable of running at two speeds: low speed for washing and rinsing and high speed for extracting. In modern commercial laundries, continuous tunnel washing machines are now used. Washing, rinsing and extraction, using the hydraulic extraction principle, occurs in the same machine.

3.6.2.8   Starching   It is customary to starch certain articles, after they have been washed, to impart a degree of stiffness, in some cases only moderate but in other cases considerable. If an article requires only a moderate stiffness, such as sheets and pillow-slips, this can be applied in the washing machine following the final rinse.

It is necessary to provide a separate starching machine for items which need to be stiff. This is because a large amount of starch needs to be used, which is expensive, and any not taken up can be reused for other loads. The processing may last up to 30 minutes and the items need to be hydro-ed before the starch is applied, to allow penetration of sufficient starch.

3.6.2.9   Tumbling   The complete drying of laundered work by means of hot air tumblers is usually restricted to such articles as bath towels and blankets, which require a 'fluffy' unpressed finish.

Tumblers are also of use in the processing of items manufactured from fabrics composed totally or partly of polyester fibres where the process has to be carefully controlled, the degree of loading reduced, the load gradually cooled down in the final stage of the cycle, and the item quickly removed and folded.

In other cases tumblers are used merely for heat conditioning which assists in removing extractor wrinkles and moisture so that items may be ironed without difficulty.

They are generally wasteful and ineffective in their utilisation of heat, since a considerable amount is blown into the atmosphere, along with the moisture which has been evaporated from the work in process. During the process fluff and loose lint will shake off the articles, so a lint trap or screen is fitted prior to the outlet trunking to prevent it blowing into the atmosphere. The trap or screen must be cleaned at regular intervals to prevent the air flow being reduced, resulting in longer drying time.

3.6.2.10   Finishing   The next stage is known as *finishing*, ie ironing or pressing according to the size and shape of the item.

The quality of finish achieved at this stage depends largely on three things:

1 the moisture content
2 pressing temperature
3 pressure.

If an item is too dry before pressing then the resultant finish will be poor, this can be remedied by the use of a spray. Too much moisture will result in an excellent finish but a long (and costly) drying time on the press, thus slowing down production. The type of equipment used for ironing or pressing depends on the type of item. Flat items such as sheets, pillow cases and table cloths are referred to as *flatwork* and may be calendered or, on a smaller scale, may be ironed by means of a rotary ironer. Non-flat items, such as uniforms, coats, shirts, etc, are finished on presses of various forms which have been developed to cater for different types of articles. Some items may still have to be finished manually with an iron, but in a large scale operation, these are few.

In commercial laundries, spreaders and feeders are used to aid the preparation of flat work for ironing, and aid economy of labour and effort to maintain continuous uninterrupted production.

3.6.2.11 Folding Calendered and pressed items are then mechanically folded. Standardised folding of each item will aid the operative, for instance when making a bed or setting a table; will certainly affect the appearance and could also aid storage and stocktaking. Items may then be mechanically stacked.

3.6.2.12 Temporary storage When all the work has been finished and folded there still remains the job of arranging the work in the correct order for packing and distribution, so the work is often temporarily stored on fixed or mobile racks for a short period of time.

3.6.2.13 Distribution The packing operation can be performed in a number of ways. Finished work may be loaded onto mobile racks or into bags, baskets or trucks, or even individual boxes for personal work.

Semi-automatic packaging machines are now being employed which use sheet polythene or polythene lined paper which is heat sealed to form instant closure, so the finished parcel, whether wet or dry, can withstand rough handling and is protected from contamination.

The finished items may then be despatched to the establishment, department, individual or central linen room from whence they came.

The objectives of the laundering process can be summed up as follows:

- to remove dirt and stains
- to prevent damage of the fibre and/or of tensile strength
- to 'finish' the item in order to prevent re-entry of dirt for as long as possible, and provide a wrinkle and crease-free item.

It is important to consider not only the fibre type and its properties, and the characteristics of the finished fabric when initially selecting an item but also the care and maintenance of the item, particularly the effects which the equipment, agents and processes involved have on it.

3.6.3 Infected and fouled linen

In a hospital, special thought must be given to the processing of infected and fouled linen. Infected linen, sometimes called *special category linen*, is that which has been in contact with patients suffering from notifiable diseases such as smallpox, anthrax, typhoid, infective hepatitis and salmonella poisoning. It is generated in isolation or infectious diseases units and usually includes staff uniforms.

Fouled linen is potentially infected because it has come into contact with blood, urine or faeces. Normally it is generated from psychiatric and geriatric patient areas, departments such as Accident and Emergency and also includes babies' nappies.

Both infected and fouled linen are usually placed in polythene bags, which are securely fastened, before placing in appropriate colour coded bags, which may be stitched with soluble alginate thread. Some infected linen might be incinerated, the rest is laundered. Some of the modern hospital laundries now have a *barrier washing* area which is physically separated from the rest of the laundry by a wall. The washing machines have two doors, so the dirty linen is placed in the machine in the barrier area and removed after prewashing and washing at 60°C for 10 minutes (or 71°C for 3 minutes) from the other door in the clean area, where it then undergoes normal treatment.

3.6.4 Dry cleaning

Some items have to be dry cleaned as laundering processes or agents may cause damage. Generally fabrics which may shrink, pile fabrics or items which may be subject to fibre distortion or colour (dye) movement should be dry cleaned even though it is an expensive process. Very large, heavy and bulky curtains may also be dry cleaned to facilitate their cleaning.

Dry cleaning is usually an off-site process but a large hospital district laundry may consider the installation of a dry cleaning plant to be a feasible proposition.

Dry cleaning is a process by which textile items are cleaned by washing in a solvent other than water. The stages involved are not unlike those already discussed for laundering, see Figure 3.17.

3.6.5 Uniform control

The provision, issue, laundering and control of staff overalls and uniforms is usually considered to be part of the linen and laundry

Figure 3.17 *The dry cleaning system*

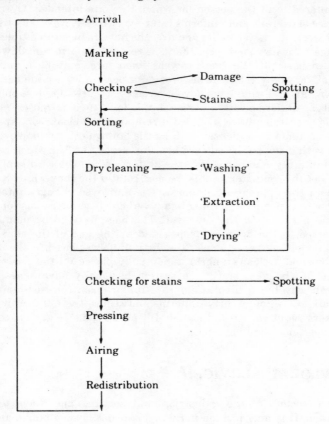

system. All employees will require either some type of protective clothing, or uniform which for operational, comfort and psychological purposes should be well designed. Often employees require a change of overalls every day or two depending on the activities they perform, and some organisations such as the NHS have a responsibility to provide clean overalls that are laundered by the Health Authorities. In other types of operations, uniforms which denote grade, status, theme, say of a restaurant, are required, which often have to be dry cleaned. A system has to be devised whereby a member of staff receives an appropriate overall or uniform which fits them, with sufficient quantities to exchange for a clean one as required according to company policy. Procedures for laundering or dry cleaning, controlling issue and distribution and reclaiming the overall on termination of employment, all have to be set up. Where an on-site sewing room operates, overalls or uniforms may at best be made to measure or at least altered to fit the person for whom they are intended. Outright purchase of overalls and uniforms can be very costly, especially where a high labour turnover exists and overalls have to be altered time and time again for new employees. For this reason, uniform rental, which works in basically the same way as linen hire, may be a feasible alternative. Many rental firms provide a personalised issue service, whereby an individual employee receives a customised supply of overalls or uniforms with a personal code for control purposes.

Some operations have installed a computerised cloakroom system and clean uniform dispenser such as the 'autovalet'. An employee is issued with a computerised card bearing a code number which corresponds to a peg number within the system. When the card is placed in the slot the computer locates the peg, rotates the conveyor belt and dispenses the appropriate uniform. The employee changes into the uniform, puts personal clothing in a polythene bag, fixes a disc on the bag and places it on the conveyor. The bags have to be manually transferred to the appropriate peg and at the end of the shift the personal clothing is reclaimed, the dirty uniform placed in the dirty linen bin and a clean uniform is manually placed on the peg to be claimed on the next shift. The system has many advantages and disadvantages but it aims to improve uniform control, ease issue of clean and collection of dirty uniforms and reduce the number or size of lockers required. An individual still needs some locker space for handbags, shoes and valuables.

3.7 FLORAL SERVICES

In some sectors of the industry, floral services may have to be organised. This may include floral or plant displays in public areas, table and bedroom arrangements or even the provision of button-holes or corsages for functions or customer requests. Seasonal arrangements for Christmas, Easter and Thanksgiving, may also be required.

In the NHS a facility has to be organised to receive floral displays on a patient's behalf, transport them to the appropriate ward and provide vases for their display. A space (flower room or utility area) is required for personnel or patients to maintain and subsequently dispose of the display and wash the vases. Floral displays may be commissioned for public areas in the hospital or special functions.

Other organisations may use a contract service. Plant hire companies provide the plants initially, and then water and tend them at an agreed frequency. Floral displays may be produced off site and then maintained by the contract florist or housekeeper, or a contract florist may produce them on site and then visit regularly to maintain them.

Few hotels these days employ a full-time florist, although a talented housekeeper may undertake the provision of this service as part of the job.

When designing the floral service the following factors will need to be considered:

- what are the establishment's and the customers' requirements?
- are plants and/or floral displays required?
- who will provide and maintain them?
- where will they be produced?
- what on-site facilities and equipment are required? Where will they be located?
- will fresh, plastic, silk or other types of arrangements meet requirements?
- how much will it cost? What is the most cost effective option?

3.8 PEST CONTROL SERVICES

All service operations have a legal obligation under the Prevention of Damage of Pests Act 1949 (or equivalent in other countries) to protect the health of the public and prevent loss or damage to their property and its contents by pests. Of course, reputation and subsequently profitability can suffer if pests are sighted or infestations occur. Buildings and contents can also be damaged if pests get out of hand and are not dealt with early on. It is, therefore, necessary for providers of accommodation service packages to ensure a pest-free environment.

Pests, which can be defined as anything which is destructive, offensive or troublesome, can carry harmful bacteria and cause damage to buildings, the environment and human beings. They can also be upsetting to customers and personnel when encountered and give them a bad impression, suggesting poor standards of cleaning and maintenance. Customers, therefore, expect a pest-free environment. Pests include:

- insects, such as bed bugs, beetles, fleas, ants, flies, cockroaches, silverfish, mites, moths, wasps
- rodents, such as rats and mice
- fungi, such as wet and dry rot and moulds.

Cats and birds, such as starlings and pigeons, can also be regarded as pests. Pests must, of course, be eradicated if present. It is necessary to deprive them of food, water, heat, shelter and time which they need to breed and multiply. More importantly measures should be taken to eliminate their entry and prevent infestations in the first place.

Good pest control involves identifying once again the likely risks and upgrading the building to prevent, as far as possible, the entry of pests through nooks and crannies, holes, damaged structures and so on. It also involves being vigilant and being able to identify pests

Figure 3.18 *Precautions to be taken to discourage pests (*PAUL *and* JONES, *Housecraft 1989)*[7]

- clean regularly and effectively and move furniture periodically to clean under and behind it
- report signs of infestations
- report any defects in the building which might encourage infestation such as cracks and crevices
- store textile items such as bed linen, blankets and pillows correctly
- do not leave food uncovered and take particular care with remains of food, remove meal trays and early morning tea trays promptly from customers' rooms. Mop up food spillages promptly
- remove waste promptly to the refuse area. Do not leave it lying about
- keep waste bins tightly covered and rubbish bins closed; clean waste bins after use
- arrange effective disposal and/or frequent removal of waste from the premises and clean refuse areas thoroughly and regularly
- check insect trays and fly killing devices or screens to see they are functioning correctly and not harbouring dead pests. Replace ultra violet tubes periodically
- inspect storage areas, boiler houses, cellars, laundry areas regularly and do not allow rubbish to accumulate.

---

and spot evidence of their presence. Pest sightings should be monitored and most operations have a 'pest book' in which sightings, locations, treatments, and dates are recorded. It is essential to know the life cycle of the various pests and the condition they thrive in, so measures to stop them flourishing can be taken.

The checklist, Figure 3.18, outlines some of the precautions which should be taken to discourage pests.

Pest control contractors, such as Rentokil, can be employed to inspect premises on a regular basis, deal with sightings and carry out necessary treatments. Obviously, the cost of such provision must be weighed against the risks involved. Advice can also be sought from the Environmental Health Office of the Local Authority if problems occur.

References

[1] LEE, R (1987), *Building Maintenance Management* 3rd edition, Collins
[2] HMSO (1972), *Report of the Committee on Building Maintenance, Department of the Environment*, HMSO
[3] HCIMA, *Technical Brief*, Sheet No. 2, 'Precaution against AIDS', April 1987
[4] ALLEN, D M (1983), *Accommodation and Cleaning Services* Volume 1: *Operations*, Hutchinson
[5] JONES, I and PHILLIPS, C (1984), *Commercial Housekeeping and Maintenance*, Stanley Thorne

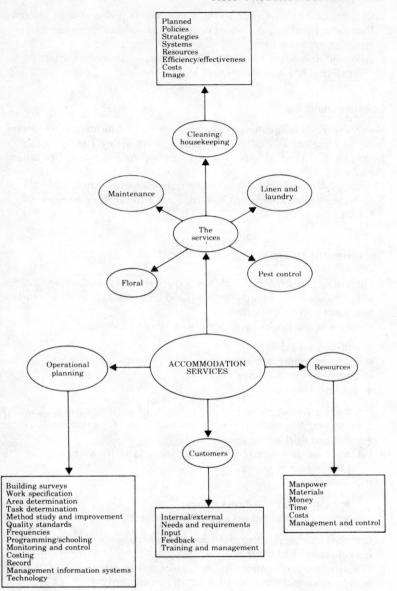

Concept Map summarizing Accommodation Services.

[6] COLLINS, B J (1983), 'The use of Chemical Disinfectants in Hospital Domestic Practice', Association of Domestic Management Newsletter, May 1983

[7] JONES, C and PAUL, V (1989), 'Housecraft – Accommodation Operations, *Mastercraft Series*, Macmillan

Further reading

BORSENIK, F, *Management of Maintenance and Engineering Systems in the Hospital Industry*, 2nd edition, John Wiley 1987

LOWBURY, E J L, et al (eds), *Control of Hospital Infection*, Chapman and Hall 1981

MAURER, I *Hospital Hygiene*, 3rd edition, Edward Arnold 1985

Key Note Report, *Contract Cleaning*, 5th edition, Key Note Publications 1990

Assignment tasks

1 Describe the provision of the housekeeping and maintenance services in one establishment and compare with the models suggested in this chapter.
2 Prepare a job breakdown for two of the following:

- making a bed
- spray cleaning a hard floor
- shampooing a carpet
- suction cleaning.

3 Produce a Room Schedule for a room of your choice and, using a chart, list the tasks to be performed, their frequencies and the equipment and agents required.
4 (a) Visit either a hospital or commercial laundry and describe the production process.
  (b) Describe the

- hygiene precautions taken
- the monitoring and control mechanism.

5 Critically investigate the provision of the linen service in a residential establishment of your choice.
6 Prepare a specification for a bedroom/bed area, sanitary area, public area and corridor of a small establishment.

Human Resources Management

Objectives

- To consider the importance of human resources.
- To identify and examine the components of the human resource system, including personnel planning, recruitment and selection and termination, induction, training and development, deployment, supervision, appraisal and staff welfare.
- To identify the consumer as a human resource to be managed and trained.

4.1 IMPACT OF HUMAN RESOURCES ON SERVICE OPERATIONS

In any organisation it is important to use people effectively and make the most of their skills and abilities, and harness their thoughts and ideas to be utilised for the benefit of the operation. voss *et al*, (page 81)[1] suggests that this is particularly so in a service operation for the following reasons:

- service operations are labour intensive
- human resources are prime contributors to success in the operation as:
  - the behaviour of personnel in contact with customers is an integral part of the service package
  - contact personnel have a major impact on the customers' view of the organisation
- human resources are a major cost element
- management have to rely on contact personnel to try and achieve good quality and consistency when their and the customers' behaviour can vary with each transaction
- the labour force can have a major impact through strikes, go slows for instance, particularly where service production and consumption are simultaneous. Extra bedrooms cannot be serviced and then stored in case a staffing crisis arises
- customers may also have to be managed, particularly if they provide a labour input.
  (See also Chapter 1.)

4.2   THE CUSTOMER AS A RESOURCE TO BE MANAGED

Customers will have to be managed:

- where they are involved in the production of the service, providing their own labour, eg carrying their own luggage, making their own beds, using a self-service mini-bar in their room or an 'honesty' coffee service in the lounge.
- where they need to pass through a number of stages in a prescribed manner, eg a new patient entering a hospital, a guest arriving at the hotel
- where they need to know how to behave appropriately, eg when entering a restaurant for the first time – do they seat themselves or wait to be seated; at breakfast in the restaurant – is it waitress service or do they help themselves from the buffet; should staff wash their own cups or will the cleaning staff do it for them
- where they are expected to provide feedback as part of the quality assurance and monitoring process, eg reporting faults, complaining, commenting on standards and satisfaction.
- where they are involved in marketing through word of mouth.

Customers need to know what to do and how to do it but have to be managed to behave appropriately without being embarrassed or made to feel resentful. For instance, the new guest entering a five star hotel for the first time might feel overawed and unsure and needs to know where to go and what to do and how to do it without being made to feel foolish.

Other instances of when customers need to be managed or trained include:

- how to use mini-bars or 'honesty' systems
- what to do in the case of fire and how to evacuate the building
- to complete customer satisfaction questionnaires
- how to complain
- where different facilities are located and how to get there.

It is necessary, therefore, to decide what customers need to know and the most effective way of communicating this information to them.

Customer interface with the product and the contact personnel is an extremely important element of the package as discussed in Chapters 3 and 6.

4.3   DEMOGRAPHIC TRENDS

It is well documented that the existing labour market in Britain will diminish in the mid 1990s due to the decline in the number of school leavers. Managers will have to consider alternative labour markets such as part-time rather than full-time personnel, employing older people, women returners, with or without appropriate experience, and other Europeans. Attitudes, routines and procedures will have to be adjusted according to the needs, requirements and capabilities of these new markets, eg a 45 year old woman returner cannot work at the same pace as an 18 year old school-leaver, although she should possess qualities to compensate, such as wisdom, more experience of life and stability.

Apparently international statistical evidence suggests that older employees are more reliable and dependable, less demanding, have less absenteeism, experience less job-related stress, are less likely to be distracted or disturbed, have fewer on-the-job injuries and are more satisfied with their jobs as pursuance of better social status within an operation is less important.

Competition for labour will obviously increase with potential personnel being more selective about employment. Conditions of service, welfare arrangements and working conditions will become more important features of the employment package. The features that managers will have to consider to attract personnel initially and then retain them are listed in Figure 4.1.

Management must focus not only on recruiting suitable candidates in the first place but also on their retention. This will have a knock-on effect on labour turnover which, if high, can be a large financial

Figure 4.1 *Employment package features*

- improve the image/conditions of service/pay rates to attract school-leavers and other markets to the industry
- provide a crèche facility or provide professional help in placing staff's children in local play groups
- give child-care allowance
- organise English as a second language for overseas personnel, and European language courses for English personnel
- improve welfare arrangements, eg staff dining rooms, lockers and shower facilities, social clubs and activities
- introduce a staff appraisal system
- improve training and staff development programmes including the over 45s
- improve management styles
- consider job share opportunities
- consider flexible hours
- improve maternity/paternity care
- provide home-based work, eg sewing repairs at home
- restructure jobs
- improve career prospects
- improve benefits package
- sponsor students with guaranteed work experience
- improve pension schemes
- offer advice on alternatives to retirement.

burden to bear. The cost of improving the employment package can be financed from savings made on labour turnover.

4.4   MANAGING THE LABOUR FORCE

Housekeeping and Maintenance Services are not only labour intensive, but may also be large in terms of numbers of personnel employed. It is generally accepted in a hospital that the Domestic Services Department rates second only to the Nursing Department in terms of numbers of personnel employed, with the budget comprising 90% expenditure on personnel and only approximately 10% on equipment and agents. In one very large 1000+ bedded district hospital, the Domestic Services Manager controls in excess of 600 'full-time equivalent' staff, contributing to a budget of some three million pounds.

In a medium to large hotel with a four or five star rating, the number of housekeeping personnel may be large in comparison to other departments.

Managing the labour force involves not only personnel management but also human resources, planning and the design of jobs; recruitment, selection and termination; induction, training and development, promotion; motivation of the work force; payment; health and safety and industrial relations.

As personnel constitute such a large resource, both in numerical and financial terms, much of the Accommodation Managers' time is spent dealing with human resource issues.

Many operations, particularly large concerns, have a Personnel Department which will be involved in, if not totally responsible for, some of the issues listed in Figure 4.2. Where a separate Personnel Department exists, close co-operation between departments must occur. The aspects of human resource management for which each department is responsible must be clarified. Generally the Personnel Department should be responsible for personnel administration – advertising, arranging interviews, dealing with all paperwork, medicals, general induction, sickness arrangements and communicating Company Personnel Policy. The Accommodation Manager will provide job descriptions, specify personnel requirements, select the most appropriate candidate and arrange departmental induction, training and supervision.

An attempt has been made to further detail the aspects involved in human resource management, using a flow chart based on the cycle of activities to be undertaken when designing a human resource system. See Figure 4.2.

Given the proportional significance of the housekeeping/maintenance labour budgets, more scope exists for increasing cost efficiency in this area than many others. Hence the introduction to compulsory competative tendering in Section 4.19.

Figure 4.2 *The human resources system*

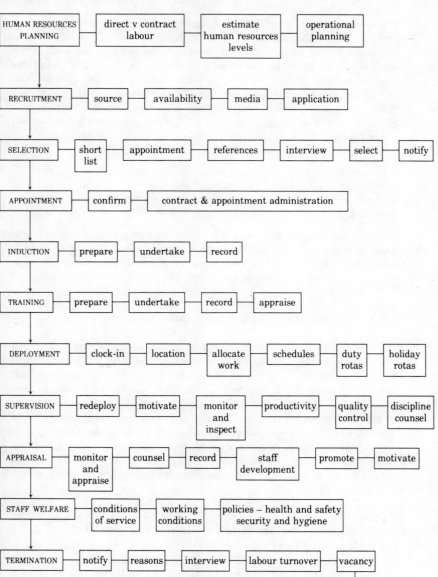

4.5 HUMAN RESOURCES PLANNING

When designing and setting up a human resources system, one must firstly have a labour plan within which to operate. This will involve forecasting optimum staffing levels, designing the jobs, allocating the work and consequently deploying the work force, besides devising the monitoring and control system (see Section 7.4.2). Cost control and efficiency and effectiveness are key issues throughout this exercise. Once the management plan is produced and agreed with senior management, the Trade Unions and whoever else must be consulted, it can be costed. Thus the human resources budget is devised.

Decisions must, of course, be taken in the light of:

● the organisation's mission statement and future plans
● the availability and capabilities of the future labour market
● the economic climate and external market (see Section 1.4.2)
● anticipated customer input.

It is useful, as a starting point, to conduct an audit of the existing human resources and customer base, if one already exists, to gain information from which predictions about the future labour availability and customer changes can be made.

4.5.1 Establishing optimum staffing levels

Too many staff will result in higher than necessary labour costs, with possibly too much time to do little work or too frequent repetition of work. Too few staff can result in stress, fatigue, low morale and high labour turnover. Both can result in falling standards, customer and staff dissatisfaction and high costs, therefore optimum staffing levels must be achieved. Business in some operations fluctuates and therefore staffing levels must be flexible to accommodate this.

It is more effective to have a model or formula to use for estimating staffing levels rather than draw the number out of a hat. The model generally used for estimating cleaning/housekeeping staffing levels will now be examined.

4.5.2 Estimating staffing levels for the cleaning/ housekeeping service

This procedure can be followed by either the in-house manager or a contractor to estimate the number of 'work-hours' required to staff a tender or job. It can be undertaken manually or by means of a computer program.

The work specification (see Chapter 3) provides the basis for estimating the work-hours required. The list of tasks to be performed in an area have already been identified (see Section 3.3.2), they now have to be quantified. In work study terms this is referred to as **Work Measurement**. This involves identifying the amount of time required to perform that task in that area, eg damp mopping 40 m^2 of unobstructed hard floor in a corridor or damp dusting 10 bed spaces in a hospital ward, or making the bed in a hotel bedroom.

The time alloted to a particular task may be based on:

- past experience of performing that task
- use of experimentation and crude time studies conducted by the Departmental Manager to establish a time value
- scientifically work studied time studies undertaken by a qualified work study officer
- MTM, ie Methods Time Measurement techniques whereby tasks are broken down into basic motions, which have already been measured and given a pre-determined time value. The time values for all motions can then be built up for a particular task without having to observe it. In other words, the time value for a task can be *synthesised*.

Some organisations commission Work Study Officers (referred to often as Management Services) or use MTM techniques to produce standard time values which can be used throughout the organisation for estimating purposes, eg District Health Authorities or hotel chains.

Unfortunately little of this kind of data is published. However, if access is gained to a company's time values, it is important to remember that they have been synthesised for tasks for a particular type of operation and may not be valid in a different type of operation. Available data is mostly in the form of synthetic time values, ie representative times for various tasks and activities gained from carrying out a number of time studies in a particular organisation, eg damp mopping takes 0.15 minutes per 100 m^2.

Once a time element has been established for each task, the time required to complete each task in a given area can be calculated. A total amount of time to undertake all tasks in that area can then be calculated. This calculation can be adjusted or weighted according to furniture and/or usage density. These densities are often coded for ease and standardisation as high, normal or low, with therefore a higher or lower amount of time allocated accordingly. See sample in Figure 4.3.

The amount of time required to complete all the tasks on a daily basis in each area is required as this will aid estimating the amount of time and number of personnel required per day. It will also be useful when developing work schedules (see Section 4.6.3) as house-keeping personnel are usually employed on a weekly basis and the amount of time required for the provision of the service is usually calculated on a weekly basis, although there is no reason why

Figure 4.3 *Density adjustments*

ROOM DATA

Room I.D. –   No. 12   Room Type – Offices
Standard Code: 1
Subdivision   1

TASK DESCRIPTION	Unit of Measurement	Dimension (m²)	Soilage Adjustment 90% 100% 110%	Furniture Density Adjustment 67% 100% 133%
1 Mop Sweep	m²	34	90%	67%
2				
3				

calculations could not be made on a monthly or annual basis. For a weekly estimation, the time element is simply multiplied or divided by the frequency to calculate the time required to perform the task over the period, eg

Task	Frequency	Time per task	Daily time	Weekly total
bedmaking	daily × 7	5 mins	5 mins	35 mins
window cleaning	monthly ÷ 4	60 mins		15 mins

The total weekly time required for cleaning or servicing the property under consideration can then be calculated.

This figure may or may not include a time element for the periodic tasks. In a hospital, for instance, where it is normal policy to undertake a proportion of periodic tasks every week, then these tasks would be included in the estimated weekly figure. Where all periodic work is done at one time, for instance during the vacation in a hall of residence, then separate figures will be calculated to establish the amount of time required for term-time and for periodic work. Another instance is where all or some periodic work will be undertaken by contractors, so a figure is not included in the normal staffing hours.

As the time elements used, particularly work study or synthetic time values, are based on actual time to complete a task only, various allowances must be included in the final calculations. These allowances tend to fall into several categories:

● a contingency allowance for collecting, returning and cleaning equipment and redoing work

- a relaxation allowance for natural breaks, working near the end of a shift, working in hot or cold conditions
- a break allowance to cover lunch and tea/coffee breaks
- an allowance to cover days off (if this is necessary)
- an allowance for holidays and bank holiday lieu days
- an allowance to cover sickness and absence.

All these allowances are not applicable in every situation, for instance in a hall of residence, where only a five day service is provided, an allowance for days off will not be included. In a hospital ward where the workload is consistent seven days a week, an allowance will have to be made to accommodate two days off per person per week. The allowance is usually incorporated on a percentage basis, eg 10% of the total working time for equipment preparation and relaxation purposes. The percentage allowance will fluctuate from one organisation to another depending on company policy and other factors such as variances on holiday entitlements, sickness and absence ratios.

The final calculation is a summation of the total number of hours per area, per week, plus appropriate allowances, eg

Area A   800 hours
Area B 1200 hours
Area C 1000 hours
                          _____
                          3,000 hours

10% relaxation   300 hours
10% sickness and absence 300 hours
11% holidays   330 hours
                          _____
                          3,930 hours

In some organisations, such as the NHS, this figure is converted to a 'full-time equivalent' (FTE or WTE whole-time equivalent), that is a figure used to express the number of staff who would be required if employed on a full-time basis, eg 40 hours (this will depend on company policy) per week, eg

$$\frac{3{,}930 \text{ hours required per week}}{40 \text{ hours worked by one full-timer}} = 98.25 \text{ FTE}$$

This is then referred to as the 'Establishment Figure' for the Domestic Services Department so, in this example, the domestic service department would require 98.25 FTE staff.

It may be more meaningful to express the total in numbers of work-hours required per week, as often a mix of full-time and part-time staff are employed.

This is the basic model of estimating from scratch. In time and with experience an estimator may be able to build up a series of 'norms'

Figure 4.4 *Estimation and staffing hours*

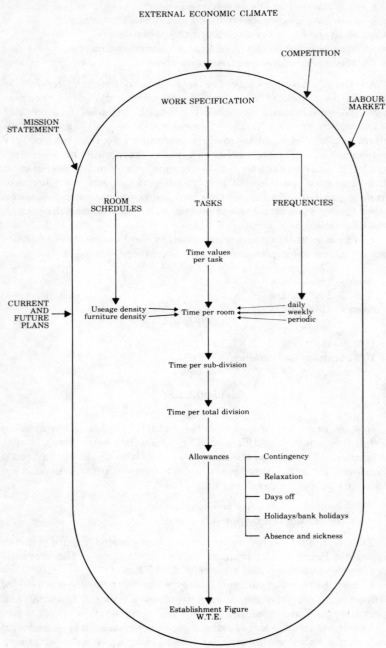

which are relevant to a particular type of operation, and reduce the amount of time and effort spent on estimating. Examples include:

- 50 m^2 per hour to clean offices
- 10 m^2 per hour to clean sanitary areas
- 70–80 m^2 per hour to clean sports halls
- 35 m^2 per hour to clean first schools and nurseries

Figure 4.4. provides a summary of the issues to be considered when estimating staffing levels.

4.5.3 Computerised estimating

A number of computerised estimating and monitoring packages are now on the market. They are designed to help with the preparation of specifications and tenders for cleaning services and also have applications in evaluation and monitoring, and control of tenders.

Generally the programmes involve defining divisions and sub-divisions of the building; room details or inventories and tasks and frequencies to be undertaken in each type of area, thus specifying the standard for that area. This database can then be used to produce a service definition print-out; calculate the workload and estimate resources, both labour and equipment, and supplies; provide a monitoring scheme, based on random sampling, and recording facility and provide management control information. Some have a modelling facility to enable the implications of variations and changes to be studied in order to be as competitive as possible.

4.6 OPERATIONAL PLANNING

It is not only necessary to determine the optimum number of work-hours, but also to plan the allocation of work to staff, and design their individual jobs. In the cleaning and housekeeping service a worker or small number of workers will need to be deployed in a specific area of the building, possibly at a specific time, to perform the allocated tasks at the designated frequency, in order to achieve the work specification objectives. This involves scheduling the work to be allocated to staff, thereby designing their jobs and then rostering to ensure that all the work is covered in all areas, as and when required. Effective operational planning at this stage helps the supervisor to deploy staff on a day-to-day basis and ultimately monitor and control performance. It also contributes to productivity (see Section 7.8).

4.6.1   Divisions and subdivisions

Before the Work Schedules can actually be prepared, the layout of the building, the approach to work allocation and the grades of staff to be employed must be considered.

Normally a building will be divided into sections of convenient size to be tackled by an individual or a small number of personnel. The type of establishment, its size, design and layout will influence the actual subdivisions or sections designated, as will the siting of cleaners' cupboards or utility rooms, sockets, water points, large scale equipment stores and lifts, the nature of the work and the times of usage of the areas. Often a building physically divorced from the rest of the premises is designated a separate subdivision. In a hospital a subdivision tends to be a ward or block of wards, a department or residence, whereas in an hotel a floor of bedrooms, or a number of public areas, such as restaurants, bars and function rooms may be regarded as subdivisions. Consideration must also be given to allocating adjoining areas to a member of staff, to avoid unproductive time walking from one area to another. Where areas are not adjoining an allowance must be added to cover 'walking time'.

4.6.2   Job design

When designing a job it is necessary to consider the range of tasks to be covered by an individual. Once again this will be influenced by the building layout and design, the type of organisation, quality standards to be achieved and the capabilities of the staff.

Provision may be made for a member (or members) of staff to be allocated a specific section, where a range of tasks, such as bed-making, damp dusting, cleaning sanitary areas and suction cleaning, are carried out in a number of rooms. Alternatively, a small number of tasks may be allocated to a small team of people. This often occurs where certain tasks require a higher degree of skill and/or knowledge or more specialised equipment, or are carried out less frequently, such as periodic floor maintenance. The team then perform this limited range of tasks throughout the building. This is known as *team cleaning* and often carries a higher wage rate. Window cleaning, floor maintenance and curtain rail teams are deployed in many hospitals. Staff may be allocated either on a permanent or a rotating basis to a team; range of tasks or subdivision. Rotation often occurs where some of the workload is boring, repetitive, strenuous, unpleasant or costed at a different rate. In a large on-site hospital laundry personnel are often rotated from one stage or process to the next on a cyclic basis, to relieve boredom and even out wages.

Specific tasks and activities must then be allocated to specific grades of staff. In most operations traditionally recognised grades of

Figure 4.5 *Job description*

Job title:	**Room Attendant**
Location:	
Scope and General Purpose:	To service allocated rooms, corridors and public areas and services on a daily basis to the standards laid down.
Responsible to:	**Housekeeping Manager**
Responsible for:	No one
Dimensions	House Porter/Laundry/Duty Housekeeper/ Maintenance Reception/Switchboard

MAIN DUTIES/ ACCOUNTABILITIES:

1 To arrive for work at the correct time as per rota, in full hotel uniform.
2 To ensure a high standard of personal hygiene at all times.
3 To ensure a good working liaison with all other departments and Management at all times.
4 To ensure that all opening and closing procedures are carried out correctly at all times.
5 To service allocated rooms to the standards as laid down in the Minimum Standard Checklist.
6 To clean appropriate service corridor on a daily basis to the standard laid down in the Minimum Standards Checklist.
7 To ensure trolley is stocked to the correct level, of all cleaning agents, stationery and guest supplies.
8 To be responsible for the laundering and upkeep of supplied uniforms.
9 To report all maintenance defects on a daily basis to the Housekeeping Manager.
10 To care for all equipment supplied and report any defects.
11 To be aware of and implement security to the standard laid down in the Induction Training Manual.
12 To be aware of and implement energy conservation to reduce hotel costs.
13 To hand in all lost property as found to the standard as laid down in the Induction Training Manual.
14 To sign the time sheets on the appropriate day to ensure payment of correct wages.
15 In case of illness to telephone and contact the Duty Housekeeper or Night Manager before 7.30 am and to produce medical certificates for periods of sickness.
16 To carry out any extra duties as requested by the Housekeeper or deputy, or Management.
17 To turn mattresses on beds as required, with the assistance of the House Porter.

Figure 4.5 *Continued*

18 To report any findings of pests or insects to the Duty Housekeeper.
19 To establish a courteous and helpful attitude to all guests at all times and anticipating and caring for their individual needs.
20 To inform the Duty Housekeeper of any guest found to be unwell.
21 To discuss with the Housekeeper any ideas and suggestions that would contribute to the profitability of the department.
22 To attend training sessions as and when required.
23 To be familiar with the hotel and company children's policy relating to Housekeeping and to ensure that it is carried out correctly.
24 To be familiar with the hotel policy regarding fire, health, safety and security in accordance with F P Act 1971 and H & S A W Act 1974.
25 To report all accidents to yourself, guest or other members of staff to the Duty Manager, so they can be noted in the Accident Book.
26 To deal with guests' comments, complaints and compliments, ensuring that the Duty Housekeeper is informed immediately of whatever action taken.
27 To carry out any reasonable request by Management.

Occasional duties:	Baby Sitting Cloakroom Attendant

Prepared by		Date
Approved by		Date
Signature of job holder:		Date

staff exist with well defined duties and responsibilities. This often breeds demarcation disputes and can result in more staff and less flexibility. Some thought should be given to the use of 'multi-functional' staff, to introduce flexibility and more variety into an individual's job. For instance the full brigade of front office personnel may be employed, with staff specialising in reception, book-keeping or cashiering duties, or a flexible front office clerk who can cover all those responsibilities. Thus it is easier also to cover days off and absence.

These decisions will subsequently affect work allocation, scheduling, shift hours and the number of part-time and full-time staff required.

Once the above issues have been considered, job descriptions can be devised. A job description is a broad statement of the purpose, scope, duties and responsibilities of a particular job. It may also explain the environment in which the job will be undertaken and the lines of communication and responsibility. An example for a room attendant is provided in Figure 4.5.

4.6.3   Work schedules

Work can be allocated to individuals or small groups of personnel by means of work schedules. A *work schedule* can be defined as a timetable of tasks to be undertaken by each individual worker within a certain period of time or 'shift'. Carefully planned work schedules should incorporate the following:

- a list of tasks/activities to be completed
- the sequence in which these tasks/activities should be completed
- the approximate times at which the tasks/activities should be completed and the amount of time allocated
- the break times to be taken by the member(s) of staff
- any special factors, eg check that windows are closed, keys handed in
- hours of duty ie the 'shift' hours.

A sample work schedule is contained in Figure 4.6.

A work schedule should ensure that an individual member of staff knows exactly what to do, where and when, thus avoiding worry, confusion and fatigue. It also ensures that all tasks, whether daily, weekly and possibly periodic are covered with none missed out or duplicated. Each member of staff should be given a fair and even distribution of work within the number of hours worked, with no overlapping of duties. Time should be saved as, in conjunction with induction and training, no staff should be left waiting for instructions. Equipment can also be scheduled to ensure a fair distribution and allow even wear and tear.

Supervisors should know where staff are at a particular time and which area or tasks can be checked. Work Schedules are also useful where a relief member of staff is covering an area; as a training aid; to help set the quality standard required by ensuring that the right amount of time needed to perform a task, and the correct sequence of tasks occurs.

Work Schedules for a specific section can then be drafted using data already collated, ie the tasks to be undertaken, the frequencies, the times per task, the required standards and special requirements. The other data to be considered includes the time span through which that section needs to be covered, the timing of tasks and their sequence.

The routines of other groups of personnel, such as bed-making by nursing staff and of the customers such as business people vacating rooms earlier than holiday makers, will influence the timing and sequencing of tasks. Other factors which may influence scheduling of

Figure 4.6 *Work schedule*

Circulation Areas

Domestic Assistant 1–4 pm Monday to Friday

Shopping Area/ECG/Porters

30	Corridor and Lobby to Porters Room
31a	Porters Room
32	ECG Room
53	Security Office
62	Main Entrance
54,55,56	Male WCs
63–66	Female WCs

Lifts

62a	Staff Lift
62b	Staff Lift
62c	Visitors' Lift
62d	Visitors' Lift
62a	Entrance Carpet

Daily Duties

1.00 pm **Clean Porters Room, ECG Room and Corridor and Lobby to Porters Room**

Collect and dispose of **Refuse**. Empty and clean ashtrays. **Damp Dust** furniture and fittings. Clean **Sinks**. Replenish soap and towels. Remove marks from doors and paintwork.
Vacuum carpet in Porters Room. **Dust Control Mop** corridor and ECG Room. **Damp Mop** corridor and lobby. **Spot Mop** ECG Room (Damp Mop ECG Monday).

1.30 pm **Check Clean Level 02**, Male and Female WCs, Lift Lobby, Coffee Area, Corridor and Shops and Entrance Carpet.

Replace Soap, Toilet Rolls and Paper Towels in WCs

Clean Lifts
Damp Dust fixtures and control panel. Wipe marks from walls and doors.
Dust Control Mop and Deck Scrub floors.

2.15 pm **Check Clean Level 02** Lift Lobby, Coffee Area and Corridor by shops.

Vacuum Entrance Carpet Level 02.

Full Clean Male and Female WCs
Collect and dispose of **Refuse**. Clean **Sinks, Urinals and WCs**. Replace **Soap, Paper Towels and Toilet Rolls**. Remove marks from walls, doors and paintwork. **Damp Mop** floors.

2.45 pm **Clean Security Office**
Collect and dispose of **Refuse. Damp Dust** fixtures and fittings. Remove marks from doors and paintwork. **Vacuum** carpet.

3.00 pm Commence **Weekly Duties**

3.30 pm **Check Clean Level 02** Lift Lobby, Coffee Area, Corridor by Shops, Entrance Carpet and Male and Female WCs.

Replace Soap, Paper Towels and Toilet Rolls in WCs

4.00 pm OFF DUTY

Weekly Duties
Porters Room, ECG Room and Lobby and Corridor to Porters Room

Monday	High dust, low dust, clean metal door plates, and door grilles, clean bins and inside paper towel holders. Wash chairs (monthly).
Tuesday	Weekly Duties in Lifts
Wednesday	High dust
	Polish stainless steel walls and doors
Thursday	Remove fluff and debris from floor channels
	Wash painted doors.
Friday	

tasks include doctors wards rounds, visiting times, opening hours and frequency and pattern of usage. For instance, hospital departments and offices only used five days a week, open say from 8 am to 6 pm, would suggest that cleaning commences after 6 pm on a five-day basis. By plotting on a time plan those tasks which can only be performed at certain times, those tasks which have to be completed before a deadline or prior to another task and meal and break-times, and then fitting in all other tasks in sequence, it is possible to highlight the peaks and troughs in activity which will help to determine when periodic tasks can be fitted in, and the shift hours when staff are required.

This in turn helps to determine the number of part-time and full-time staff required. Sources of recruitment and availability of personnel in the locality will affect the decision to employ full-time or part-time staff.

4.6.4   Human resources budget

It is now possible to project the labour costs over a period of time and thus produce the human resources budget. The following information will be required:

- the number of personnel required within each grade
- the hourly rates of pay
- the shift hours and duty rotas to estimate the enhanced payments to be paid for alternating shifts, weekend work, etc
- anticipated overtime (although this is not allowed in some operations)
- employer's statutory contributions.

Other costs, such as recruitment, training, labour turnover, over-alls and uniforms, meals on duty, paid breaks, must also be projected to produce the human resources budget figure. The budget may also include supervisory and management costs, although these may

***Figure** 4.7 Operational planning*

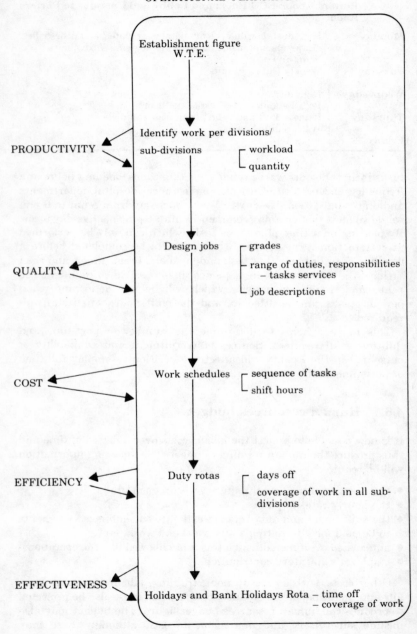

OPERATIONAL PLANNING

be included elsewhere. Figure 4.7 outlines the issues involved in operational planning.

4.7 RECRUITMENT AND SELECTION

The aim of recruitment and selection is to choose the right person for the job, using methods which are cost and operationally effective, and at the same time acceptable to the candidates.

4.7.1 The vacancy

The Accommodation Manager is very rarely going to recruit and select the whole team at once unless a completely new venture is being undertaken. Normally the recruitment and selection process commences when a member of the team has terminated employment and hence created a vacancy. All specific details of the vacancy must be identified, such as place of work, shift hours, grade, and off-duty arrangements. In a large department where a number of Assistant Managers are involved in the recruitment and selection process confusion can arise and all details of the vacancy must be documented. On reviewing the vacancy a decision may be taken not to fill it.

If a Job Description (as explained in Section 4.6.2) does not exist for the vacancy or the job is to change then one should be prepared or amended. A technique known as *Job Analysis* can be used which involves direct observation of the employee and interviewing them and the Supervisor to determine the duties and responsibilities involved in that job. Job Descriptions must be kept up to date. They are not only invaluable at interviews for explaining the job but form the basis of an individual's training programme.

It is also useful to define, as accurately as possible, the desired attributes of the individual required to fill the vacancy. These individual requirements can be collated in the form of a Personnel Specification covering the following set of headings against which candidates can ultimately be assessed:

- age and physical requirements
- educational qualifications and special skills
- experience pattern
- personality requirements for proper integration within the team or organisation
- special considerations, eg need for a language
- potential for individual development in line with planned growth of responsibilities
- interests.

The specification is intended to describe the person who is capable of doing the job adequately, not an impossible ideal. See example in Figure 4.8.

Figure 4.8 *Personnel specification*

Job Title	Essential	Desirable	Contra-indications
Physique			
Attainments eg Schooling Qualifications Experience			
Special aptitudes			
General intelligence			
Interests			
Disposition			
Present circumstances			

4.7.2   Sources of recruitment

Consideration must be given to the source(s) of recruitment most appropriate to the type of vacancy to be filled. Candidates may be recruited internally by recommendation, internal advertising or even from an on-going waiting list of possible candidates. Internal recruitment can boost morale, create a promotional structure and ensure than existing talent is not overlooked. Job Centres and employment agencies may be considered as an external means of recruitment, the latter are used extensively by London hotels to overcome staffing shortages. Advertising in the national or local press; trade or professional journals; magazines; shop windows or any other appropriate media, is another external option. When external recruitment is necessary, the most appropriate media, and times to attack the labour market required, should be selected. Good advertising copy must be created in order to gain attention, through say a distinctive title and layout, hold interest with information about the company, create desire by describing the job, the type of person required and the benefits, and promote action with a simple application procedure. Costs must be considered, some organisations have an Advertising Budget, and measure the effectiveness of advertising by the number of respondents, the cost per application, per interview or per vacancy filled.

4.7.3 Selection

Interview costs can be reduced by considering an initial screening of the application letter and/or standard application form (see Figure 4.9) to eliminate unsuitable candidates or, conversely, select the most suitable candidates to be called for interview. It is courteous to acknowledge receipt of all requests and inform the candidates of success or failure to attain an interview.

References may then be taken up for those candidates to be called for interview. There are basically three alternative methods of procuring a reference, each with its own particular advantages and disadvantages:

- by letter asking for a reference
- by postal questionnaire, asking specific questions (see Figure 4.10)
- by telephone.

Individual, ie one to one, interviews are effective for operative and supervisory levels to speed up the decision making process and attain consistent judgement from the specialist (Accommodation Manager), whereas multi-individual or panel interviews are more appropriate for managerial levels, particularly to give a cross-section of opinions.

4.7.4 Interview structure and techniques

It is best to structure an interview to ensure that all relevant areas are covered, but the structure itself should not be too apparent or inflexible. In order to maintain rapport the discussion should be informal but the interviewer must ensure that all the following areas are covered and assessments made:

Figure 4.9 *Sample application form*

APPLICATION FOR EMPLOYMENT

NOTE: Please complete in type or in block capitals in black ink
(*denotes delete as appropriate).

FOR OFFICE USE ONLY

POST APPLIED FOR	LOCATION
SURNAME	*MR./MRS./MISS/MS/OTHER (please specify).
ADDRESS	FIRST NAME(S)
	FORMER NAME (if applicable)
	DATE OF BIRTH
TELEPHONE NUMBER	Do you have a current clean driving licence? *YES/NO
DAYTIME TELEPHONE NUMBER (if applicable)	Do you own your own car? *YES/NO

SECONDARY EDUCATION

Schools Attended	Dates From	To	Examinations Passed (with grade)

FURTHER EDUCATION
(If applicable include details of apprenticeship)

Establishment Attended	Dates From	To	Examinations Passed (with grade)

EMPLOYMENT DETAILS Enter your present job. ALL previous employment (most recent first) and periods of unemployment.

Employer's name and address	Where employed	Job held	Dates From	To	Wage/ Salary	Reason for Leaving

- impact
- education
- intellectual capacity
- experience
- motivation
- adjustment/compatibility
- personal background.

Despite the failings of the selection interview, if it is properly conducted it can be a potent tool and every manager should be skilled in its use. The following aspects should be considered:

HEALTH   Please note that you may be required to undergo a medical examination before any offer of employment is made.

A disability or health problem does not preclude full consideration for the job and applications from suitable disabled people are welcome.   All information will be treated as confidential.

Do you suffer/have you suffered from any serious illness ?   *YES/NO
If Yes, please give details

Do you have any physical disabilities ?   *YES/NO
If Yes, please give details

Are you a Registered Disabled Person ?   *YES/NO
If Yes, please give your registration number

REFERENCES   Please give the names of two people — these should normally be representatives of your present and last employers, not friends or relatives — to whom we can apply for references

	NAME	OCCUPATION	ADDRESS	TELEPHONE NO
(1)				
(2)				

References will normally be taken up prior to interview.   If you do not wish us to do so, please state here:

Please give details of how you came to know about this job:

Please use this space for any further information you would like to give in support of your application:

DECLARATION
I understand that the appointment, if offered, is subject to the information given above being correct.

Signature...   Date ....

Please return this form, without delay, to:

● Application forms
Wherever possible these should have been completed prior to the interview and are a valuable aid as a means of comparison against the personnel specification, as a basis for screening and, in the interview, as a basis for question formulation.

● Appointments
Consideration should be given as to when the interviews are to take place, if all candidates are to be expected at the same time, or appointments are to be staggered on one day or over a few days.

● Waiting Area
Candidates will need a designated area in which to wait until called for interview. The area must be well sign-posted, have enough chairs

Figure 4.10 *Example of a reference questionnaire*

FRAZER CLEANING

REFERENCE REQUEST
Reference from _____
Designation _____
Candidate's name _____
Candidate's address _____

Date of Employment – From_____To_____
In What Capacity _____
Was candidate dismissed? If so, kindly give details _____

Please give your opinion of the candidate's suitability for the post, including so far as you are able your assessment of:-
(a) His/her professional knowledge and skills _____

(b) His/her relationship with both senior colleagues and subordinates _____

(c) The main features of his/her character and personality _____

(d) Any other information relating to candidate's ability, manners, integrity

As far as you know is candidate:-
(a) Honest and Trustworthy _____
(b) Punctual _____
(c) Industrious _____
(d) Efficient _____

This post is not protected by the Rehabilitation of Offenders Act 1974. Have you any knowledge of any criminal convictions of the candidate? If so, please give details.

Does candidate suffer from any disability? If so, please give details _____

Did candidate lose much time through ill health? _____

Is the candidate receiving any medical/hospital treatment? _____

Would you re-employ? If not, please give reasons _____

Please give below any other relevant information likely to be helpful _____

Signed_____Date_____

and be near to toilet facilities. Candidates should not be kept waiting for any longer than necessary as it only increases anxiety and apprehension. An apology and explanation for any delay is only courteous.

• Venue for the interview
It is essential to consider where the interview is to take place and how the seating and furniture is to be arranged to encourage an informal and relaxed interview. Telephone calls and other interruptions should be stopped whilst interviewing is in progress.

• Structure
A definite time plan is useful for each type of interview, especially if several occur one after another. For instance, 20 to 25 minutes is about right for a domestic assistant with:

- 5 minutes for the introduction
- 5 minutes for giving information about the post
- 10 minutes for fact finding and discussion
- 5 minutes for drawing the interview to a close.

The candidates will be nervous and anxious so the interviewer should try and put them at ease initially and create a rapport to achieve a relaxed candidate who will talk freely. The interview should be constructed in a chronological sequence, for instance, working through the application form to the present day and retracing steps where inconsistency or disagreement with the application form occurs. The reference may also be used to highlight inconsistencies. Questions soliciting a 'yes/no' answer should be avoided, and comment and expansion should be encouraged. The interviewer's role is to prompt, record and listen, and the interviewer should try not to be flippant, off-hand or offensive. It is useful if the interviewer can also be aware of non-verbal communication. Does body language, for instance, reinforce oral communication or contradict it?

A conducted tour prior to or after the 'formal' interview may be required. Supervisors and Assistant Managers can play a valuable role in this.

Thought should always be given to the concluding procedure. Is the successful candidate to be informed immediately or in writing, or are outstanding references to be awaited? The interviewer should be consistent and ensure the procedure indicated to the candidate is carried out. The candidates should be treated as the interviewer would wish to be treated under such circumstances, and the interviewer should remember that candidates will take away an impression of the interviewer and the organisation which could be favourable or otherwise.

4.7.5 Assessment

Brief comments for assessment should be recorded immediately after each interview as the memory is fickle. Simple headings, such as appearance, personality, mental capacity, experience, may be used rather than those given in the Personnel Specification. Some kind of rating scale may be required, a convenient one being:

A – exceptional
B – good
C – satisfactory
D – below standard
E – unsuitable.

Candidates not meeting essential qualifications and experience, as set out in the Job Description and Personnel Specification, will be unsuitable (E). Compatibility with others in the team or organisation must be considered, potential for growth and career development may well be required attributes.

4.7.6   Administration

It is essential, particularly with regard to public relations, to inform both successful and unsuccessful candidates by the date stated at the interview. A starting date will have to be confirmed with the successful candidate and arrangements will then proceed for uniform provision, medicals, induction, notification of all relevant departments, provision of a Contract of Employment and preparation of a personal file. The Personnel Department may have made all the arrangements and the Accommodation Manager purely interviewed and selected the most suitable candidate.

4.8   INDUCTION AND TRAINING

Induction

Induction is the introduction of a new employee to the working environment, the existing members of staff and the purposes, practices and policies of the organisation. It can be seen as a continuous process as existing staff have to be introduced to new environments when they are moved.

The purpose of the induction process is to relieve anxiety and provide the new employee with a better understanding of the organisation. It should be designed to help the new employee settle in and quickly feel part of the organisation, enabling them to develop confidence and contribute to the organisation more speedily. Induction is beneficial to both the employee and the employer, not only as a basis for formulating relationships and communication links but also as a means of potentially reducing labour turnover which, in the long term, can be very costly. Many staff leave their employment after a relatively short period – a few days to a few weeks, which is an expensive burden for any operation. A good, well planned induction programme should help to alleviate this occurrence as it tends to create a good first impression, which often encourages staff to stay longer.

In a large organisation, particularly where a Personnel Department exists, induction can be split into two stages:

Stage 1 Immediate (pyschological) induction to the work environment, colleagues, the actual work to be undertaken and performance standards, all of which are psychologically important.

Stage 2 Background induction to the wider organisation, its objectives, structure, policies and condition of service.

Stage 1 is usually organised by the Departmental Manager, immediately the new employee commences, whereas **Stage 2** may be undertaken some time later by the Personnel Department, when the new employee has settled in, and often consists of a mixture of personnel from the whole organisation.

When planning the immediate induction programme, the Departmental Manager should consider several questions:

- **When will the induction commence?**
  The beginning of the normal shift is often inconvenient to the organiser and the employee may be asked to start later or earlier than the normal shift time. For instance, in a hospital a new employee may be asked to start at 8.30 am or 9.00 am instead of 7.00 am on their first morning to allow the supervisor to ensure coverage of all work areas before giving undivided attention to the new employee. On the other hand, if a new evening domestic assistant commences who will only work a three hour shift and the evening supervisor has a high ratio of personnel to supervise, it is feasible for the new employee to start an hour earlier than the rest of the employees.
- **How long will the programme last?**
  It may be two hours; the first day; split over a two or three day period. A balance has to be reached, with time to cover the essential material, but not so long that employees, especially manual staff, feel that they will never actually perform any work.
- **Who will be involved?**
  Departmental Managers, Assistants, Supervisors or a combination may be involved.
- **Where will it occur?**
  The manager's office, a training room, or the work environment may be selected. A tour may be incorporated.
- **What will the content be?**
  There are certain essential areas which have to be covered and a well organised department may produce a checklist to ensure that nothing is missed out.

Figure 4.11 *A typical induction programme*

Reception	Welcome and Introduction
Administration	Completion of appointment forms, contracts, confidentiality/bribery forms, P.45s
Essential places	Canteen, toilets, locker areas, time clock, wages department
Conditions of service	Working week, rates of pay, period of notice, absence, sickness, holidays, time-keeping, security, fire procedure, grievance and disciplinary procedures
Departmental information	Organisation structure, who's who, objectives, role within organisation, liaison
Introduction to the job	Job description, hours of work, duty rotas, expected performance standards, check skill level, check familiarity with equipment, training arrangements
Health, safety and security	Health and safety arrangements, fire procedures, personal hygiene, infection controls, legal implications, security awareness
Welfare arrangements	Canteen, toilets, lockers, protective clothing, occupational health, medicals, pension scheme, social clubs
Remuneration	Rates of pay, calculations, payment arrangements
General tour	

   The content of a typical induction programme is contained in Figure 4.11, the order of priority or sequence will vary according to the situation and the level of personnel involved.

   The programme should stimulate interest and provide information in an efficient and systematic manner. Many organisations develop Staff Handbooks as an aid to conveying initially the information and as a suitable source of reference for the new employee.

Training

Once the initial stages of the induction programme have been completed, training can commence. Under favourable conditions, training allows management to make more effective use of human resources – the most costly of all resources. Training not only provides the means for enhancing performance of personnel working at less than their best but also for making better use of personnel already working well. The training process should aim to develop good working methods, habits and skills, together with a better understanding of the purpose of the job, the objectives of the various tasks and the expected results or performance level. This provides the employee with a feeling of mastery over the work and increased confidence and job satisfaction, besides eliminating confusion, stress and fatigue.

Other benefits of training could include:

- increased production
- higher quality output
- lower wastage
- reduced labour turnover and increased morale
- lower accident levels
- fewer complaints
- reduced absenteeism, sickness and lateness
- greater labour flexibility
- better talent identification
- improved labour relations
- improved safety and hygiene
- increased job satisfaction
- better security
- energy conservation.

The approach to training
A systematic approach to training can ensure that it is carefully planned and supervised and the costs involved are commensurate with the benefits achieved. The following approach is recommended:

Identify the need for training
Training is usually required in response to some event such as:

- the appointment of a new employee
- the installation of new equipment or the introduction of a new product, both requiring new or improved skills, eg hyperspeed floor maintenance machine or sanding machine
- installation of new technology, eg computerisation
- a change in working methods or practices, requiring new skills, or knowledge, eg spray burnishing, bonnet buffing
- an increasing number of complaints or accidents, eg standards of cleanliness or maintenance, breakages, spillages, poor quality laundry
- improving the quality of the provision and inadequate peformance, eg hygiene control or equipment care
- the introduction of new legislation or codes of practice, eg Health and Safety, fire, COSHH
- as part of the staff development plan to improve job satisfaction, staff retention and prepare for promotion.

Thus a training need has been created. Any training which occurs as a matter of routine, such as the training of new employees, must be reviewed frequently to ensure that the purpose, methods and standards are always relevant.

Analyse the training need
It is possible, having identified a problem which seems to suggest a training need, that on further investigation the problem was a

management or organisational one, and training is not actually the solution. For instance, the recruitment and selection policy may need revising, the ratio of supervisors to personnel may need improving, large scale equipment may require more effective scheduling or maintenance, or stores selection may be inadequate.

If training is considered to be the solution, then it is necessary to consider the overall aims of the training required, which may be to:

- develop an understanding of information and ideas and show how these can be applied to different situations
- develop a skill or series of skills or procedures in order to carry out a regular pattern of sequential activities
- change existing attitudes and ideas or develop new ones
- remember facts, figures or technical terms
- a combination of all these.

Setting training objectives
For each section of the training programme, clear learning outcomes, in terms of what the trainee should be able to accomplish at the end of the training programme, should be set.

For instance the trainee will be able to:

- use a specified make of high speed burnishing machine
- spray burnish any floor in the establishment to the specified standard
- clean the equipment down after use.

An acceptable minimum standard of achievement or performance in terms of quality, speed, safety, cost must be established which can then be conveyed to the trainee during the training process.

Devising the training programme
The training programme devised will be as simple or as complex as required, according to the training needs. For instance, it may comprise a single session, such as how to use the new high-speed burnishing machine or it may comprise a larger number of sessions for say a new room attendant covering the range of tasks and duties included in their job description (see Figure 4.12). In the latter case, consideration will have to be given to such issues as:

- how many sessions are to be undertaken?
- how long will each session last?
- will the programme be an intensive continuous course, eg a one week course or will it be spread over a number of weeks, eg one session a week for several weeks?
- when will the sessions take place? Before, after or during normal work time; at the quietest time of the day or week?
- where will the sessions take place? On-the-job; in a quiet/empty area, or in a specially designated training room?

Figure 4.12 *An example of a training programme for a new room attendant*

Room cleaning
– Constituent tasks – Bedmaking; vacuuming; dusting; ledges; paintwork; walls; telephones; bins and ashtrays; stains
Washing the teapots
Replenishing room stocks, soft furnishings and bedding
Frequencies
Standards expected – appearance, hygiene, layout when completed
Time allowed per room

Bathroom cleaning
– Constituent tasks – Cleaning bath; shower and curtain; basin; mirrors; bidet; toilet; floor
Replenishing stocks
Frequencies
Standards expected
Time allowances

Services – eg how to serve early morning tea
Laundry arrangements
Waste disposal
Care and usage of equipment
Hygiene
Health and safety
Fire and security
Social skills and attitudes to customers
Energy conservation

- who will be involved in training? The Manager; an outside speaker; a company representative; the supervisor?

Carrying out the training programme
For each session within the training programme to be successful, careful planning should be undertaken. The objectives and content of each session must be determined and also due consideration given to the format, duration and training techniques to be used.

Content
The content should be relevant for the level of intelligence of the trainees, being neither too simple nor too complex. It should be broken down into logical divisions of knowledge to be conveyed to the trainee by the most appropriate instructional method, and for the trainee to master. Key points affecting quality, safety, costs should be stressed.

Format
Thought should be given to the introduction to the session in order to gain attention, put the trainees at ease and motivate them to want to learn. It is a good idea to state the job or subject and explain the

format of the session so the trainee will initially have an idea of what to expect.

A logical sequence of events should follow at a suitable pace, with a range of varied activities wherever possible, to promote participation, stimulate interest and maintain concentration. Information should be summarised at appropriate stages. It is important at the end of the session to recap, test understanding of knowledge or skills acquired in order to encourage a deeper understanding and retention of information before drawing the session to a conclusion. The following maxim is worth remembering:

Tell them what you are going to tell them.
Tell them, and tell them what you have told them.

Where a practical skill has been included, some time should be allowed for practise and correction of errors.

The duration of the session should be given careful thought, particularly where manual staff, such as room attendants are concerned, as they are not used to sitting and concentrating for long-periods of time, so 20–30 minutes only is preferable.

Instructional techniques

Before deciding on which one or more of the alternative instructional techniques or activities to use consider the following:

I hear and I forget
I see and I remember
I do and I understand.

The alternative instructional techniques and activities include:

- telling
- showing or demonstrating (live or video)
- question and answer
- discussion groups
- quizzes
- case studies
- exercise/problems
- practical
- brain storming

To facilitate the transference of information and ideas, visual aids may be used such as charts, handouts, pamphlets, overhead transparencies, slides, films, videos or photographs. Teaching equipment such as overhead projectors, slide and film projectors, videos, computers, flip-charts, chalk boards, magnetic boards and wall mounted clip boards may then be required.

The content of the session will, to some extent, dictate the techniques, aids and equipment appropriate but a variety of techniques and a variation in activities will enhance the training process.

All equipment must be in good working order, and the trainer must be able to operate it correctly.

Methods of training

Training may be on-the-job, that is given by the trainer in the normal working situation with the trainee using the actual tools, equipment, materials or documents that will be used when fully trained. However, the trainee might find this stressful in a very busy, noisy area and learning may well be inhibited, equipment could be damaged, and an amount of spoilt work could occur.

An alternative system not highly favoured, but not uncommon, is the method known as *Sitting with Nellie* or *The Buddy System*, where a member of the peer group will train a new employee. This type of training is often used when staff shortages occur. This may be satisfactory if the 'trainer', who may in fact receive a training allowance, is trained to train. On the other hand, this 'trainer' may be a poor trainer and the trainee may be exposed to poor practises and shortcuts and thus pick up bad habits.

Off-the-job training may take place away from the normal work situation in a specially designated training room, within the establishment. The trainee, in this case, is not regarded as a productive worker during the training process. Specialist training of a higher quality should occur and as the trainee can learn in planned stages, higher standards of quality and speed could well ensue. Difficulties may be experienced when changing from the training environment to the production environment.

Off-the-job training may also take place at a company training centre or a college but higher costs will be incurred to cover travelling and subsistence expenses.

The trainee

The trainee must also be considered when preparing the training programme.

The number of trainees to be trained will influence the format of the session, the range and type of activities, the number of handouts required and the seating arrangements and the layout of the area. The latter in turn influencing the effectiveness of the training process.

The background of the trainee is also important. The application form and personnel specification can be used to identify the extent of prior knowledge and experience and the age and sex of the trainee which again may affect the approach and training techniques used. An example of a training plan is contained in Appendix 3.

Training records

During the training period it is necessary for training records to be kept up to date, as a management control and aide-memoire to record what took place, and provide information on staff and their progress. Records are especially useful to record illness or absence; for health and safety purposes or in the occurrence of accidents (see Figure 4.13).

Figure 4.13 *Training record*

| NAME | GLADYS SMITH | | DEPT | DOMESTIC | | | |

| ORGANISATION | **GRASSFIELD GENERAL HOSPITAL** | | | | | | |

TRAINING RECORD CARD

NATURE OF TRAINING	DATE & DURATION	EMPLOYEES SIGNATURE	DATE & DURATION	EMPLOYEES SIGNATURE	REMARKS	TRAINING COMPLETED SUPERVISOR
To clean toilet	4/7/85 30min	G Smith	5/7/85 10min		Well organised	J V P
To clean handbasin	9/7/85 10 min	G Smith			No further instr. needed	J V P

4.8.1   Assessing the effectiveness of the training programme

Once the training programme has been completed it is necessary to evaluate it and, if possible, measure its success. Sometimes this is possible in practical terms but intangible results such as better co-operation or changes in attitude should also be noted. In the short term, it is necessary and possible to monitor the trainee to see if the instructions given are being carried out. This ensures that the instructional methods being used are correct. In the mid term it is possible to see that standards are being maintained and, in the longer term, to monitor any benefits to the business, effects on other departments, staff or the customer and changes in the number of complaints, absence, sickness and lateness, labour turnover, productivity, reduced costs or increased revenue.

It is necessary to determine whether training was worthwhile, in relation to the individual, the department, the unit, whole organisation and the customer and establish whether the training achieved its objectives and satisfied the originally identified need. This is particularly important when comparing it with such alternatives as:

● carrying out no training
● sending the trainee away for training by another body
● improving recruitment and selection policies by recruiting already trained staff at a higher cost.

During the evaluation of training, strengths and weaknesses of the programme or techniques used can be assessed and where necessary remedial action taken to improve future training.

4.8.2   Calculating the cost of training

It is often difficult to establish where training commences and finishes and as many of the costs involved are intangible, it is somewhat difficult to calculate the cost of training. If attempting to calculate the total cost of training the following must be considered:

- **Labour costs** — trainer's salary
  - wages of staff whilst training
  - outside speakers' fees and expenses
  - preparation time
  - technician help

- **Equipment costs** — audio-visual equipment and associated costs

- **Accommodation costs** — training room
  - hiring of accommodation
  - overnight costs
  - loss of revenue if area is taken out of commission

- **Administrative costs** — duplicating/printing
  - stationery

- **Subsistence** — food and beverage costs.

Unfortunately trainees may leave during or after the training programme hence other organisations may benefit from your investment.

4.8.3   Training packages

It may be of value for a large company to develop or commission the development of customised training packages for various types of personnel.

The benefits of such a concept are that the costs of formulation and production are shared by a number of users over a period of time, thus resulting in more economic training. Standardisation of training and content material, and a systematic approach to training will also result. The training package must be piloted initially in order to eliminate teething problems and be evaluated and updated on a regular basis. It must be flexible to amend to meet local training needs and allow for learners with different learning rates.

The development of a training package involves initially identifying a large scale training need which will warrant the time and effort of formulation, the expense of production, and provision to the end user. The formulation, usually undertaken by a small group, will involve defining the aims and objectives, writing the content and suggesting suitable training techniques and aids to use. Suggestions for organising and running the training package may also be included.

The NHS Hotel Services Training Directorate has developed a *Domestic Supervisor's Training Kit* covering all technical aspects of a domestic services or housekeeping department. Although primarily designed for health care establishments, it can be used in all sectors of the cleaning industry. The kit is in two parts:

- **The Manager's Pack** – including a guide on how to use the kit and help supervisors to learn, and a reference book of the modules, with further technical notes and learning activities.
- **The Supervisor's Pack** – which comprises stand-alone booklets to encourage supervisors to use them for their own benefit and for on-the-job training. It contains the following 11 modules:

- Introduction
- General principles of cleaning
- Cleaning agents
- Equipment
- Furniture, fixtures and fittings
- Sanitary areas
- Walls, windows and ceilings
- Hard floors
- Textile floor coverings
- Isolation and special risk areas
- Hotel services

4.8.4   National Vocational Qualifications (NVQs)

It was suggested in an official report in the mid 1980s that there was a link between investment in training and development and commercial success but that this perception was lacking in the UK and must be improved.

Subsequently the National Council for Vocational Qualifications was set up to act as a catalyst for change, and work towards developing an accreditation system through a comprehensible system of vocational qualifications, having responsibility also of moving towards competence-based qualifications. The NCVQ has worked closely with the now Training Enterprise and Education Department (TEED) to establish Industry Lead Bodies, eg The Cleaning Industry Lead Body, Health Care Consortium or the Hotel, Catering and Training Company. The Industry Lead Bodies (ILBs) have been charged with defining standards of competence for that Industry which will form the basis of the NVQs. Awarding bodies such as City & Guilds and HCIMA have been working with the ILBs to develop the NVQs and provide the assessment and certification system. There are five levels, ranging from the basic operative grade, Level 1, to Senior Management, Level 5 (see Appendix 4).

The NVQ framework aims to make a comprehensive training and education provision for everyone to cover all significant occupations and work activities. The NVQs are unit based (see Appendix 4 for definition) and units are offered for separate assessment and certification. Assessment will take place in the workplace wherever practicable. Therefore individuals can achieve credit towards a qualification which can then be built up to progress onto the next level, so a career route has been opened up for all.

Companies will have to become familiar with the relevant NVQs and develop a system to allow access to all personnel who have potential to reach the standard, be assessed and certified. Advisor/ Assessors within a Company will have to be identified and trained, and internal and external verifiers will endeavour to ensure that standards are consistent across the Industry. The system should provide the opportunity to enhance professionalism in the Industry.

4.9 ROSTERING

Managers must ensure that staff are on duty to undertake the tasks and services specified for each subdivision in the work specification at the appropriate times. This will involve rostering staff to cover all subdivisions as and when required, but at the same time planning for staff to have their off-duty allocation on a fair and rational basis. When a seven-day service is required, then 'relief' staff must be rostered to cover the two days off, to which a full-timer is entitled, or two part-time staff may be employed, for instance one to cover four days and the other to cover three days. This involves the preparation of a duty roster indicating on a weekly and/or monthly basis, which members of staff are on or off duty at any particular time and which subdivisions are to be covered by which named members of staff. When preparing the duty rota the needs of both the personnel and the subdivisions should be considered.

When designing duty rotas there are a number of options for allocating days off. These include:

- a fixed rota – where staff work the same hours and have the same days off every week. Their days off may or may not be covered depending on whether a seven-day or five-day service is required.
- a rotating days off rota – where the days off rotate each week. In the following example, see Figure 4.14 two consecutive days off are given. The staff have to work no more than seven days before having a day off. Alternatively, rotation may be based on the first day off, whereby a member of staff would have Monday and Tuesday in week 1, then Tuesday and Wednesday in week 2, and

Figure 4.14 *A duty rota showing rotating days off for seven staff over a four-week period*

WEEK 1   WEEK 2

Names	M	T	W	T	F	S	S	M	T	W	T	F	S	S
1	D	D								D	D			
2			D	D								D	D	
3				D	D			D						D
4	D					D		D	D					
5		D	D								D	D		
Relief 6			D	D									D	D
Relief 7					D	D	D	D						

WEEK 3   WEEK 4

Names	M	T	W	T	F	S	S	M	T	W	T	F	S	S
1					D	D		D						D
2	D						D	D	D					
3		D	D								D	D		
4				D	D								D	D
5					D	D	D	D						
Relief 6	D	D									D	D		
Relief 7			D	D									D	D

so on. This system also usually applies where staff work the same shift hours every day.

• an alternating shift rota – where staff may cover different shifts each day. For instance early one day and late the next or even early one day, middle shift the next day and late the day after. In this system staff may have worked late one evening and be expected to be on duty early the next day. A financial allowance is often given for working alternating shifts.

In some cases staff may be expected to work split shifts, but this may not be very popular, particularly if staff live out, as it may cost twice as much in travel expenses or there may not be time to go home and return between the shifts. However, a split shift allowance may be paid. It may be more economical to recruit two part-time members of staff. In circumstances where the operation is geographically isolated and staff live in, a room attendant may be expected to work a split shift to cover the turn down service in the evening.

Duty rotas have to be documented and communicated to personnel well in advance so they know when their off-duty will occur. A systematic cycle, such as alternate weekends off where a seven day cycle exists, will simplify arrangements for all concerned. An allowance has already been included in the calculation if days off have to be covered, and often a 'relief' member of staff is allocated to a particular subdivision on a regular basis, to cover days off, so becoming a 'permanent' relief, always covering the same subdivision.

The effects of occupancy trends should be reconsidered at this stage, for instance, if hotel room occupancy is low at the weekend, then less staff are required and days off may not have to be covered, or in a hospital where offices are only used from Monday to Friday, provision is made for a five-day rather a seven-day service.

In circumstances where enhanced payments are made for shift or weekend coverage, consideration should be given to allocating lower priority tasks and weekly and periodic work at the lower pay rate during the week. For instance, in a hospital if periodic floor maintenance was undertaken on Sunday when double time is paid, then the cost of the work is doubled.

There is a tendency, therefore, in some service operations particularly where provision fluctuates regularly, to employ part-time rather than full-time staff to increase flexibility. Part-time staff are cheaper to employ as employer's statutory contributions are less.

Where holiday and Bank Holiday allowances have been made in the calculation, a pool of non-allocated hours must be kept available to employ relief cover for these occurrences and again a fair and rational system must be devised for allocating and covering holiday entitlements.

Programming of maintenance activities has already been covered in Section 3.2.5.

4.10   SUPERVISION

Business success or failure is dependant upon good, bad or indifferent supervision. Supervision is the keystone of any enterprise. There is no substitute for it. (SYSKA and HENNESSY).[2]

No matter how well methods and procedures are developed, results cannot be satisfactory unless management makes sure that work is performed as it should be, at the time it should be done, and to the quality standard required. Management cannot, personally, ensure quantity and quality especially where a large number of personnel are working in all parts of the building. So, Management's responsibility for quality, quantity and cost must be largely met through proper direction of the supervisory level.

The fact that housekeeping, domestic and often maintenance personnel are scattered, individually or in small groups, throughout the premises to perform their duties makes constant, direct supervision impossible. This phenomenon can affect the motivation and morale of personnel and create feelings of isolation and insecurity. It also means that a high proportion of supervisor's time can be unproductively spent travelling from one area to another. Management must consider firstly, the ratio of staff to supervisor. This is an attempt to achieve the optimum number of staff that a supervisor can adequately train, supervise and monitor.

In the National Health Service, the ratio is 1:25 domestic services personnel. Secondly, the physical division of the premises into subdivisions will reduce travelling time. These problems do not apply to supervising front office or even laundry personnel who are confined to a comparatively small area of the building.

Even though attempts may have been made to allocate a particular number of personnel, in a specified subdivision of the building, to a supervisor, the very nature of housekeeping activities means that the supervisor has to rely, very heavily, on the individual employee to ensure that the work is performed as it should be, at the right time, to the required quality standard (see Chapter 7). The supervisor's responsibility for quality, quantity and cost are, therefore, met through the direction of personnel and the control of other essentials of production such as equipment, agents, methods and time.

The six primary functions of a supervisor, according to The American Hospital Association (1966)[3] are to:

1 organise the work assigned to them
2 plan the tasks to be performed
3 direct the work of those responsible to them
4 co-ordinate the resources under their control
5 control staff and resources
6 evaluate the total job performance and that of the individual staff.

The most difficult task of the supervisor is time management – their own and that of the staff in their team or section. Their success will be largely measured by their ability to lead others and motivate them to meet the specified quality standards. Supervisors must earn the respect and co-operation of the staff in their team.

Supervisors at any level may be either autocratic or democratic (American Hospital Association, 1966).[3]

● the *autocratic supervisor* directs, commands and controls by driving, demands complete obedience from inferiors in spite of hard feelings and dissatisfaction and often gets good production

- the *democratic supervisor* avoids being overbearing, deals with workers fairly and patiently, with humour and understanding, treats them as associates in a joint undertaking, is liked and respected by group members, is seldom referred to as boss and is successful in encouraging people to the greatest intelligent effort possible.

A good supervisor will ensure that staff understand clearly what is expected of them, guide and advise them in performing their work, recognise good work and correct poor work.

Management must recognise that the supervisor plays a somewhat invidious role as a mediator between management and the work force and, in some situations, with their trade union representatives. Adequate training and management support is vital if the supervisor is to function effectively and with confidence.

Supervisory training may be in-house or externally conducted, according to the type and size of the operation. If externally conducted, it may be college based, eg day release City & Guilds; organised by the company on a group basis, eg housekeepers within an hotel chain, or organised by outside agencies such as the HCTC, eg 'Training the trainers' certificiate, or suppliers of equipment, agents or systems. Ideally the training should not only include developing technical skills and competencies but also the following:

- human relations and personnel control
- effective communications
- quality assurance, control and monitoring
- how to train
- health and safety, COSHH and other appropriate legislation
- hygiene and infection control
- cost efficiency and productivity
- dealing with day-to-day problems and situations and customer complaints.

4.11 INCENTIVE BONUS SCHEMES

Incentive bonus schemes have, in the past, been implemented in some sectors of Accommodation Management, namely domestic and laundry services in the NHS. They were originally introduced to solve such problems as:

- low productivity resulting from low pay
- little pay differential between grades of personnel
- lack of opportunity to earn overtime
- poor financial control
- poor supervision
- poor management structures
- poor motivation

- poor utilisation of the labour force, particularly in labour intensive operations.

Three main types of incentive schemes were considered:

1 *variable incentive schemes* – where earnings are directly related to pay
2 *measured day work* – where a fixed addition to the weekly or hourly rate is paid if a set target is reached. This scheme was generally adopted for domestic services
3 *productivity agreements* – based on the acceptance of improved methods.

Incentive schemes can also be based on piecework, profit-sharing or points systems.

However, many problems were encountered with the implementation of such schemes, bearing in mind that their efficiency depended to some extent on how they were managed. In the context of compulsory competitive tendering in Britain they have lost popularity. They were found to be time consuming and more expensive to administer, requiring clerical assistance. Monitoring of standards could easily slip and consequently quality could be reduced. They were not acceptable to all employees and often conflict existed between Management Services and Domestic Services managers. The bonus payment tended to become an accepted addition to the weekly pay packet and was no longer perceived as a bonus for improved productivity or quality.

Productivity may be improved by offering an incentive or reward scheme for:

- lack of absence, sickness, lateness
- constantly maintaining high quality standards of performance
- increasing sales (see Sections 6.5 and 6.8)
- safety and lack of accidents.

Sometimes competitions for 'the best employee of the month' may be effective.

4.12   APPRAISAL

A manager needs to develop a team and the individuals in that team. This would involve ensuring that the team members are fully conversant with their job description and then setting the targets or standards to achieve this. The achievement of these targets or standards, which must be meaningful and also challenging, can then be monitored. This means that the targets or standards must be specified, communicated and understood and be achievable and realistic and, above all, measurable.

A supervisor might be given the target, over the next period, to improve the cleaning cost per bedroom (marginal cost) by 0.20p; an advance reservation clerk the target to increase room occupancy at weekends by 20%, and a domestic assistant or room attendant would be given defined quality standards to accomplish (see Chapter 7). At the same time staff generally want to know how they are doing and where and when they can improve, particularly at supervisory level and above.

Appraisal aims to improve performance and develop people. Appraisal should not just be about reviewing past performance but about planning for future actions based on what has been learnt in the past. It is also about developing people to provide the organisation with those qualified to step into higher positions as they develop and also to help the individuals acquire the skills, knowledge and abilities to be eligible for promotion. Appraisal can be used for promotion, demotion, transfer, retention, retirement, executive development, identifying training needs, improving relationships and other organisational purposes.

The objectives of an appraisal system, as suggested in the LEAP *Training Manual*[4], are as follows:

- give all employees a formal opportunity to discuss and gain from their superior, information and feedback on how they are doing
- identify what assistance can be given to each employee to improve, as necessary, their performance in their current job
- identify future promotion potential
- identify what development assistance needs to be given to employees thought to have potential, to prepare them for future promotions
- give employees the opportunity to discuss their future career
- relate salary or pay to performance in some instances
- negotiate and agree standards of performance for the coming year and identify immediate priorities for action.

Figure 4.15 serves to explain the context of appraisal.

Appraisal is, of course, on going, on an informal day-to-day basis but it also usually involves a formal interview with one's immediate superior, no less than once a year. This interview must be given careful consideration and must be well planned, taking into account the aspects suggested when interviewing personnel already discussed in Section 4.7. Appraisal interviews are not easy to conduct and need skill and expertise to manage them effectively. There are many problems and pitfalls associated with conducting appraisal interviews, including:

- lack of skill and expertise on the appraiser's part
- lack of planning and forethought on the appraiser's part
- personality clashes
- appraiser's personal value system
- lack of time to conduct properly
- failing to look at causes behind results.

Figure 4.15 *The context of counselling and approval (LEAP* Training Manual)[4]

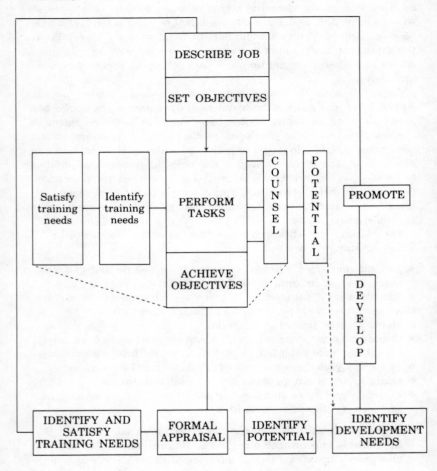

It must be remembered that the outcome of the interview will be recorded and an individual's career prospects could be affected by the appraiser's opinions and judgements, which may, of course, be biased. Outcomes may vary from one appraiser to another.

The objectives of an appraisal interview, as suggested in the LEAP *Training Manual*[4] are basically to:

● ensure that each individual understands their duties and responsibilities and expected targets or standards to be performed. This involves reviewing last year's performance and looking to fulfil next year's business plan

- recognise 'better than average' performance, and identify weaknesses and areas where performance fails to meet standards and needs improvement.
- negotiate and construct jointly, development plans to improve weaknesses and further develop strengths and then to summarise the individuals development plan
- to build goodwill and better understanding.

A suggested format for appraisal is:

- for the individual to discuss their job description with their supervisor and agree the content and relative importance of major duties/ tasks
- for the individual to establish performance targets for the next period
- to discuss these targets with their superior
- establish checkpoints for evaluating progress and ways of measuring performance
- meet at the end of the period to discuss targets previously set.

Although appraisal is generally more usual above operative level, it is probable in the future, with the introduction of NVQs (see Section 4.8.4) and changing demographic trends (see Section 4.3) that appraisal will be applicable at all levels in an organisation, including operative level.

The appraisal system can also be used to provide an audit of human resources and as a means of testing personnel procedures. For instance, are personnel specifications and job descriptions acceptable for a particular job or role in the operation?

It has been suggested that appraisal is not easy and there are many pitfalls to be overcome. When setting up an appraisal system it must be treated seriously by all concerned and given appropriate resources to undertake it effectively. This includes training and developing both appraisers and appraisees. It should be remembered that it is a time-consuming and therefore costly system to operate. When designing the appraisal system consider its purpose, format, timing, personnel, acceptability, outcomes and how they are to be recorded and used, the criteria for measurement, and on which criteria judgements will be made.

4.13 COUNSELLING

The Accommodation Manager or the Supervisor may have to counsel personnel for many reasons, for instance during appraisal, grievance or disciplinary interviews, or because an employee seeks assistance with a work or a personal problem.

The policy to be adopted, should be decided such as:

Figure 4.16 *Features of staff welfare*

FACILITIES

Residents
Bedrooms
Sitting room
TV lounge
Pantries/kitchens or
  meal provision
Laundering provision
Hairdressing
Use of organisation's
  facilities, eg swimming pool
  cinema
Staff bar

Non-residents
Shower/locker facilities
Staff dining rooms/
Sitting rooms/
Smoking areas

Health and medical services
First aid
Accident procedure
Health screening
  – commencement
    periodically
Chest X-rays
Cancer screening
Occupational health
  centre and services
Compassionate leave
Stress management
Well-person clinics
Keep fit activities

Health and safety
Hazard spotting
Accident prevention
Safety of buildings
Safe procedures
Training
Supervision
Hygiene and
  infection control
Sharp's policy
AIDS policy

Working conditions
Induction and training
Well organised jobs and
  work schedules
Adequate supplies
Well maintained equipment
Overalls/protective clothing,
  rubber gloves, hand creams
Clean and pleasant working
  environment

Security
Personal – in grounds
         – in building
Belongings

Social activities
Bingo
Social club
Trips and visits
Parties/dances
Sports – table tennis, squash,
         football, swimming
Films

Counselling and advice
Staff appraisal and
  development policy
For – work problems
    – personal problems

- an open door policy, where an employee can call any time
- a 'limited' open door policy, where the employee can call between certain hours each day or week
- an appointment policy either through the supervisor or the secretary.

As with any interview, it must be well planned. Listening is an attribute to be developed on the interviewer's part and any positive help which can be given to the employee in terms of advice, where to get further information, actions to take to solve the problem or even just sympathy, may not only help the employee but also develop a better relationship between Manager/Supervisor and employee. The Counsellor should be careful not to 'gossip' about the employee as confidentiality is an important feature of counselling. Training in counselling skills should feature in both management and supervisory training programmes.

4.14 STAFF WELFARE

Staff welfare involves looking after the physical and emotional needs and requirements of the staff. The aim being to improve morale and thus reduce labour turnover and absenteeism, and improve staff retention, and at the same time create a greater feeling of identification with and loyalty to the operation. It is a valuable way of communicating the ethos, attitude and management style of the operation to employees.

Welfare embraces the provision of facilities for resident and non-resident staff; health and medical services; health and safety arrangements, security, working conditions, counselling and advice and social activities. A more detailed list of aspects which may be considered under the above headings is outlined in Figure 4.16.

Good conditions of service, including pay rates, sickness and holiday entitlements, pension schemes, and staff development programmes, are also important features of staff welfare.

The cost of welfare provision must be viewed in terms of reducing labour turnover, the ease of attracting potential personnel, reduction in absenteeism, retention of staff and the development of a well motivated, happy and stable work force.

4.15 TERMINATION

The Accommodation Manager must clarify the extent of their authority with regard to the termination of an employee's employment for whatever reason. In some organisations only the personnel manager or general manager can terminate employment. Employment may be terminated for the following reasons:

- **Dismissals**   (i) unsuitability
                   (ii) disciplinary action
- **Redundancy**   (i) seasonal fluctuations (prevalent in resort areas at end of summer season)

184 Human Resources Management

(ii) economic pressures

- **Unavoidable resignations will include:**
  - marriage
  - maternity
  - to further career prospects (to gain experience of another company's systems)
  - transport difficulties
  - to move to another part of the country or abroad
  - illness or accident
  - domestic responsibilities
  - retirement
  - death

- **Avoidable resignations:**
  - pay
  - conditions
  - hours
  - dissatisfaction with the work
  - personal frictions between staff
  - promotion prospects
  - failure to achieve acceptable work standards

- **Other reasons unknown**

Usually, the employee has to complete a termination form or submit a letter of termination, but an exit interview is invaluable if an attempt is being made to establish the real reason for termination. If an employee terminates their own employment, it is useful to know the real reason, which is often different to the reason actually given. This may highlight a particular or a recurring problem which may be affecting labour turnover and hence labour costs. It can only be rectified if it is identified.

4.16 LABOUR TURNOVER

Labour turnover subsequently increases labour costs as selection, recruitment, personnel administration, induction and training costs will increase. Costs may also be incurred in the initial period of employment as a new employee is more prone to a higher percentage of errors, wastage and breakages.

Labour turnover can be measured in a variety of ways. It is usually measured on an annual basis.

- **Staff turnover rate**

  $$\frac{No.\ of\ leavers\ per\ annum \times 100}{Average\ no.\ of\ employees\ per\ annum} = \%\ per\ annum$$

  eg $\frac{10}{100} \times 100 = 10\%$ labour per annum

Figure 4.17 *Survival curve*

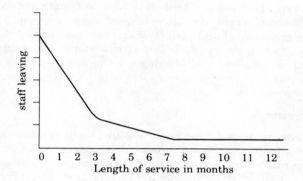

- **Survival curves**
  This chart indicates the length of time a new recruit survives in their employment.
  The example given in Figure 4.17 indicates that the majority of employees left within the first two to three months of their employment.

- **Length of service chart**
  This indicates how successfully an operation has established a stable core of employees.

Some labour turnover is vital to the healthy growth of an operation as it allows new staff to take a fresh look at the operation and its policies and practices and bring in new ideas.

There are many often unavoidable reasons why employees leave their jobs, but ideally the large majority of the labour force should remain settled and only a few leave each year. Often staff leave for no apparent reason. In fact they may even just fail to report for duty and are never seen again. As suggested in the section on termination, an attempt should be made to identify reasons for termination of employment.

Abnormally high levels of labour turnover must be investigated as they are disruptive. With a high influx and outflow of employees it becomes increasingly difficult to create a team spirit, engender good working relationships and motivate staff. Supervisors are under stress and often lose motivation as they are constantly involved in induction of new personnel. It takes time for any new personnel to settle in and make a fully productive contribution and quality, besides expenditure, can obviously be affected. In some situations, a loss of sales or reputation could result.

A vicious circle is created by high labour turnover. When staff leave inevitably extra pressure is placed on those who remain and morale begins to suffer. If several staff leave in quick succession it may take time to replace them all and even loyal and conscientious employees may begin to feel pressurised. Relatively new employees could then be involved in inducting and training even newer employees. It is difficult to recreate a stable labour force once high labour turnover has been experienced.

- **Absenteeism**

  Productivity is affected when personnel are absent as other personnel have often to cover 'extra' work. Absenteeism can be planned for if accurate records are maintained, as an appropriate allowance can be included when estimating work hours. However, there may be a tendency to over-compensate resulting in over-staffing. Where compensation is made, a relief pool of personnel may exist to cover days off, holidays, sickness and unknown absence. It may be more appropriate to have a pool of hours rather than employed personnel, so that casual staff can be appointed or overtime can be paid only when required and thus relief staff are not idle.

- **Lateness**

  This obviously affects the individuals productivity and the performance of the whole subdivision besides the quality achieved. Thought should be given to disciplinary procedures to prevent its occurence or reoccurence. It also raises the issue of whether personnel should clock in at a central point before proceeding to their place of work.

  Whenever potential changes which affect personnel, either individually or as a whole, are deemed necessary, thought must be given to their acceptability to personnel, the Trade Unions, where appropriate, and the customer.

4.17 PERSONNEL RECORDS

Another control measure, whether undertaken by the Personnel or the Accommodation Department, is to keep effective personnel records. To be of value these records must be necessary, relevant, accurate, up-to-date, in a useful format and summarised, often in a statistical format on a regular basis. Labour turnover, sickness and absence ratios lend themselves to statistical analysis. Figure 4.18

Figure 4.18 *Personnel records*

Staffing requirements	– Number required*; vacanices*; grades*; shifts*; location*; Job Descriptions*; Work Schedules*
Recruitment	– Adverts; response statistics; applications*
Selection	– Shortlist*; application forms*; personnel specification*; interview form; confirmation/ rejection letters
Appointment	– Personal file – appointment form; contract of employment; references; medical
Induction	– Induction programme; record and progress*
Training	– Training programme, record and progress*
Deployment	– Clock-cards/register*; Work Schedules*; duty rotas*; holiday and bank holiday records
Supervision	– Quality control*; disciplinary
Appraisal	– Interview records; absence and sickness*; progress*; disciplinary*; problems*
Staff welfare	– Conditions of service; policies; sickness, occupational health
Termination	– Reasons*; labour turnover*

* Indicates those to which the Accommodation Manager must have access or keep within the Department.

suggests the personnel records which need to be kept either by the Personnel or the Accommodation Department.

4.18 DIRECT VERSUS CONTRACT LABOUR

Managing a direct labour force is a very complex business and thus contracting out some or all of the accommodation services can be an attractive proposition, particularly when the provision of such services is secondary to the main mission of the operation as in a hospital.

A decision may have to be taken then at some stage to provide a direct or in-house service or employ a contract service. This decision will be influenced by company policy or the prevailing circumstances such as compulsory competitive tendering or isolation of the property and the nature of the service or constituent part of the service, such as window cleaning in a high rise office block.

When establishing a new operation the extent to which contract services will be utilised must be determined at the outset. This decision may be reconsidered many times. The advantages and disadvantages of contract services in general, and the types of services available is discussed in Chapter 5.

A full contract service may be considered as an alternative to a direct service in the following situations:

● when economic or accounting advantages may be achieved eg savings in the cost of provision can be made

- when reduction of administrative work load is sought
- when staff availability is difficult
- when high levels of sickness, absence, labour turnover are occurring
- when capital equipment, involving a large expenditure, needs replacing
- when a new unit is being opened.

However, when the costs of monitoring and controlling a full contract service are higher than the resultant savings, it is not a feasible proposition.

When changing from a direct labour force to a full contract service, the following factors must be considered:

- what happens to the departmental manager?
- what redundancy arrangements will be made?
- will the contractor re-employ the existing labour force?
- what will happen to all equipment and agents in stock?
- who will monitor the contract?

4.19   PRIVATISATION AND THE TENDERING PROCESS

In some organisations, such as the NHS and now Local Government, privatisation policies have been introduced to test the cost of 'support services', eg catering, domestic, laundering, portering, to discover whether savings could be made and resources released, eg for improved patient services or simply to reduce the cost of provision. Such a policy, first introduced in the early 1980s, resulted in the process known as *compulsory competitive tendering*. A *Health Circular* (HC(83)18)[5] in 1983 stated that:

> *District Health Authorities are accordingly asked to test the cost effectiveness of their domestic, catering and laundry services by putting them out to tender (including in-house tender). Where these tenders show that savings can be made, a contract should be let.*

The whole Domestic or Cleaning Service is an ideal service for putting out to tender because it is labour intensive, labour costs being the highest element of the domestic services budget (80–90%) and unlike catering and laundry services involves relatively little capital investment in equipment, plant and premises. However, such aspects of domestic service as pest control, security, floral arrangements can also be contracted out.

4.19.1   The tendering process

The tendering process usully involves the following stages, laid out in Figure 4.19 and outlined below.

Figure 4.19 *The tendering process*

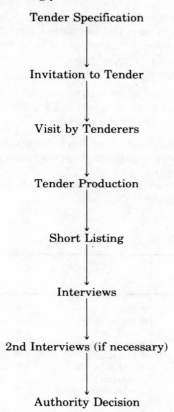

Tender Specification

Invitation to Tender

Visit by Tenderers

Tender Production

Short Listing

Interviews

2nd Interviews (if necessary)

Authority Decision

● **Tender specification**

This involves the production of the specification of work, as outlined in Section 3.3.2.1. The specification generally includes a statement of the cleaning procedures, although the expected frequencies are not always specified, allowing the tenderer to make this decision, schedules of accommodation (room schedules and plans), and general information such as hygiene, health and safety, and security policies to be followed by the tenderers. The monitoring and control system to be operated should also be specified at this time.

This stage is very time consuming particularly in a large establishment where it could take six to nine months to prepare. The technical specification should be prepared by parties not involved in the production of the in-house tender.

● **Invitation to tender**

A decision will have to be made as to whether Selective Tendering (where a shortlist of desirable companies are invited to tender) or Open Tendering (where any company who so desires can tender) is most satisfactory. Prospective tenderers will normally be issued with three documents:

- ● conditions of tender, ie what to tender for and how to tender
- ● contract documents, ie the contractual rules
- ● the specification of work documentation.

This often results in one very large document which is costly to produce, hence some organisations are actually charging potential tenderers a fee for it.

Figure 4.20 outlines more specifically the type of information contained within the three documents.

Figure 4.20 *The tender specification documents*

Conditions of tender	Contract document	Specification of work
What to tender for ● types of service ● tasks/services to be produced ● areas to be included **How to tender** ● information to provide ● format/breakdown ● procedure to follow ● deadlines ● contract price – (precise composition to be defined)	● control of assets ● ownership of supplies ● period of contract ● inflation ● variations to contract, ie (deletions and inclusions) ● payments to contractors (how and frequency) ● default and termination ● receipting ● supevisory and management cover ● no. of inspections ● security arrangements ● uniforms ● welfare arrangements ● storage areas ● office space ● transport arrangements ● emergencies ● insurance liability	● accommodation schedules and plans ● tasks/services required ● frequencies ● definitions of technical terms ● hours of coverage ● access ● standards statement ● equipment/agents ● health and safety arrangements ● infection/hygiene policy

In fact, the Department of Health (1989)[6] suggest using the following checklist to ensure completeness of the specification documentation:

- have pretender enquiries and the selection of contractors been satisfactorily completed?
- have dates for the following been set and issued to contractors?
  - briefing meeting
  - closing date for return of tenders
  - evaluation panel meetings
  - interview dates
  - estimated date of decision
  - contract commencement
- are all definitions clear?
- has any ambiguity been rectified thus minimising the risk of misinterpretation?
- has each type of area been defined?
- are measurements provided for all areas?
- have quantities and details of beds, furniture and fittings been included for each work area?
- are the procedure codes, treatments and frequencies realistic and achievable and can these be cross-referenced throughout the documentation?
- have precise details of other non-cleaning duties and services been included, eg meals and beverage times?
- have tenderers been asked to provide a cost for additional work?
- has the quality assurance and monitoring policy been included?
- has a summary list of the documents to be returned by each tenderer been included?
- is it clear how increase to the contract price will be implemented after the first year?
- is it clear what should be included in the first year tender price and the date on which the tender price should be based?

- **Visit by tenderers**

  All tenderers (including the in-house services) may be invited to visit the premises in order to undertake their own building survey and ask questions. For fairness and expediency this should be conducted at the same time by the same person.

- **Production of tenders**

  Production of the tender, whether by the contractor or the in-house service manager, will involve making such technical decisions as:

  - how will each task be performed?
  - how often will each task be performed? (if not specified)
  - what equipment and agents will be required? types and quantities.

  It will also involve:

- estimating the total number of work-hours required to fulfil the tender
- a breakdown of staffing requirements to cover the work when access is possible, days off, holidays and absence
- producing work schedules and duty rotas
- a cost breakdown of labour, equipment, supplies and other expenditure such as supervisory cover, profit margin, etc
- supervisory and management cover
- quality assurance and monitoring procedures to be implemented.

- **Shortlisting and interviews**

To achieve comparable tenders, tenderers must be aware of precisely what information to include in their submission. The documentation should include a summary which lists the standard forms to be completed and documents to be submitted as part of the tender.

The following list based on suggestions by the Department of Health (1989)[6] indicates the type of information required from contractors in order to evaluate and compare tenders submitted:

- tendered price per annum
- tendered price per week
- worked hours per week for operative staff
- notional cost per worked hour, ie

$$\frac{\text{tendered price per week}}{\text{worked hours per week}}$$

- supervisory hours per week
- supervisory ratio, ie

$$\frac{\text{worked hours per week for operatives}}{\text{supervisory hours per week}}$$

- management hours per week
- cleaning equipment and materials cost per annum
- cleaning equipment and materials as a percentage of the tendered price per annum
- allowances for absence, holidays and sickness
- basic hourly pay rates of individual groups of staff
- operatives and supervisory duty rotas
- conditions of service including holiday entitlement, sickness benefit scheme, bonus payments and other staff benefits
- certificates of collusive tendering and canvassing
- guarantee from parent company
- bankers and trade references
- company accounts for the past three years
- insurance and VAT certificates
- breakdown of cleaning equipment and materials
- quality assurance and monitoring
- training plan
- staff uniforms and personal identification

- health and safety and control of infection policies
- equal opportunities policy
- disciplinary and grievance procedures
- industrial relations record and contingency plans in the event of an industrial dispute
- unit cost for additional/non-contracted work.

Standard formats aid evaluation of tenders particularly at the shortlisting stage and should be contained wherever appropriate in the documentation supplied to the tenderers.

The interview obviously allows both parties to ask questions and clear up problems and misunderstandings. If necessary the panel may wish to invite one or two companies back for a second interview before a final decision can be made and the tender let. The in-house service will follow the same procedure. Again to avoid bias the in-house manager involved in the in-house tender production should *not* be involved in the evaluation process.

Negotiations with the appropriate Trade Unions should occur as and when necessary throughout the procedure. Once the tender is let the tender price becomes the budget for the service (whether in-house or contractor) and the contractual arrangements specified in the documentation are enforced. Continuous liaison throughout the term of the contract is of mutual benefit to both parties.

4.19.2   Quality assurance and monitoring

Quality assurance and monitoring of the tender are very important and financial penalties may be incurred if the standards are not achieved and the work not undertaken for whatever reason. The principles of designing a quality assurance and monitoring system are dealt with in Section 7.4.

References

[1]   VOSS, C, ARMISTEAD, C, JOHNSTON, B, MORRIS, B, *Operations Management in Service Industries and the Public Sector*, John Wiley and Sons 1985

[2]   SYSKA and HENNESSY, 'The Housekeeping Supervisor – Keystone to Success', *American Training Manual*

[3]   AMERICAN HOSPITAL ASSOCIATION *Housekeeping Manual for Health Care Facilities* (1966)

[4]   LEAP *Training Manual, Appraisal*, British Junior Chamber and P A Management Consultants Ltd

[5]   DHSS *Health Circular* HC(83)18 'Health Service Management – Competitive Tendering in the Provision of Domestic, Catering and Laundering Services, (1983)

[6]   DoH (1989)

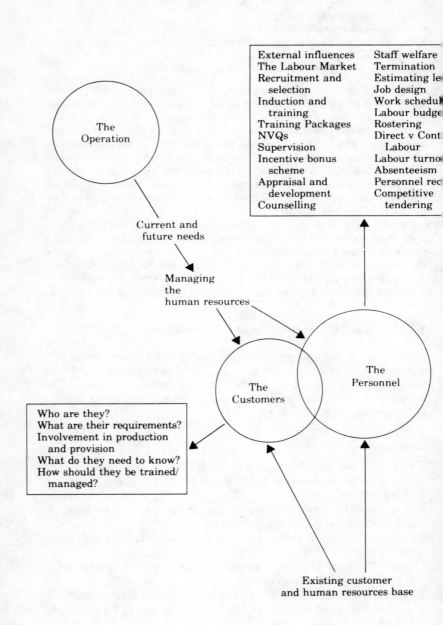

Concept Map summarising Human Resources Management.

Further reading

HCITB, *A guide to Systematic Training,* 1982

International Labour Office, *Introduction to work study,* 2nd revised
    edition, 1969

GULLEN, H V and RHODES, G E *Management in the Hotel and Catering
    Industry,* Batsford 1983

Domestic Supervisors Training Kit, NHS Hotel Services Training
    Directorate 1989

Assignment tasks

1 Find out how much time has been allocated to undertake such
    tasks as bed-making, damp mopping, cleaning a toilet, etc, in an
    operation of your choice.
2 Compare the 'establishment figure' and staffing structure in two
    or three different operations. Evaluate in relation to the size ie
    square meterage of the property.
3 (i) Produce a job description and personnel specification for the
        following types of staff:
        a maintenance engineer in a four-star hotel
        a hospital domestic supervisor
        a receptionist in a three-star hotel
  (ii) Find out the hour rate of pay for:
        an hotel and college porter
        a room attendant
        a hospital domestic assistant
        a college cleaner.
4 Determine how many work-hours are required for a small opera-
    tion or a subdivision of a larger operation. Compare, if possible,
    with the actual figure.
5 Prepare an interview for either
  ● an appraisal session with a Domestic Supervisor or Floor
    Housekeeper or
  ● a termination interview with an operative who has just com-
    pleted all their training.
6 (i) Design an induction programme for one of the roles listed in
        Question 5.
  (ii) Prepare a training programme for either:
        a floor housekeeper
        a receptionist
        a hospital domestic assistant.

5

Materials Management

Objectives

- To demonstrate the need for good materials management within the accommodation department(s).
- To explain the overall value of different purchases made in this sector.
- To demonstrate the need for a problem-solving approach, prior to the actual purchase of goods.
- To analyse and apply the stages in the selection process.
- To evaluate sources of supply.
- To evaluate the relative merits of hiring or buying in a given situation.
- To identify the methods and value of effective stores control with respect to the role of the Accommodation Manager.

The need for good materials management

In manufacturing industries, materials, of one sort or another, represent an important and expensive resource. In some supply industries, materials are the main resource and may represent 75% of sales revenue. In services industries, such as Accommodation Services, the main resource is labour, and on-going material costs are commonly only around 10% of the operating costs.

This is not to say that materials management is of little importance in Accommodation Management. Of a large budget 10% can itself be a considerable figure and, also, the costs of the goods themselves do not reflect their value to the organisation.

Without the appropriate equipment and supplies available at the right time and in the correct quantities, labour costs can increase significantly, as staff try to 'make do', and quality is likely to suffer. The 'knock on' costs of **not** having a good materials management system in operation will be much greater than the costs involved in maintaining a good system. Some of the possible benefits achieved through a good choice of cleaning equipment, for example, are shown in Figure 5.1.

Figure 5.1 *Possible benefits achieved through a good choice of cleaning equipment*

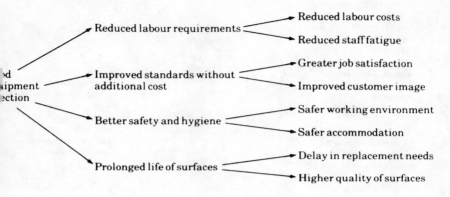

5.1 THE SYSTEMIC ROLE OF MATERIALS MANAGEMENT

It is not difficult to appreciate the systemic role of materials management within the overall system of Accommodation Management. Whether the materials in question are for the purpose of replenishing stocks or extending plant, the needs of the users are the key issue.

Figure 5.2 shows the elements of the Materials Management subsystem, the constraints imposed by the main system and, also, the significance of the 'needs of the user'. The 'user' could be a domestic assistant who requires a floor polish which will assist maintenance of the surface, a badminton player who needs a slip-resistant floor surface on which to play, a leisure centre manager who requires, within cost constraints, an impressive and well-kept appearance for all surfaces. All will make certain demands which have materials management implications.

5.2 ITEMS TO BE PURCHASED

As the specific role of the Accommodation Manager varies from one establishment to another, so the items to be purchased or hired will also vary. They might include items from the following categories:

- those forming part of the product, eg furniture, furnishings, linens, surfaces and fittings
- those involved with the production process, eg uniforms, energy supplies for equipment

Figure 5.2 Materials management subsystem

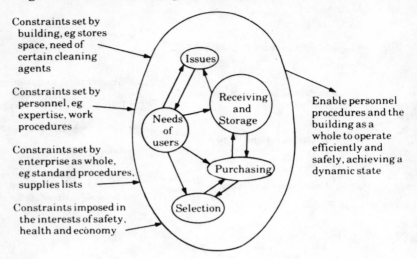

Constraints set by building, eg stores space, need of certain cleaning agents

Constraints set by personnel, eg expertise, work procedures

Constraints set by enterprise as whole, eg standard procedures, supplies lists

Constraints imposed in the interests of safety, health and economy

Issues

Receiving and Storage

Needs of users

Purchasing

Selection

Enable personnel procedures and the building as a whole to operate efficiently and safely, achieving a dynamic state

- items providing the production facility, eg cleaning agents, machines and other equipment
- items for maintenance, eg spare parts or equipment servicing contracts
- items for management and administration, eg stationery or computing facilities
- items for support services, eg recruitment, equipment trials, pest control or consultancies.

Different establishments categorise materials differently, depending on the accountancy system used, eg there may be a category for 'consumables' or revenue items, ie those items usually costing less than a certain figure, and being an on-going expense. Above that figure items might be classified as 'capital' items.

It should be stressed that the cost of a particular item does not indicate the value of that item to the establishment. Lack of sufficient bed linen could, for example, mean that significant losses of room revenue are incurred, disproportionate to the cost of the linen itself.

5.2.1   Pareto* analysis

Costs which might be misleading, when determing the relative importance of particular goods to be managed, is the unit cost of these

---

* Pareto was an Italian/American scholar of the nineteenth century, who discovered that 80% of the wealth was owned by 20% of the population. It was later found that this 80:20 ratio occurred in many situations.

Figure 5.3 *Pareto curve showing comparative annual value of stock items*

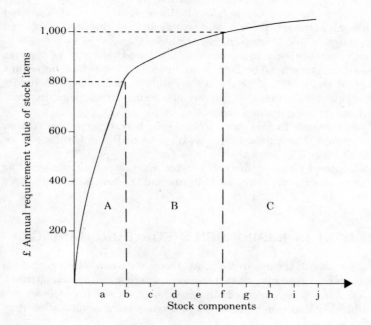

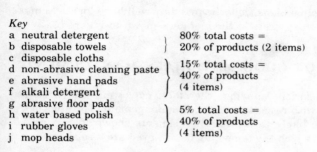

Key
a neutral detergent
b disposable towels   } 80% total costs =
                              20% of products (2 items)
c disposable cloths
d non-abrasive cleaning paste
e abrasive hand pads   } 15% total costs =
f alkali detergent   40% of products
                              (4 items)
g abrasive floor pads
h water based polish
i rubber gloves   } 5% total costs =
j mop heads   40% of products
                              (4 items)

goods. If the Accommodation Manager were planning to replace, after five years, a carpet and upholstery shampoo machine costing several hundred pounds, it is likely that investigations would be made to determine the best machine for the work to be done with the money available. Considerable managerial time and effort might go into such a purchasing decision.

In the same establishment, when placing an order for neutral detergent, costing only a few pence per litre, an automatic reorder procedure may well be followed.

In operational and financial terms, it is not so much the unit costs that are important, as the total annual usage costs of those items. In-use costs of apparently very similar products can vary enormously, as for example, with two neutral detergents. One may have a dilution rate of 1:20, the other a dilution rate of 1:10.

It should also be remembered that there are always costs incurred by placing an order. Their extent will depend on the time associated with selection and other purchasing processes.

With respect to inventory control, it is found that 80% of supplies investment is incurred by 20% of products. It is, therefore, important to target these 20% of products for careful management, including development of clear specification of needs, careful sourcing and purchasing, storage and distribution.

This approach to inventory control can be further extended into three groups. These groups are identified as **A**, **B** and **C** (hence *A, B, C Analysis* as it is known).

Here, items representing the greatest overall costs are classed as **A items**, the middle range as **B items** and the low, as **C items** (see Figure 5.3).

5.3 WHO IS RESPONSIBLE FOR PURCHASING?

In some small organisations, the Accommodation Manager, as a departmental head may have a free rein where selection and purchasing of stores are concerned. In larger organisations, however, the likelihood is that a central stores and purchasing organisation may be functioning.

In many organisations, departments may well have inputs to make to the purchasing process in the manners shown in Figure 5.4.

5.4 AIMS OF GOOD MATERIALS MANAGEMENT

The Accommodation Manager, therefore, may well have a shared responsibility with respect to materials management. The aims of the subsystem are likely to include the elements shown in Figure 5.5. The means by which the aims may be achieved are also shown.

Figure 5.4 *The involvement different departments may have in the purchasing process*

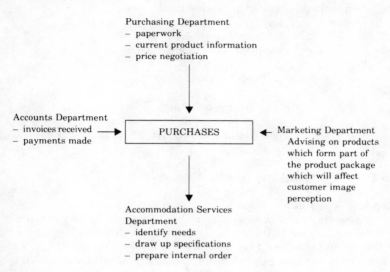

Figure 5.5 *The aims of the purchasing process and how those aims are achieved*

Subsystem aims	Achieved through
Ensuring correct goods are available at point of use at lowest cost	• detailed specifications • good sourcing, vendor rating • value analysis • stores issues system • follow-ups • standardisation of stock
Continuity of supply	• good relationships with suppliers and good sourcing • good stores controls
Maintaining stocks in good condition at lowest costs	• ordering suitable quantities at correct time, economic ordering • storage conditions • stock rotation and stores controls • standardisation and simplification of stock
Provision of information on new products	• access to and knowledge of current product developments

5.5   THE PURCHASING PROCESS

The purchasing process can be summarised as follows:

Problem identification and
identification of product need
↓
Product Specification
↓
Source Selection
↓
Purchase of Product

5.5.1   Identifying the product need

Step one – problem analysis

Purchasing can be a means of solving a problem. The purchasing process commences with the analysis of a problem, and problem-solving techniques should be applied.

A problem may be perceived, for example, low stocks of neutral detergent, hotel guest complaints regarding inaccurate billing, accidents involving slipping.

When a possible problem has been identified, the manager should not immediately prescribe a solution, but, rather, investigate the matter, looking at such factors as frequency of occurrence, severity, possible causes and effects of the problem; indeed, find out what actually is the true problem. This will enable the manager to put the problem into perspective.

In some instances, as in the case of the neutral detergent, a supplies need might be immediately diagnosed. This may or may not be justified. Problems should be investigated. In some cases, such investigation is automatic; in others, the idea that there might be some alternative solution to the obvious is not considered.

The first stage in the purchasing process is, therefore, to identify, not just that a problem exists but, specifically, what the problem is.

To return to the example of the low stocks of neutral detergent, it may be found that, in fact, no problem exists, that the stocks are low due to normal usage and an effective reorder system will come into effect when the stocks reach a specified level. It could be that the particular brand of detergent in question is being replaced and stocks, therefore, are being allowed to run out. Alternatively, there could be a problem. The basic problem or 'root problem' could be any of a number, for example:

- excessive usage due to inadequate training, pilferage, exceptional workloads
- a poor reordering system

- unreliable delivery patterns by the supplier
- an inadequate stores issuing system where excessive stocks are developing at the point of use.

Many alternative root problems might exist, probably a combination of factors will be seen to be acting but, in any case by investigation, the root problem can be addressed and not just the symptoms.

Step 2 – solutions identification

It can be seen that tackling the 'wrong' problem or merely the symptoms of a root problem can serve to prolong the problem. For example, again looking at the neutral detergent, simply ensuring that stocks were replenished, when the root problem is lack of staff skills in the use of the product, could lead to further problems such as:

- damage to hands, due to strong solutions being used
- slipperiness on floor surfaces
- waste disposal problems due to excessive lather in water
- overspending on budget.

Similarly, reordering stocks does not solve a pilferage problem.

When the root problem has been identified, the right solution must be identified. Again, there could be several from which to choose. If inadequate staff skills has been identified as the root problem, alternative solutions could be identified such as:

- reducing skill requirements by directly controlling dilutions of the product
- improving staff training
- stopping staff from using the product by changing the job or job process
- employing staff with different skills.

Step 3 – solution selection

In some cases, having identified the root problem and possible solutions, the selection of the solution may be outside the authority of the Accommodation Manager; in others, only one possible solution will be identified. If no appropriate solution is identified, there must be a process of reiteration.

Step 4 – solution requirements

When a solution (or combination of solutions) has been chosen, the requirements of this solution must be identified. In the example of the neutral detergent, to take the first listed solution, ie 'reducing skill requirements by directly controlling dilution of the product', the requirements would include:

- the appropriate neutral detergent
- some means of directly controlling the solution, eg supervisory staff, automatic, mechanical or packaging method of proportioning.

Step 5 – performance specification
The final stage in the selection process is to develop specifications of performance or 'performance attributes', for the requirements listed in stage 4. This calls for analysis, where other stages have called for enlargement and development.

In the example given, two performance specifications are needed; one for the detergent itself and one for the method of dilution control. The specification for the detergent might include:

- pH level
- ability to remove grease, water soluble soilage and carbon stain
- low foam
- within in-use cost limit
- available in 4-litre containers
- minimum shelf life of three months
- non-irritating
- biodegradable
- effective in cold water
- non-streaking
- non-corrosive

The specification for the dilution control might include:

- not involving additional labour
- cost effective
- usable in domestic staffs' peripheral store
- no maintenance required
- varied, regulated dilutions possible
- not specific to one detergent type
- hygienic

The list of performance attributes can then be compiled as a performance specification and, to assist in the final selection of a product, the attributes can be ranked, eg essential, highly desirable, desirable.

Performance specifications may be relatively simple, as above, or extremely complex, such as might be prepared prior to the invitation to tender for a complete cleaning service (see Chapter 4).

5.5.1.1 Value analysis In the process of developing a performance specification the technique of value analysis can be applied. This is a means of cost reduction whereby the functions of a product are identified. Frequently it will be found that products have more than one function and, in the process of value analysis, the primary function is highlighted. Unnecessary attributes are identified so that only essential qualities will be specified, and unnecessary details omitted from the specification.

To return to the neutral detergent example above, in the performance specification, the primary function will be seen to be the 'ability to remove grease, water soluble soilage and carbon stain'. Other attributes such as 'low odour' will be seen to be more subjective and, in any case, secondary to the basic requirement. Other attributes, not listed in the specification above, such as colour and viscosity, would not be seen as relevant to the ability of the product to fulfil its primary objective.

5.5.2 Selecting cleaning agents and equipment

In preparing specifications, consideration must be given, not just to the efficiency of the product but its suitability for that particular situation. Some general aspects to consider in preparing specifications for cleaning agents and equipment might include:

- **site characteristics,** eg floor coverings and their conditions, soilage types and rates, furniture densities, service points, power sources available, storage facilities, access facilities (ramps and lifts), geographical layout of site, use of building and special requirements (low noise, electrical suppression, vacuum filtration, etc).
- **Labour considerations,** eg numbers sharing one machine, training aspects, strength of operatives, working hours, supervisory cover, effects on productivity levels and agreements, health and safety.

Performance attributes of cleaning agents and equipment must be considered with respect to the characteristics of soilage.

Another aspect which may be considered in specifying characteristics, particularly of cleaning agents, is that of the associated environmental implications. Many chemicals used in large scale cleaning have for some years now been biodegradable but other aspects are also being addressed by some manufacturers.

Alternatives to aerosols containing CFCs are now commonly available. Some manufacturers supply products free from phosphates, enzymes, optical or chemical bleaches, synthetic perfumes or colourings. Other products use recycled materials in their composition, eg toilet paper and stationery or in their packaging, eg products contained in recyclable plastic. Packaging, or lack of it, may be something else which may be included in a specification. Unnecessary packaging, in terms of product protection, will cause a waste disposal problem for the buyer, as well as being wasteful of global resources.

5.5.3 Selecting surfaces, linens, fittings and furniture

In Chapter 2, consideration has been given to the performance attributes required of such items as floors, windows, soft furnishings, heating and lighting installations. In general terms three aspects must be considered:

- the purpose and overall function of the establishment, eg non-profit orientated, health care facilities, commercially orientated leisure centre or rapid turnover fast food operation
- the standards aimed for within the organisation
- the integrative nature of design.

The application of the problem-solving approach outlined in 5.5 above is also valid. If a problem of, for example, insufficient seating in a conference hall is identified, rather than just place an order for more chairs, the root problem should be examined. Why is there insufficient seating? Are bookings exceeding the capacity of the room? Have chairs been removed? Is this a recurring problem or a 'one off'? When the root problem has been established, the possible solutions can be identified and so on.

5.5.4   Selecting contract labour

Selecting contract labour or selecting services, as opposed to supplies, is a complex operation, particularly where total facilities management contracts are being considered. Basically, however, the process is the same as that described above. The selection process must be followed and a performance specification prepared before tenders are invited. Contracting of labour is discussed more fully in Chapter 4.

With the development of a performance specification, the manager is part way to solving the problem. The selection process is time-consuming but, in the long run, may save management and staff time. The true problem will have been identified and the best solution chosen. The next stage is to purchase that solution (or the nearest fit).

5.6   WHERE TO BUY

Having determined that there is a purchasing need, the next logical step is to determine the best source for the goods. It may well be, particularly in larger organisations, that the Accommodation Manager does not have a free choice here. Central purchasing and supplies units may be in operation, or the organisation may have negotiated contracts with certain organisations, or have a list of approved sources. Nevertheless, it is worth following through the process logically.

The purchasing process continues with investigations as to what is available on the market which appears to be broadly similar to the products required or, alternatively, a list of suppliers who deal broadly in the field of interest needs to be drawn up. Such information, in either case, may be gathered from trade literature, manufacturers' leaflets, trade exhibitions, manufacturers and suppliers.

5.6.1 What makes a good supplier?

Some of the aspects worth considering in making a selection with respect to suppliers are:

- prices quoted, including quantity discounts and other special rates
- contract terms, eg 'lead times' (how long orders would take to be delivered), frequency and timings of deliveries, etc
- financial record of the supplier, eg is it a stable organisation?
- capacity, would the size of order match the size and nature of the supplier?
- technical competence – what sort of record does the supplier have with respect to effectiveness of goods and what backup systems do they offer?
- quality assurance – what is their system of quality assurance, ie to ensure that all goods supplied will be of a similar quality
- proximity – is your distance from the supplier likely to have any detrimental effects on deliveries and backup services? On an international front, considerations would need to be made for fluctuations in trade cycles, exchange rates and tariff barriers. Cultural barriers too would need to be addressed.

Other criteria for assessing suitability of suppliers will be identified in particular circumstances.

It may well be worth determining the relative importance of the criteria listed, in order that suppliers can be chosen in the most objective way. For example, in the case of linen supplies, a particular hotel might weight criteria as follows:

Criteria	Weighting (to total 10)
Price	3
Reliability of delivery time	4
Quality of finish	2
Ability to hire extra stock	1

Each supplier would be rated using the above weighting and the supplier scoring highest would then be selected. In the case of new suppliers, it may be difficult to acquire the information, other than price, on which to rate the supplier. However this may sometimes be available from current customers of that firm.

Such a process is called *Vendor Rating*.[1]

At this stage, either a supplier must be selected to whom a specification can be given for the product to be made to order, or a product, which is the 'nearest fit', must be selected from those available on the market.

5.6.2   Sources of supply

Sources of supply open to the Accommodation Manager, subject to company policy include:

- retail
- cash and carry
- wholesale purchasing organisations
- central purchasing departments
- manufacturers

A comparison of these is shown in Figure 5.6.

5.6.2.1   Retail   This includes shops and supermarkets and is really only a suitable source of supply to solve unforeseen situations or, in an hotel situation, for purchasing goods on behalf of *guests*. Stocks available are limited in quantity, unsuitable for large scale use and expensive. Usually cash must be paid, and money from petty cash is used.

5.6.2.2   Cash and carry   The main advantages that cash and carry suppliers have over retailers are that goods are available in large quantities and generally cheaper. Generally the stocks are designed for the domestic market rather than for large scale use, and usually, they do not offer the same convenience as the retailer due to their, frequently, more remote locations.

5.6.2.3   Wholesale   This usually involves buying from some agency warehouse, or purchasing body, which stock a range of products suitable for large scale use. The supplier may specialise in the products of just one or two manufacturers, or may have a more varied range. Often deliveries can be made more quickly than by placing an order with a manufacturer whose factory or base is some distance away. In addition, the purchasing organisation buys in bulk, and may pass on some of the discount achieved to customers. This may be an advantage, particularly to customers placing smaller orders involving, for example, a standard pack being split.

5.6.2.4   Purchasing departments   Many large organisations, such as the example of the NHS already discussed, set up their own central purchasing departments which, to the individual units of the organisation, act almost as a wholesaler, but with further advantages:

Materials Management   209

Figure 5.6 *A comparison of the sources of supply*

	Retail	Cash and Carry	Wholesale	Central Purchasing	Manufacturers
Choice of goods	Wide	Wide	Selected choice (though special orders may be arranged)	Selected choice (as Wholesale)	Widest choice
Suitability of goods for large scale use	Usually unsuitable	Often unsuitable	Suitable	Suitable	Suitable
Relative cost	Expensive	Less than retail	Less than retail or cash and carry	Usually relatively cheap	Much depends on quantity
Quantities available	Small	Large	Large	Large	Large
Amount of notice needed	None (except for special orders)	None (except for special orders)	Order must be placed	Order must be placed. Delivery may be quicker than wholesale	Order must be placed
Delivery	Rare	None	Normally made	Normally made	Normally made
Customer service, eg training	None	None	Possibly some and manufacturers may be contacted	May be some and manufacturers often involved	Usually offered

- the central purchasing departments are not profit orientated. They provide a service within their organisation and therefore users may gain the advantages of lower prices
- products stocked are specifically selected for use in that particular type of organisation.

Restrictions may be placed by the central purchasing departments in that individual managers lose freedom in the choice of products. They may be required to buy only those products named on the department's supplies lists. In such instances savings are probably being made through standardisation, but, to an individual manager, the restrictions may in fact be costly. They may otherwise, for instance, have the opportunity to take advantage of a special offer or a superior product.

5.6.2.5 Manufacturers Buying products direct from manufacturers can give the manager the maximum freedom of choice in one sense, the restrictions however are on the manager of the small organisation. Without sufficient purchasing power, list prices on some items can be relatively expensive, and the manager may not be able to buy much in bulk if storage space is limited, and, in any case, this does not make for good stores control or cash flow. Conversely, a very large organisation may be purchasing by specification direct from the manufacturers. In this case, the revenue involved makes it worthwhile for manufacturers to produce a product specifically for one customer.

Other advantages of buying direct from the manufacturers are that customer services of various forms may be available and, if goods are faulty, there is a direct line between user and manufacturer.

In most instances, more than one source of supply may be used. To achieve effective purchasing, the buyer must develop an effective stores, ordering, and control procedure. A balance must be achieved with respect to quantities purchased, bearing in mind administrative costs, storage costs and quantity discounts.

5.6.3 Final selection

When the market has been surveyed a limited number of the most appropriate products may be considered further until the choice has narrowed down to two or three. At this stage it may be valuable to approach manufacturers or suppliers with a view to a demonstration of equipment or materials or to the viewing of samples of fixtures, fittings, furniture, furnishings, linens and other similar items.

5.6.3.1 Demonstrations Demonstrations, or the examination of samples, should be viewed as serious undertakings if they are to be of true value. It may well be useful, if not obligatory, to seek other opinions from within the buying organisation, eg when buying staff uniforms in a hospital, people who might be invited to see and comment on samples include:

- supervisory grades and representatives from staff
- unit manager
- a member of the Health and Safety Committee
- a member of the staff's trade union
- control of infection officer
- linen services manager

Inviting such varied opinions may well be constructive and highlight aspects which the Accommodation Manager may otherwise have overlooked or underestimated. It can also promote goodwill between the Accommodation and other departments, and between management and staff. Conversely, of course, inviting comments and apparently encouraging participative management on the one hand, then, apparently, ignoring comments made, could also create staff difficulties. The balance is aimed for.

When equipment, particularly cleaning equipment, is being purchased, competitive demonstrations may be set up. Two or three manufacturers are invited to demonstrate their products simultaneously. Direct comparisons can be made, eg noise levels, ease of handling, efficiency. Care must be taken not to be influenced by the quality of 'salesmanship'.

To be of full value demonstrations, competitive or otherwise, must be well planned. Planning should include:

- site of demonstration. Somewhere which will be uninterrupted to create minimum inconvenience to other building users and yet to provide suitable and representative conditions, eg when testing floor maintenance machines, a variety of floor coverings may be required
- decisions must be made as to whom to invite to the demonstration
- adequate notice, both to suppliers and to the other interested parties, must be given
- a checklist should be prepared of criteria to be measured and some scale must be attached. This scale may simply have two values, satisfactory and unsatisfactory or, alternatively, criteria might be measured on a scale of 1 to 10.

Following the demonstration or viewing of samples, prices and *in-use costs* of products must be determined. Hidden costs, as well as quoted prices, must be considered, eg prices of accessories, service costs, delivery charges, life expectancy, dilution rates of cleaning agents, must all be considered.

5.6.3.2 Field trials In some instances, the value of demonstrations is fairly limited. Much more information regarding the suitability of a product can be gained by testing the product on site by the operatives who will be using it. It is not sufficient, however, to acquire a piece of equipment for a week or two, or a small quantity of a new polish and give it to the staff to 'see what they think'.

To be safe, as well as efficient, field trials need to be carefully set up and monitored. Before a final decision is made, and following any demonstrations, the product may be tested or perhaps two or three may be used on site, so that comparisons can be made. Some of the planning to be done, and decisions to be made when setting up field trials, are as follows:

- in which areas of the building are the products to be tested, eg if a trial was to be conducted to compare duvets with conventional bedding, double, as well as single, beds must be included in the trial
- which staff are to be involved? Are these staff representative of the others who will be using the product?
- is training needed before staff can use the product? If so, will this be given by the supplier?
- for how long are trials to last?
- who else, besides those carrying out the test, need to be informed of the trials?
- a means of evaluation must be prepared, eg checklists, comments from supervisors and others who have been affected. In the case of some cleaning products, bacteriological tests may have to be set up. In the case of linens, certain in-house testing may be valuable.

The format of the evaluation checklist might be as shown in Figure 5.7.

In carrying out field trials, as with any scientific testing, it is important to ensure that only one variable changes at a time. In testing floor maintenance machines, for example, measures need to be taken to ensure that similar pads and floor maintenance products are used. It is the efficiency of the cleaning machine which is being measured, and all other variables should remain constant. In the case of detergent testing, dilution rates must be carefully monitored, manufacturer's instructions must be followed and in-use costs calculated. When testing fabrics, usage, laundering or other cleaning processes and cleaning agents must all be controlled.

Before a final decision is made, and an order placed, the manager must also discover details of deliveries, and customer services that may be require, such as training and installation.

In this purchasing process, the buyer is choosing from the market the product most suited to the requirements documented in the performance specification. It is unlikely, in fact, that the manager will find a product which exactly meets the criteria and will usually have to settle for the best compromise, (hence the importance of grading elements of the specification). In the case of very large organisations, due to their 'purchasing power' or volume of trade, products may be

Figure 5.7 *Checklist for suction cleaner field trials*

Machine manufacturer: ....

Model: ....

Area/s tested: ....

Floor types and soilage: ....

Product characteristics	**Rating**		
Ease of use	*Good*	*Satisfactory*	*Poor*
Training needs			
Ease of assembly			
Manoeuverability			
Weight for carrying			
Cable length			
Stability in use			
Ease of emptying			
Ease of adding attachments			
Storage of attachments			
Capacity of collection bag			
Ease of cleaning			
Variety and effectiveness of attachments			
Efficiency			
Apparent soilage removal — on pile carpet			
— on low pile carpet			
— on hard floors			
Real soilage removal — on pile carpet			
— on low pile carpet			
— on hard floors			
Efficency on other surfaces			
Environmental factors			
Air disturbance			
Air filtration			
Noise level			
Acceptability by users of area			
Appearance of machine			

Acceptability by user

Safety aspects

Durability expected

Users name .... Other comments:
Supervisor ....

custom made by specification (manufacturers make up products to meet the actual specification). Regardless of the size of the organisation, drawing up a specification is not a once-and-for-all exercise. Circumstances are always changing and thus specifications need updating.

Where services, as opposed to supplies, are to be purchased, field trials are of course difficult. Even if one small unit could be isolated and the services completed there to give a sample of standards, running two systems, ie direct and contract labour, in harness within the same organisation, is almost bound to cause labour unrest and in any case may not give a true picture. The best chance of 'sampling' work is to visit other establishments already serviced by interested firms.

5.6.4   Sources of advice

There are many sources of advice from which valuable information is available, guidelines set, and, in some cases, strict rules laid down with repect to purchasing supplies. Particularly on safety, where data is available, the manager is well advised to seek this information. Some of the relevant bodies include the following:

British Standards   British Standards, prepared and published by the British Standards Institution (BSI), are technical agreements on such matters as safety, comfort, efficiency and dimensions on all manner of aspects. These standards broadly follow agreements set by the International Standards Organisation (ISO).

With respect to purchases the Accommodation Manager might make, there are British Standards for some items of cleaning equipment, some detergents, furnishings, wallpaper, colours, chairs and many others. The Standards describe criteria needed to ensure that items are fit for the purpose for which they are intended. Products which are made to BS will be marked with the relevant BS number and this is the manufacturer's claim that it is made according to the documented standard. In addition, the BSI license some manufacturers to use BSI Kitemark (mark of safety) indicating that BSI inspectors have inspected the manufacturer's quality control system as well as sampling products.

British Electrotechnical Approvals Board   The British Electrotechnical Approvals Board is related to the BSI, but specialises in electrical items. Again, the BEAB mark on products, given under licence, is a sign of safety (design, construction and endurance).

The Design Council   The Design Council is government sponsored, and aims to promote good design within British Industry. It assists in many ways, including the provision of direct advice and assistance to manufacturers. The Design Advisory Service has been established by the Design Council, to assist in the diffusion of knowledge, with respect to technological development and design skills. Member companies subscribe to this service.

The Council's design index is an illustrated record of modern products which have been selected by the Council from British products, as being of above average design. Products are checked, where the relevant BS exists, and Design Centre labels can be bought by the manufacturers of items selected. (The object of these labels is to promote the product and so aid marketing.)

Public Authority and Private Organisations Standards   Local Authorities, Government bodies, and large organisations, take advantage of their large purchasing powers, and set up central purchasing supplies departments which can buy largely by specification. To prove that specifications are met, manufacturers may need to submit samples to independent testing houses before tenders are considered. (These testing houses include such bodies as the Building Research Association (BRE) and the British Textile Technology Group, for textiles.) When products are accepted, they are included in the products information circulated to member organisations of the purchasing body. The products are then known to be of a certain standard, specifications can be viewed, and probably a reduced price will have been negotiated.

Other Associations   Other organisations from whom advice may be available, with respect to purchases, include the manufacturers' own associations, eg Contract Cleaning and Maintenance Association, Contract Furnishings Association. These are professional bodies with agreed Codes of Practice for members. They may provide valuable information in the area of their own expertise.

5.7   HIRE OR BUY?

After a formal selection has been made, a further choice of hire or buy may be open in the case of services, eg labour, and many supplies, eg machinery, linen and, in some cases, furniture items.

5.7.1   Supplies

Some of the occasions when hiring or buying may be appropriate, are shown in Figure 5.8. In addition to these factors, the policy of the purchasing organisation and its accounting system, may well determine whether items are bought or hired.

5.7.2   Equipment

The types of equipment, which may be hired in preference to buying, include larger items of cleaning equipment, particularly those used periodically, high cost laundry equipment and office equipment.

Figure 5.8 *Occasions when hiring or buying may be appropriate*

Hiring appropriate	Buying appropriate
1 Infrequent use is likely, storage difficult/expensive	Daily or very frequent use
2 Maintenance, laundering, etc, likely to cause problems	Own maintenance department/ laundry or service contract taken out
3 Equipment is unreliable, linen or furniture usages highly variable and hirer may have alternatives available in case of breakdown or backup stock	Suppliers or servicing company may make short term loans to cover breakdowns or shortages
4 Short term cost advantages	Long term cost advantages
5 Short life expectancy. Many factors may speed up obsolescence	Technological advances or fashion trends expected only gradually

5.7.3 Linen

Whether linen is hired or bought will be closely linked with the laundry process planned. A decision to buy linen, rather than hiring it, cannot be made independently of the choice of laundry and repair system, nor the type of linen service overall which is to be established. The main types of linen systems have been considered in Chapter 3. Figure 5.9 shows some of the advantages and disadvantages of hiring or buying linen.

Figure 5.9 *The advantages and disadvantages associated with purchase or hiring of linen stock*

	Advantages	Disadvantages
Purchase	Freedom of selection of fibre, fabric, colour, quality, cost manufacturer. Capital asset	Require storage space High capital outlay Strict control required Repair costs Replacement costs
Linen hire	No heavy initial cost No replacement costs No repairs No staff Short term loan arrangements Charges may be no greater than depreciation and laundering costs No repair or replacement costs Easier budgeting	Limited choice of style, quality and colour Still have to purchase bedding and soft furnishings Constant control Pay for excessive loss and damage Subject to contract price rising Pay monthly charge even if less numbers May be delivery problems

A decision to hire or buy linen stock must be considered closely with respect to the servicing of that stock.

5.7.4 Furniture

Furniture hire is becoming increasingly popular, particularly:

- where replacement cycles are planned to be short
- where circumstances, eg conferences, exhibitions make abnormal demands
- where labour problems associated with maintenance are experienced, and the hiring firm can offer a maintenance contract, along with the furniture.

5.7.5 Services

The Accommodation Manager has a very wide range of contract services available. These include:

- carpet shampooing
- cleaning services
- decorating
- degreasing
- drain cleaning
- dust control mats and mops hire
- equipment maintenance
- floral arrangements
- hand towel provision and laundering
- laundering
- management services
- night security
- pest control
- telephone cleaning
- uniform hire
- upholstery cleaning
- wall washing
- window cleaning

Recent years have seen a growth in contract services. Occasions where contract labour may be appropriate are as follows:

- when staff availability of direct labour is low; perhaps through sickness, holidays or vacancies
- when infrequent tasks occur which would require expensive equipment and/or expertise in the completion of that task. (These might in any case be outside the job description of existing staff.)
- when a reduction of administrative work is sought to enable an organisation to concentrate on its primary function
- when economic or accounting advantages can be achieved.

In any of these circumstances, contract labour may well be preferable to direct labour. Contract labour can, nevertheless, have its drawbacks. Problems may be encountered with contract staff due to difficulties of their split loyalties to their employer on the one hand, and the establishment on the other. Difficulties may be encountered with low standard of work which arouses complaint from other building users. This in turn necessitates management communicating the problem to the contractor. This all takes time. Other difficulties may be the inflexibility of the service, concern over safety standards, confidentiality of staff, security lapses. Employment of contract labour is not justified when the cost of monitoring the contract is excessive.

One means by which the risk of many of the above difficulties can be minimised is by the preparation of a tight specification before tenders are invited (see Chapter 4).

5.8   HOW TO BUY

In making purchases for large organisations, there are various methods which may be adopted, and usually more than one will be employed by an organisation depending on:

- the products or services
- the expected frequency of subsequent orders (if any)
- policy decisions

Frequently, there are at least two levels of buying goods and supplies:

1 minor items (consumables)
2 more expensive items (capital purchases).

In addition to this, as has already been seen, the Accommodation Manager is likely to be purchasing services. These may be restricted to window cleaning or equipment maintenance, or may run to complete cleaning systems (see Chapters 3 and 4).

Minor items
The actual cut off price, which would determine whether an item was minor/revenue or capital expense, varies from one establishment to another. In one establishment the figure could be £20, in another, £200. Products within the minor items category can usually be purchased at the discretion of the Accommodation Manager (subject to any sourcing restrictions).

Capital items
For more expensive items, costing more than the upper limit for minor items, the manager may need to have budgeted separately. If they are to be bought on the open market, the manager may need to be able to justify the selection of supplier by submitting, with a requisition for the order to be placed, more than one quotation. In some cases, specific approval for the purchase may need to be sought from a more senior level of management. These restrictions will vary with the authority and responsibility held by budget holders.

5.8.1 Buying supplies by contract

When a product is to be reordered frequently, and substantial quantities bought in a year, often more favourable prices can be arranged if a contract is drawn up between supplier and buyer. The buyer agrees to purchase certain quantities over a period of time, and the supplier agrees a fixed price for that period. Contracts for supplies might be drawn up by an individual unit, eg an hotel, a number of units, eg a number of hotels in a certain area, or a central purchasing organisation.

When a contract has been drawn up at a level higher than unit level, individual managers may or may not have that individual product imposed on them. To maintain the purchasing power of their contract negotiating body, officers will be encouraged to a greater or lesser degree to buy from the contract list.

It is in the interests of economy that all managers should be encouraged to utilise such contracts. In so doing, this will:

- maintain the purchasing power of the parent body
- reduce variety, ie simplify the materials management process through standardisation, eg by reducing:
  - the numbers of suppliers dealt with
  - the numbers of orders to be placed
  - price negotiations
  - numbers of deliveries to be managed and processed
  - the numbers of stock items
  - the number of suppliers to be paid, etc.

5.8.2 Buying services by contract

The purchasing of services involves the development of a specification and the drawing up of a contract (see Chapter 4).

Once a contract has been made, the Accommodation Manager will still need to monitor the work being carried out. It may not be necessary to be too concerned with how the work is being done. This might, in any case, be outside the field of expertise, eg selection of chemicals for pest control. The Manager will need to monitor standards. Waiting for complaints or accidents is not sufficient. Whilst many routine and mundane matters may have been passed on to a contractor, the Accommodation Manager is still responsible for standards within a certain sphere of control.

Monitoring a contract will involve physically viewing standards and, perhaps, work in progress, on a regular basis and receiving regular reports from the contractor. It should not involve supervision of the work (see Chapter 7).

5.9 STORES CONTROL

The aim of any stores control system must be to have, at a minimal cost, goods available in sufficient quantities, and of correct type and quality for staff to carry out their work safely. As has already been discussed, equipment, materials and linen do not represent a very large portion of the housekeeping budget. Labour is the costly element and if labour is available and unable to work, due to failures in the stores control system, much money will be wasted. Other reasons for developing an efficient and effective stores control system are as follows:

- shortages, or poor stock rotation will reduce standards. Linen shortages may mean reduced room availability and, therefore, directly reduce revenue
- when supplies are lacking, items may need to be borrowed from other sections (or staff may even bring items from home). This may well constitute a safety risk, eg borrowing inferior equipment, and, in a hospital, could constitute an infection risk
- excessive stock may constitute a safety risk, a fire risk, be costly in storage space (through lost opportunity costs), be time consuming to operate and reduce cash flow
- 'losses' may occur which must be identified, causes established, and controls implemented
- good store control is necessary to implement Health and Safety procedures, eg maintenance of equipment, care of substances hazardous to health
- monitoring of use and product evaluation is better achieved
- budgetary control is facilitated
- standardisation of quality is facilitated.

5.9.1 Storage requirements

Some items should not be kept in stock at all for safety reasons, eg plastic floor seals, or solvent based detergent wax removers, which may well constitute a fire hazard. Their use is infrequent, and purchases can be made for a specific operation. Other items should not be stocked in any quantity due to their limited shelf life, eg some chemical disinfectants.

Many products need to be kept in stock if an efficient accommodation service is to operate. The levels of this stock needed to provide an efficient system will vary with circumstances from one establishment to another, eg reliability and proximity of supplier, degree of variance in work patterns, and levels of staff, eg are annual spring cleaning programmes operated, or a more regular process of periodic maintenance?

The stores area required will depend on the overall stores system of the organisation, eg is a central store operated, or does each department have its own stock room? Frequently, a combination of systems operate. The advantage of having different levels of stores areas within the establishment is that goods are available at close proximity to the point of use. Operatives do not waste time in requisitioning or collecting stores when, perhaps, the storekeeper is not available, or perhaps they themselves would be involved in some productive work which must be interrupted. Conversely, too many peripheral stores areas will increase administrative and control procedures in other ways, and the stores themselves may be utilising potentially valuable revenue earning space. A balance between too many and too few stores areas must be reached which is economical with respect to space and work-hours.

In general terms, the requirements of domestic stores are similar to those of most other stores areas. They include:

- a good situation, which facilitates the delivery of goods throughout the establishment. Ground floor sites, with close proximity to service lifts are common
- stores need to be easily and effectively secured
- space and fittings need to be adequate to enable safe storage, ease of stock taking and effective stock rotation, eg island shelves
- environmental conditions must be suitable to work in, (though, usually, for only short periods), and also for storage, eg controlled heating, adequate lighting (though not necessarily daylight), suitable ventilation
- surfaces need to be easy to maintain to appropriate hygiene and safety standards
- clerical equipment will be needed though the types will vary
- stores areas are particularly vulnerable to fire outbreaks, and must meet the appropriate fire precaution standards
- hand washing and drying facilities will probably be required
- a stores location system will be required.

Other requirements of domestic stores areas vary with the different commodities stocked, eg cleaning and maintenance stores, linen stores, furniture and equipment stores.

5.9.1.1 Hazardous substances

There are potentially many chemicals associated with housekeeping services which constitute health risks. Some are toxic, corrosive, irritants or flammable. Some cause skin irritation, others produce irritating fumes, others are poisonous. In Britain, the Control of Substances Hazardous to Health (COSHH) regulations, part of the Health and Safety at Work Act (1974), has implications here.

For legal reasons, as well as common sense safety, where such substances are deemed to be necessary to use, they should be readily identified as hazardous and records kept of:

- name, stores record number, and any synonym
- ingredients and physical properties
- supplier and details of supplier's Hazardous Data Sheet
- issues made and items returned
- copies of procedure details for their safe use.

Examples of such hazardous substances which may be found in Domestic Services products' lists, might include:

- acids, eg toilet cleaners, concrete etching chemicals
- toxics, eg stain removers
- flammables, eg solvent based polishes or seals, chewing gum remover
- alkali detergents, eg water based polish stripping agents (which may cause skin irritation)
- chemical disinfectants, eg hyperchlorides.

5.9.1.2 Requirements peculiar to cleaning and maintaining stores

- non-porous surfaces to facilitate cleaning of spillages
- closed cupboards for some chemical disinfectants which may need to be protected from sunlight
- no excessive temperature variations as this will cause deterioration of some chemical products, eg water-based emulsion polishes
- electric sockets needed for some equipment
- sink, slop sink or sluice
- hanging space for storing vacuum hoses and other items
- drying space for cleaning cloths, floor pads, etc may be required
- dispensing aids may be needed for issuing chemicals, eg detergent proportioners or drum stands
- flame proof cabinets for flammable and highly flammable materials, eg chewing gum remover, solvent based polishes, as directed by the Fire Authority
- slatted shelves to aid air circulation around certain items, eg impregnated mops and mats to, minimise the chance of spontaneous combustion.

5.9.1.3 Requirements peculiar to linen stores

- slatted shelves to assist air circulation around linen and prevent dampness
- strict pest control to prevent damage by moths and rodents
- protection from sunlight for some items, eg linen
- use of colours and textures in the area, such that they are easy to maintain in a hygienic condition but do not cause excessive glare for storekeepers working in the area. (Glare is a fairly common problem in linen stores, where much of the stock is white and surfaces are chosen for hygiene and hygienic appearance)

- sewing and fitting rooms may adjoin the linen stores
- separate areas for clean and dirty linen may be required, depending on the linen system
- large working surfaces for sorting and folding, etc.

5.9.1.4 Requirements peculiar to furniture and equipment stores

Furniture stored in these areas will be items not in constant use, eg in hotels, cots may be stored to meet customers requests, seminar tables may be stored for temporary conversion of bedrooms to meeting rooms, banqueting tables and chairs may be stored. Equipment stored may be just items used infrequently, eg carpet shampooing machines, or a central room may be used for all equipment storage. (This greatly assists planned servicing of that equipment, also security can be tighter, though, the disadvantage is that equipment is less accessible to staff.)

Furniture stores, in particular, rarely receive the same frequency or amount of use as the previous stores areas. Apart from periodic cleaning and maintenance, the working involvement of staff in these areas is usually restricted to the collection and return of stocks. Conditions, therefore, do not have to provide a working environment. Such stores must not be subjected to excessive temperatures; they must be dry and ventilated, clean and well protected from fire outbreaks and damage from pests.

5.9.2 Stores administration

To enable good stores administration, the physical requirements of the storage area must be satisfactory and, in addition, systems for the monitoring and control of incoming and outgoing stock must be devised. The first decision to be taken is to determine which items should be stocked. This information can be collated from work procedures. The next decision is with regard to quantities to be kept. This decision is much more difficult to determine, and is reached on the basis of:

- quantities required for one operator
- frequencies of operation
- degree of variance between peaks and troughs in the work load
- minimum quantities supplied at one time
- reliability of supply
- storage space available
- issuing system
- shelf life of product and any associated storage problems
- economics related to bulk purchase.

5.9.2.1 When to buy

With economic material management in mind, it must be remembered that the process of placing orders, even

Figure 5.10 *Purchasing questions and means of answering those questions*

Questions to ask	Information source
Expected rate of use	Forecasting assisted by historic data, target occupancy levels, job breakdowns, work schedules
Stock level	Stock taking and records
Ordering time	Past experience and any performance targets set
Delivery lead time	Contractual agreements and past experience

placing an identical order to that placed previously, costs time and money in terms of administrative time, telephone and correspondence costs. By placing large orders economies can be made in office time as well as through quantity discounts. There is, though, a balance to be reached, as large orders have stores implications, if not deterioration costs. Storage costs money in terms of space, in terms of lost opportunity, heating, lighting, insurance costs and in terms of the capital tied up in the stock. These are known as *holding costs*.

In deciding when to make purchases and how much to purchase at once, some of the questions which must be asked and the means of answering these questions are shown in Figure 5.10.

Economic Order Quantity

The Economic Order Quantity is a mathematical formula applied to show the optimum (in terms of economy) size of order to place.

$$\text{EOQ} = \sqrt{\frac{2 \times \text{average annual demand} \times \text{cost of placing order}}{\text{cost of holding one item of stock}}}$$

The formula can be applied to items of stock which are used independently, for example neutral detergent, mop heads, paper towels. It is not appropriate to apply to items which are used in conjunction with others, for example lambswool applicators or thinners for use with solvent-based floor seals. In this case, as floor sealing operations are planned, the materials implications of the whole operation are assessed in a process called *Materials Requirement Planning*.[2]

Applying the EOQ formula to stock control in a large organisation will call for careful planning and forecasting but can save considerable time in the long run. It would be most appropriately applied to commonly used stock items but there are drawbacks, which may render the formula unworkable in some cases. These drawbacks include:

- a predictable demand is required
- a constant rate of demand is necessary
- no allowance is made for 'lead time', ie the time between the placing of an order and delivery
- the cost of holding stock and of placing an order are difficult to calculate.

Fixed order cycle/topping up system

This system is also known as the *Periodic Review* or *Imprest System* and involves checking of stock at fixed intervals. A minimum stock level is fixed and when that level is reached, an order is placed.

The formula for calculating the quantity to be ordered is as follows:

Maximum stock level $= D(P + L) + S$
    Where D = expected rate of demand
              P = review period
              L = lead time
              S = safety allowance

In the case of water-based floor polish, for example:

the expected rate of demand might be 1×5 litres per week
the review period might be two monthly (say, eight weekly)
the lead time might be two weeks
the safety allowance might be 1×5 litres

In this case the formula would read:

Maximum stock level $= 1(8 + 2) + 1$
                              $= 11 \times 5$ litres

At the end of the review period, ie month 2,
if the stock level was 2×5 litres,
the order would be for 9×5 litres

Fixed order point/two bin system

Another system used to determine how much stock to order and when, is the fixed order point system. As with the fixed order cycle, a re-order level is set, ie a minimum level to which stocks are allowed to fall, before a new order is placed. Rather than a fixed period being left between assessment of stock levels, stock is monitored constantly and when the reorder level is reached, an order is placed.

In some operations, literally two bins or containers are used. These bins hold set levels of stock and when issues are made they are all drawn from the same bin. When that bin is empty, the new bin is started and, at the same time, a new order is placed. The system might be used in a small operation for, say, rubber gloves. Limitations can be seen with respect to its application, though the simplicity of the system can in itself be labour saving.

The fixed order point can also be applied to computerised stores control systems. Here the level of stock can be monitored constantly by the computer. As an item is removed from stock, the stock level on the computer memory is reduced by one and when the reorder level is reached the need to place a new order can be signalled.

The use of computers makes this system much more widely applicable to a whole range of domestic services stores.

Carrying too much stock then, is seen as similar bad practice to carrying too little. Indeed, in the Japanese *Just in Time* system,[3] stock items are strictly controlled. Only those quantities required within the given order period are placed. Buffer stocks are seen as wasteful.

5.9.3 Other stores controls

To develop and maintain efficient stores controls, systems are also required for the following:

- filing correspondence
- receiving, checking and receipting deliveries
- authorising payment
- recording stock types, including hazardous substances
- recording batch numbers, model numbers or other identifying data
- recording and monitoring issues
- recording defective stock and product evaluation data
- recording details of stock returns
- recording details of replacements
- stock taking.

5.9.3.1 The stores cycle A flow chart of the stores cycle is shown in Figure 5.11, together with the clerical and administrative implications.

As can be seen from the chart, official orders are frequently sent by an administrative section, rather than from the stores themselves. These orders are, however, initiated by stores and details of goods, supplier, quantities required, and any other relevant information is shown on the requisition. When goods are delivered, they are accompanied by a delivery note, a signed copy of which is generally returned to the supplier, so initiating their invoice; another copy is sent to the finance department, as an authority to pay. Ideally, goods should be checked for quality and quantity when they are delivered, so that any defective items can be returned at once, and discrepancies in quantities can also be dealt with.

Financial dealings are not often the responsibility of the Accommodation Manager, stores invoices are often sent to administrative sections and payment dealt with by a financial department. A point worth noting here is that the Accommodation Manager, as budget

Figure 5.11 *Flow chart showing a stores cycle*

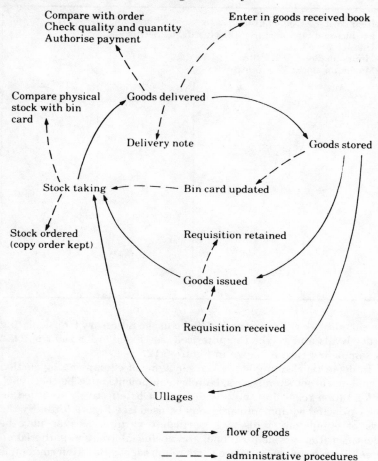

flow of goods

---- ►   administrative procedures

holder, must be kept informed of expenses incurred. In some cases, invoice totals will vary from the expected value, eg annual price increases, periodic reduced price offers, discounts for quantity.

When goods have been accepted by the storekeeper, the details are entered in the goods received book, and the stock is stored appropriately. Stores areas are of particular fire risk, due to their infrequent occupancy. Goods must not be stored against hot pipes, against light fittings and so on. They must be stored in a manner which will facilitate retrieval for use, and also enable stock rotation.

Bin cards are frequently used as a means of keeping a quick check

Figure 5.12 *A bin card*

Item: Water-based emulsion polish Product and manufacturer: 'Floor brite' by Sel Units: 5 litre Minimum stock: 2 × 5 litre Maximum stock: 12 × 5 litre			
Date	*In*	*Out*	*Balance*

on current stock. They provide data on usage necessary for calculating order levels and maybe computerised (see Fixed order point p. 225). A sample bin card is shown in Figure 5.12.

In domestic cleaning stores, larger items of equipment, eg suction cleaners, carpet shampooers, laundry equipment, must be controlled. Information regarding these items cannot be effectively recorded on bin cards and equipment cards may be used (see Figure 5.13). By the use of equipment cards, one particular vacuum cleaner may be identified from an identical one, and useful information gathered on breakdown frequencies, spare parts required, etc. Such information is vital in the process of equipment evaluation when cost efficiencies can be measured and depreciation of future items assessed.

When periodic stock taking takes place, quantities counted on shelves should, in all cases, equal balances on the bin cards. Any discrepancies should be investigated.

5.9.4 Issue systems

A variety of issue systems and their advantages and disadvantages are shown in Figure 5.14. Often a combination of systems is used, depending on the goods and the situation. The main aims of distribution systems are to facilitate stores control by:

Figure 5.13 *An equipment card*

Machine: .... Model: .... Serial No: ....

Manufacturer: ....

Date purchased: .... Purchase price: ....

Date commissioned: .... Date condemned: ....

Accessories: .... Price: ....

....

Usual location of machine: ....

Date	Service details	Date	Service details

- ensuring sufficient goods are available for operatives at all times, and to minimise time wasted, due to insufficient supplies, broken equipment or any other reason
- minimising labour time spent on stores matters
- control of the use of stores such that deviations from the norm are quickly identified, and can be investigated. Such investigation might identify training needs, particular operational problems, wastage or pilfering
- provision of information for budgetary control
- provision of information on product evaluation.

Stores control can be a complex matter, but an efficient system is crucial to the effective running of the department. Good stores control can have a significant effect on wasted work-hours. It must be remembered that the system of stock control must, itself, be cost effective. Control must be directed towards cost efficiency. For example, a system which causes staff to reduce neutral detergent needs by 10%, may save tens of pounds over a year, but, to achieve this, stores administrative costs could be much higher, and goodwill

Figure 5.14 Methods of stores issue

System	Operation	Advantages	Disadvantages	Comments
New for old (or counter exchange)	The user must return the old mop head, empty bottle, etc before a replacement is given	Tight control is achieved over usage	Time consuming for each member of staff to go to the store room. Not a hygienic method collecting in dirty items	Need specified time for stores collections
Topping up/imprest	Each domestic assistant's store has a predetermined stock level. Items are topped up to this level on a weekly basis by a supervisory grade	One person can be made responsible for stores distribution. Excessive variations in usage can be identified and investigated. There should always be sufficient stores. There is some flexibility	Setting the level can be difficult to allow for justifiable variations in use	Commonly used for linen as well as cleaning stores
Set amount	A set quantity of stores is determined for each cleaner's store and that amount is issued weekly	Stores distribution is simplified and record keeping minimised	Excesses can build up and encourage misuse. Alternatively, if the level is set too low problems will occur	Periodic stock checks in each point of issue are necessary
Requisition	Users complete requisition slips for goods required. The requisitions are recorded by the storekeeper	Usage is recorded and excess easily identified. Some restriction in use though to some extent staff set own limit	Time consuming. Level not controlled normally by supervisory grade	Need specified time for requisition to be handed in and items collected

might be lost. Control must be kept in perspective, and labour costs, incurred by stores control, must be accounted.

Computerised stock control is an effective means of reducing labour costs, as has been shown. Orders, product prices and costs, Pareto analysis, bin cards, product specifications, details of suppliers of hazardous substances, goods received, goods issued, ullages and budget details can all be recorded.

5.10 EVALUATION OF STOCK

It may be that having gone through the processes listed above, a stable stock of products can be maintained for a short period of time. The need for change will become apparent in time.

- there may be a need to reduce costs for budgetary reasons
- new products may be needed to maintain new surfaces
- product developments may make current items obsolete or less desirable
- problems with existing stocks or suppliers may be experienced

Regular product evaluation process may operate whereby any of the above are identified prior to a problem being perceived, the process, therefore, begins again!

References

[1] BAILY P, and FARMER D, *Purchasing Principles and Management*, 5th edition, Pitman 1986
[2] LYSONS C K, *Purchasing*, 2nd edition, Macdonald and Evans 1989
[3] VOSS C A *Just in Time Manufacture*, Kempston, IFS Publications 1987

Further reading

BSI, BS 5415 (1985 and 1986) *Safety of Electrical Motor Operated Industrial and Commercial Cleaning Appliances*
BS 3762 (1986) *Analysis of Formulated Detergents*
BS 808 *Chick Martin Test*
GAGE W L, *Value Analysis*, McGraw-Hill 1967
GULLEN H V and RHODES G E, *Management in the Hotel and Catering Industry, Batsford* 1983
KASAVANNA M L, *Hotel Information Systems*, CBI Publishing Company 1978
LOCK D, *Project Management*, 3rd edition, Gower 1984
MORRIS C, *Quantitative Approaches in Business Studies*, 2nd edition, Pitman 1989
STEADMAN C E and KASAVANNA M L, *Managing Front Office Operations*, 2nd edition, Educ. Inst. American Hotels 1988

Concept Map summarising Materials Management.

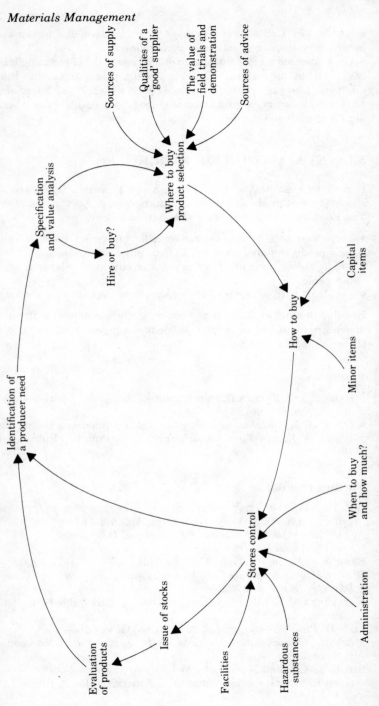

TUCKER C and SCHNEIDER M, *Professional Housekeeper*, Cahners 1975
WALKER D and CROSS N, *The Man-Made World*, Open University Press 1976

Assignment tasks

1 Draw a systems map of the subsystems within the Materials Management System of an accommodation department known to you.
2 Explain means by which the relative value of a product to the accommodation department could be assessed.
3 Discuss the aims of good materials management and the benefits to the Accommodation Manager.
4 Taking a particular accommodation department as an example, find out which are the sources of supply and how those sources could be evaluated.
5 Following a problem solving approach, a need to purchase a suction drying machine has been identified. Describe the process of selecting the product and supplier and include a product specification and a check list for the field trials.
6 Giving specific examples, show the relative benefits of hiring or buying equipment or services within the field of Accommodation Management.
7 Devise a stores control system for the accommodation department of a named establishment and emphasise the health and safety implications within that context.

6

The Front Office Dimension

Objectives

- To highlight the Guest Cycle concept as a basis for determining the Front Office activities to be undertaken and improving the customer experience.
- To identity issues relevant to designing or improving the Front Office system.
- To analyse and develop the accommodation service packages.
- To consider how the volume of sales can be increased through a marketing, sales and customer care orientation.
- To consider how performance, both in occupancy and revenue terms, can be measured and monitored.
- To discuss ways of maximising potential, including yield management, selling conference space, and income generation.
- To identify the issues involved in managing conferences.
- To determine the value of computerising front office activities and the factors to consider when doing so.

6.1 THE IMPACT OF THE FRONT OFFICE OPERATION

As suggested in Chapter 1, any service operation involves a 'front of house' dimension, where customers interface with the service package and the operation or, more precisely, individuals within the operation. The Accommodation Service Package is no exception. Customers interface with the Accommodation Service Package at many stages during its production and provision.

Each point of contact is a critical point in the total process, as the customer's, or potential customer's, perception of the service package, the operation and the personnel can be influenced favourably or adversely by the contact experience. The behaviour of both customers and personnel is variable and therefore each transaction is a unique experience. Whilst the behaviour of personnel can be partly controlled through training and monitoring, for instance, the behaviour of customers is less predictable.

It is the potential customer's initial contact with the operation which has far reaching consequences on space utilisation, occupancy and revenue levels, reputation and profitability. The potential customer may in fact be deterred, for many reasons, from ever becoming an actual customer. In most Accommodation outlets the customer's initial contact will either be with the telephone operator or reservation clerk or, on arrival, with the commissionaire, porter or receptionist.

Some Accommodation Operations, such as medium and large hotels, have a well defined 'front office' operation, designed to provide a focal point of contact for the in-house customer and deal with a whole range of customer transactions from the initial contact through to the customer's departure, thus covering such functions as reservations, reception, room allocation, billing and accounting, and communication functions. This type of operation has its own organisational structure and is managed as a department or subsystem in its own right.

However, in other operations, such as a hospital, these 'front office' functions will be fragmented under the jurisdiction of different departmental managers.

For instance, in a National Health Service hospital:

a patient

- has to be registered by out-patients, admissions or the accident and emergency unit
- has to be allocated a bed, which involves:
  — making enquiries
  — checking documentation
  — allocating a specific bed to a specific patient
  — recording bed status
  — controlling bed occupancy
- has to have a file opened, recording details of services and treatments received
- has to receive services and facilities besides medical treatments, such as meals and beverages, snacks, magazines, telephone calls
- will incur costs which have to be monitored and paid by someone, whether the patient or the general practitioner.

nursing and medical staff

- will have to request accommodation, if they want to be resident
- be allocated the accommodation
- be allocated keys
- register on arrival
- be shown where the room is
- pay their account on a regular basis.

visitors

- will have to be informed about visiting times
- be directed to the appropriate location of their friends or relatives.

Whereas in a Contract Cleaning Company, the 'front office' may simply be the switchboard-operator-cum-receptionist.

Managing the front office, however, involves more than the 'mechanistic subsystem' of processes and procedures to manage the customer interface. It also involves analysing, improving, selling and marketing the service package and maximising both potential and profitability.

6.2   MANAGING THE CUSTOMER INTERFACE

The activities of the Front Office, indeed of the total operation, revolve around the activities of the customer, whether hotel guest, hospital patient or sports hall user.

It is possible to plot the sequence of the customer's activities by using a flow chart, commencing from when the potential customer first makes contact with the operation until the final transaction is completed. This concept is referred to as *the Guest Cycle*, which KASAVANNA (1978)[1] suggests is 'an effective means for enabling management to better monitor, chart and control the guest's transactions'.

It means that the activities which must be undertaken by the Front Office at the time appropriate to the customers' activities, and the flow of information, can be readily determined. In simple terms, the Guest Cycle activities tend to fall into three sections, with a number of activities occurring in each section.

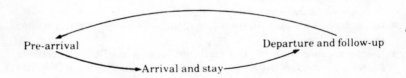

Figure 6.1 is a more detailed flow chart showing the customers' activities which occur in each section of the cycle.

Figure 6.2 is a further development of the customers' activities showing the Front Office activities which have to be undertaken to satisfy the customers' requirements.

Although the Guest Cycle outlined in Figures 6.1 and 6.2 refer to a typical hotel, the concept can be used in other types of establishments such as hospitals, halls of residence or conference centres, to plot the sequence of customers' activities.

The Front Office activities outlined in Figure 6.2 can be grouped under the following headings, thus the basic functions of the Front Office system are defined:

Figure 6.1 *Flow chart to show guest activities*

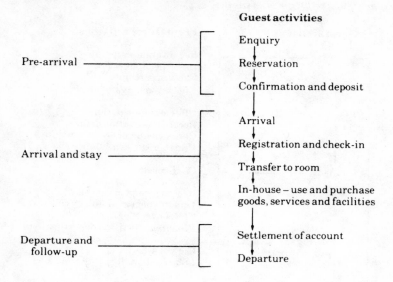

- advance reservations
- reception and check-in
- accounting (and check-out)
- sales and selling
- information and communication services
- security.

It is possible also to focus on the resident consumer and analyse the pattern of their day which will also suggest activities to be organised and services and facilities to be made available. An example is given in Figure 6.3 and often particular consumer patterns emerge, for instance in an hotel catering for business people, a high proportion will leave each day usually fairly early in the morning.

6.3 DESIGNING OR IMPROVING THE FRONT OFFICE OPERATIONS

There are many texts available that describe the alternative Front Office processes and procedures. It is the intention here to provide, for each Front Office function, a checklist which poses a series of basic questions to be asked when initially designing or appraising the total Front Office operation.

Figure 6.2 *Flow chart to show the Front Office activities which must coincide with the guest activities*

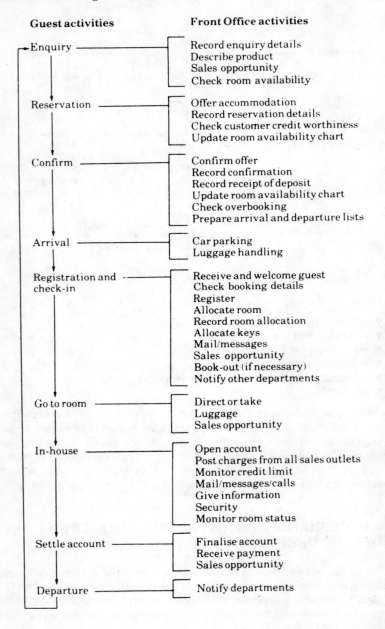

Guest activities	Front Office activities
Enquiry	Record enquiry details Describe product Sales opportunity Check room availability
Reservation	Offer accommodation Record reservation details Check customer credit worthiness Update room availability chart
Confirm	Confirm offer Record confirmation Record receipt of deposit Update room availability chart Check overbooking Prepare arrival and departure lists
Arrival	Car parking Luggage handling
Registration and check-in	Receive and welcome guest Check booking details Register Allocate room Record room allocation Allocate keys Mail/messages Sales opportunity Book-out (if necessary) Notify other departments
Go to room	Direct or take Luggage Sales opportunity
In-house	Open account Post charges from all sales outlets Monitor credit limit Mail/messages/calls Give information Security Monitor room status
Settle account	Finalise account Receive payment Sales opportunity
Departure	Notify departments

Figure 6.3 *Checklist – the pattern of the consumer's day*

The pattern of the consumer's day

What time does the guest awake?	Do they ask for a wake-up call? Do they order early morning tea? Do they require newspapers?
What time do they have breakfast?	Do they eat in the breakfast room? Do they eat in their rooms?
If checking-out — when do they do so?	
If staying on — do they leave the hotel?	Do they require packed meals? Do they return at meal times? What time do they return?
— do they stay in the hotel?	Which facilities and services do they use? Do they go back to their rooms? Do they eat in the hotel or go out for meals?
What time do new arrivals arrive?	Do they generally want meals/snacks or drinks on arrival?
Do consumers stay in/go out in the evening	Do they use the restaurants? Do they use the bars? Do they use room service?
What time do they generally retire to bed?	

6.3.1   Advance reservations

- **Enquiries**
  - How do potential customers communicate with the operation – by letter; telephone; fax; computer terminal; personally or through an intermediary?
  - What characteristics does each means of communication possess which has to be accommodated by the Front Office system? (See Figure 6.4)
  - What does the enquirer wish to know?
  - Who enquires – an individual, a personal secretary, conference organiser?
  - How long in advance will enquiries be made, ie what is the normal lead time for a reservation?
  - What data must be recorded and how?

- **Availability of accommodation**
  - Which means of checking accommodation availability is most appropriate – diary; traditional reservation chart; density chart; room rack/Whitney system; computerised system? (See Figure 6.5.)

— Does accommodation availability need to be summarised at regular intervals to aid speed and efficiency and highlight heavy demand periods?

— How will the accommodation availability system be kept up-to-date and monitored?

— Is an overbooking facility required in the accommodation availability system adopted?

- **Reservations**
  — Does the product require selling to the enquirer – if so will the personnel involved need to possess product knowledge and be trained in marketing and sales techniques?

  — Do special requirements need to be ascertained, eg disabled facilities required; baby minding, etc?

  — What reservation details will be recorded and how?

  — Will accommodation be reserved by room number or room type?

  — If the potential customer does not accept the offer, are reservation records still to be retained?

  — Will it be necessary to analyse why enquiries are not converted to sales?

  — If accommodation of the type requested is not available will an alternative offer be made? Will a waiting list be opened or will over-booking occur?

  — Must an over-booking policy be adopted?

  — Is a 'time release' for accommodation to operate to create the opportunity to achieve full potential? If so, how is the potential customer to be informed?

  — Will the potential customer wish to guarantee a room reservation by credit card?

- **Credit worthiness**
  — How is customer credit worthiness to be evaluated? It is necessary to know how the potential account will be paid, eg by cash, credit card, cheque, Euro-cheque, travellers cheque, foreign currency, charge account.

  — Is it necessary to know who will pay – the individual, a company, or will it be a complimentary room?

  — Will a blacklist be required from the local hotel association, police, credit card company?

  — Is a guest history index required to ascertain if a customer has previously stayed and been able to pay?

- **Filing**
  — How will reservation data be filed – alphabetically under the date of arrival?

- **Confirmation and deposits**
  — Is written confirmation of the reservation transaction required? If so, by whom (hotel in the case of a telephone request; the

customer in other cases) and how is it to be given? By standard letter/card; computer printout; individually typed letter; carbon copy of the reservation form? How expensive will the confirmation process be?

— Will a credit card guarantee be acceptable?
— Is a deposit required? If so, how much? What accounting record has to be completed?
— Is the room availability system and the reservation record to be updated on receipt of confirmation or deposit?
— How is a cancellation to be dealt with?
— When is the reservation to be retrieved – a month in advance; a week in advance; a day in advance or all three?
— Is an arrival and departure list required – if so, in what format, by whom, and are confirmed and unconfirmed reservations to be segregated?
— Will an occupancy forecast be required – if so, by whom, what period in advance?

The advance reservations system devised must possess the flexibility to cope with the various means of communication and incorporate the facility to:

● check the availability of accommodation
● check customer credit worthiness
● make an offer and form a contract
● confirm the reservation request
● identify repeat customers to enable a guest history trace to be undertaken.

6.3.2   Reception, registration and check-in

● **Arrival**
— When will the customer generally arrive? Will there be a peak period?
— By what mode of transport will the customer arrive? – car; plane/ train and/or taxi
— If the customer arrives by car, where will it be parked?
    — in the hotel car park? or the local authority park?
    — how will the customer know where to park?
    — will parking be free or is a charge to be made?
    — is the car park well signposted?
    — how many cars can be parked?
    — will a discount arrangement be negotiated with a local authority car park?
    — will a temporary parking area be allocated for registration and unloading?
    — will a section be allocated for disabled customers?

Figure 6.4 *The advantages and disadvantages of the various means*

Communication means	Advantages	Disadvantages
Telephone	Allows guests to find out very quickly if accommodation is available	Difficult to sell accommodation over the telephone – must remember that every enquiry is a potential sale
Fax	Combines speed with permanence of a letter Written message is received Instant reply can be sent Communicate easily with international companies – overcoming expense and time difference Message can be received even if no one on duty	Expensive to install Space required Photocopy as original fades in time
Correspondence	Often contains special requests More enforceable as a contract particularly with reference to 'no-shows'	If not answered quickly may lose the sale
Personal or chance	Unique opportunity to sell the hotel and the facilities	Inherently suspect very short lead time Little information about the potential guest Unable to check customer's credit worthiness (unless credit card number taken at registration)
Computer terminal	Speedy service Often gives alternative room, types or room numbers within price range	

Requirements of system	Usage
Must allow check on room availability at a glance Standardised preprinted enquiry card or telephone call sheet to record all information Guest must confirm in writing (credit card number may be accepted by some hotels as a guarantee of accommodation) Analyse carefully the hours of staffing the reservation office Provide 'hot-line' telephone number for regular customers	Most common – particularly where there is a short lead time
Analyse need carefully – especially if fair proportion of business from industry and commerce and international business. Siting and space Follow up 'leads', ie names and addresses given by fax in an endeavour to increase sales	Most large hotels particularly catering for business people and conferences
Letter to be stamped and initialled on opening by clerk or secretary Send through internal mail to Advance Reservations for processing Check details and code main requirements in abbreviated form at top of letter with alternative or negative instructions for typist. Answer within 24 hours Consider alternative means of replying, eg individually typed letter, standard pro-forma, carbon copy of reservation form Follow 'leads' from letter head etc to gain further business	Where the lead time is much longer, eg resort hotels
Must offer accommodation under The Innkeepers Liability Act Accept one of the following in advance to ensure receipt of payment: a deposit; full payment of the first night's accommodation in advance; an imprint of the credit card Show the guest the room types during a quiet spell Issue a colour coded identity card to ensure cash sales only Impose 'credit limit'	Commercial, motor hotels
Easy and quick to use Visual display of room availability Offer alternative room types/dates Print out availability Print out offer/reservation letters Customer to confirm in writing or credit card guarantee	Computerised links with other hotels in the chain, centralised Reservations Office, referral systems, travel agents, car hire

Figure 6.5 *Comparative details of the alternative systems, which may*

System	Advantages
The hotel diary	Entries in date order
Room rack and Whitney system	Flexible system according to requirements Colour coding introduced to denote guest or room status or room type Remove slip for cancellation
Traditional reservation chart	Separate chart for each month Suitable if great variation in room type Allocate specific room no. on reservation
Density chart and density reservation chart	Speedy Suitable for short lead time, short stay
Computerised system	Alternative formats, eg by date, by room type, room price, room number Visual display or printout if required

  — Is the customer likely to arrive by train or plane? If so,
    — is a courtesy car/minibus service required?
    — will it be a free service?
    — how will the customer know about this service?
  — Is a commissionaire (linkman) required to receive, meet, greet customers, hail taxis, etc?
  — Is a baggage handling system required? If so,
    — which personnel are required and how many?
    — will a separate luggage entrance and storage area be required – where will it be located, how large will it need to be, what security arrangements are required?
  — Will the courtesy car driver and the commissionaire require training in social skills?

● **Reception**
  — Will customers be met at the entrance?

be used for checking and recording room availability

Disadvantages	Possible usage
Entries per page not in alphabetical or room order May need to physically rule each page Cross out cancellations if entered in ink	Small establishments
Takes up space especially if used for advance reservations Difficult to insert rack slips if too many racks	Medium to large establishments
Large sheet or several sheets per month if large hotel Messy if have to rub out, eg cancellations Limited room for information May be difficult to trace one room across whole month quickly Difficult to trace availability of one room across two months Space required	Medium to large establishments – especially those with great variations in room types and tariffs
Must include an overbooking facility into system Slight difficulty remembering to record and cancel over several days No guest information included Must file density charts in date order If peg board used, pegs may be knocked out	Medium hotels with few room types where one room is much like another
May be difficult to read on VDU May be difficult to trace one room over several days May not have an effective over-booking check	Medium to large hotels

— Is the reception easy to find, well signposted and welcoming?
— How many customers may arrive at the reception desk in the same time period?
— Is a traditional reception desk/area required? (some hotels expect the Front Office personnel to sit down with arriving guests in the front hall and complete the registration process)
— Is an alternative reception area required for tours and conferences?
— Will a 'speedy' check-in be devised for regular customers?
— Who will be the first person the customer has contact with? – courtesy car driver, commissionaire or receptionist?
— How much emphasis is to be placed on the importance of the reception/registration process and the establishment of a relationship between Front Office personnel and the customer?

● **Registration**
— What registration details are to be recorded and in what format

— card, book, computer printout? How much data is to be completed by the customer and how much by personnel?

— Is any marketing/administrative data to be ascertained and recorded at this time?

— How long has the data to be retained after the customer has left?
— where and in what format?

● **Room allocation**

— When will room allocation take place? – on reservation, the day before arrival, the day of arrival, at arrival?

— How will rooms be allocated?

— will a priority order of rooms be required, eg will rooms with views, larger or upgraded rooms be allocated prior to smaller or older rooms, and will rooms with disadvantages be allocated last?

— will a priority order of customer be required, eg confirmed before unconfirmed; long stay before short stay; VIPs and regulars and guaranteed reservations before others; company accounts and sources of potential future business before individuals.

— Will customers with special needs, eg the disabled, single women/ business women require special specific rooms?

— How will room allocation be recorded, ie when, what data, in what format? – is a room letting sheet/bed sheet; Whitney system; traditional reservation chart; computerised system the most appropriate?

— Who will require this data – housekeeping, telephonist, reception personnel?

● **Room status**

— How will room status be monitored to ensure that the state of every room, ie whether let (and by whom), vacant and ready for reletting; vacant and dirty; out of order, be known at any one time?

— Which system (eg Whitney, electronic or computerised system) will be the most appropriate?

● **Key allocation**

— Who will issue room keys – eg porters, reception personnel?
— Where will room keys be stored, eg out of sight for security?
— How will room keys be stored – pigeon holes, key board?
— Will a key card for identity purposes be required? If so will it be colour-coded to denote customer status, eg conference delegate, VIP, chance customers (chance sales only)?
— How will mail and messages awaiting customer arrival be stored and distributed?

● **Room direction**

— How will the customer be directed to their allocated room?

— Will the customer be directed? – if so,
  — how will the receptionist know where every room is allocated?
  — will the room numbers be well signposted?
  — are the signs legible?
  — are the room numbers logically allocated?
— will the customer be taken? – if so,
  — by whom?
  — what procedure will be followed on arrival at the room?

● **Luggage handling**
— Will a luggage handling service be offered? – if so, who will do it?
— Will an identity system be required?
— How will mass luggage be dealt with?

● **Booking-out**
— If over-booking occurs how will it be dealt with?
  — who will be booked-out? Will the same priority list apply as for room allocation?
  — where will alternative accommodation be reserved – an hotel in the same group, the nearest hotel, a similar class of hotel?
  — how will the customer get there? – will a map be provided, a taxi arranged, courtesy car?
  — who will book out? – the Duty Manager, Front of House Manager, Head Receptionist, Duty Receptionist?
  — will a reciprocal arrangement be negotiated with a competitor hotel?

● **Chance custom**
— What proportion of chance custom is usual?
— How will chance customers be dealt with?
— Will they be expected to pay in advance? – if so – the normal deposit; the first night's accommodation, each night's accommodation in advance, or give a credit card imprint?

● **Tour business**
— What proportion of tour business is usual?
— How will mass arrivals be dealt with?
— Will a separate reception area be required?
— Will it be necessary to prepare a room list in advance?
— Will it be necessary to allocate rooms in advance?
— Can registration cards, keys and hotel information be distributed quickly, eg in envelopes in a separate reception area, an empty function room or the coach?

6.3.3 Accounting

● **Opening the account**
— When will the customer's account card be opened? – on receipt of deposit, day of arrival, or on arrival?

— How and when will the deposit be entered on the account card?

● **Posting charges**
— In which sales outlets will residents accumulate credit sales?
— What sales data will be recorded at the point of sales? – and how?
— How will details of a specific sale be communicated by the point of sales to the point of customer billing (Front Office) – by person or point of sales terminal?
— How often will sales information have to be transferred from the point of sales to the Front Office?
— How up-to-date will customer account cards need to be at any given time?
— Is a docket/voucher system required? (see section for control features.)
— How will dockets need to be stored at the Front Office to await posting and for how long?
— Will dockets need 'actioning' after posting to prevent reposting and what happens to the actioned dockets?
— What sales information will need to be transferred to a customer's account card? eg identified sales outlet; date; amount.
— When will accommodation charges be posted? – for new arivals and stay-overs? Who will undertake this and who will monitor?
— When will Front Office accounts be balanced? – at the end of a shift or once a day?
— What procedure will be required if the Front Office accounts do not balance?
— What management information and statistics are required and how often?

● **Credit control**
— Will any credit checking of customer account cards be required?
    – if so,
      — why, when and by whom?
      — will a credit limit have to be imposed on the customer at any time? – how much, by whom?

● **Accounting system**
— Which accounting system will be the most appropriate? – manual tabular ledger; electronic accounting machine or a computerised system.
— By what alternative means may the customer pay their account? eg by cash; credit card; cheque; Euro-cheque; travellers cheque; foreign currency; travellers agents' vouchers or transfer to company accounts (transfer to the ledger) (see Appendix 5.)
— Who will require a copy of the finalised account card? – the customer, the accounts department, the customer's company?
— Will a proportion of customers wish to depart in the same time period? – thus creating a peak period

— How many staff will need to be on duty and when?
— Is a referral system for booking future accommodation a necessary service to be provided?

Whichever accounting system is selected it must incorporate the following features:

- keep the customer's account card up-to-date
- identify all sales from all sales outlets
- allow cash sales (eg chance meals, drinks, function payments) as opposed to credit sales to be recorded separately
- balance as required
- provide the following data for analytical and management purposes:
  — a sales summary from each sales outlet, incorporating a breakdown of all individual customer transactions
  — a summary of all sales (identified) attributable to one room (customer)
  — a total figure of business done (ie the total revenue from the shift or day's transactions) by each sales outlet
  — a total of each customer's expenditure (ie normally by room)
  — a grand total of all business done from all sales outlets – identifying the amount already paid for and the amount still outstanding
  — a grand total of customer expenditure, highlighting the total of the accounts paid and the total of those still outstanding
  — other information as required such as a segregation of VAT, disbursements (VPOs), allowances made, credit card transactions
- incorporate control features, including a procedure for rectifying mistakes and making allowances.

- **Check-out**
  — How will Front Office accounting personnel know which customers are to depart?
  — When will customer account cards be finalised? – prior to departure or at check-out?
  — How will customer account cards be checked to ensure all last minute credit sales are included?
  — Will VAT and service charge have to be entered as separate charges?
  — How will a customer query be dealt with?
  — Will customers be able to check themselves out – at a public VDU or in room?

6.3.4 Communications

- **Incoming**
  — How will incoming mail, messages and telephone calls for customers have to be dealt with?

— How will the telephonist know who is in which room?
— How will customers who are in-house but not in-room be contacted? – what type of paging system will be required?
— Are free 'house' phones required? If so where and how many?
— How will incoming mail be sorted, stored and distributed? and by whom?
— How will messages be recorded? Is a standard format required including the date, time and signature of the message taker?
— How will the customer know that a message is waiting?

- **Outgoing**
  — How will customers' outgoing mail, messages and telephone calls be dealt with?
  — What telephone switchboard system is the most appropriate?
  — Is an efficient, speedy and not too expensive telephone service required?
  — What attempts will be needed to prevent the telephone service from being a loss maker?
  — Will telephone charges be transferred automatically to customer account cards, how frequently and how will 'too late' charges be prevented, particularly with a manual system?
  — How much will customers be charged per unit to cover overheads and telephone charges?
  — Will a wake-up call or line-barring facility be necessary?
  — Is a public telephone system required? If so, how many facilities, where will they be located?
  — Will stationery, stamps and a post-box for outgoing mail be required?

- **Information services**
  — What type of information will customers require? – about the hotel; about the locality?
  — What importance is to be placed on this service?
  — What reference books/materials must be kept at Front Office?
  — Will it be more effective to present some of this information in a written format, eg hotel directory of services or 'What's on' in town?
  — Who will be responsible for the dissemination of this information? – reception personnel; an enquiry clerk; the hall porter?
  — Will theatre tickets, car hire and tourist agencies be required?
  — Who will deal with customer complaints?

- **Security**
  — What key controls are required?
  — How will the safe custody of customers' valuables be dealt with?
  — What is the hotel proprietor's liability for loss of customers' property within the Hotel Proprietors Act 1956?
  — Will the entry and exit of all building uses be monitored? – if so,

how and by whom? – constant portering; security guards; closed circuit TV?
— Will single women be allocated rooms in a 'safe' section of the hotel?
— Will main doors be locked at a particular time at night?

6.3.5 Guest history

Is a guest history system required? If so, what information will be recorded, how, by whom and how long will it be held before deletion?

6.4 CONTROLLING THE FRONT OFFICE OPERATION

Designing appropriate systems, procedures or processes to meet both the requirements of the customer and the operation is crucial to the effective operation of the Front Office. With forethought, control features can be incorporated into procedures and processes at the design stage, becoming an integral part of the system. As many of these features have been mentioned or inferred already, a summary chart has been included to highlight them and indicate their relevance. (see Figure 6.6)

Figure 6.6 *Some Front Office control features which can be incorporated as an integral part of a system*

Feature	Relevance
ADVANCE RESERVATIONS	
Visual, up-to-date Room Availability chart	Speedy offer
Standard system of recording using pre-printed reservation card	All information recorded. Personnel aide-memoire
Realistic overbooking policy – based on past statistics with a contingency plan for 'booking out'	To maximise revenue but prevent major crises – but have a plan in case
Check customer credit worthiness/ability to pay/guest history	Prevent bad debts or fraud; identify specific requirements
Confirmation and deposit procedure	Increase possibility of guests showing-up. Written evidence of offer and acceptance
Time release	Maximise revenue

Figure 6.6 Continued

Feature	Relevance

RECEPTION AND CHECK-IN

Feature	Relevance
Training in social skills and guest care	Welcome, first impressions
Registration	Legal
Standard procedure for chance guests	Prevent bad debts
Well designed, up-to-date room status system	Ensure state of every room known at any time
Priority rating of customers for room allocation	Foster goodwill Prevent booking out certain categories of guests
Identity cards	Security Guest status Control of credit sales
Siting of keys to prevent guest access or viewing	Security

ACCOUNTING

Feature	Relevance
Docket/Voucher control — issue to specified personnel — account for each consecutive docket — speed of transfer from sales outlet to front office — store effectively prior to posting — action after posting — file in case of customer queries — forward to Control Office	Security Prevent fraud Accurate accounting
Posting of charges — ensure all charges correctly posted — ensure accommodation charges posted — regular and frequent posting — post systematically — identify sales outlet — speed and method of transfer — action docket after posting — accommodation posted at specific time — adjustment feature for errors	Security Prevent fraud Accurate accounting
Regular balancing	To ensure accurate accounting Find inaccuracies All totals agree
Sales summary	Analyse sales revenue, guest expenditure, outstanding business

Machine accounting controls

Feature	Relevance
Audit roll	The machine will not operate without it Only access with a special key to change it Provides a clear audit trail of each transaction Consecutive numbering of all transactions
Voucher control	Overprints voucher in 'proving' slot to indicate actioned

Machine controls	Show number of transactions during a shift to each of the analysis keys
	Increases every time the machine is cleared
Cash control	
Signing in and out of floats	Security
	Inaccuracies traced to an individual
Limiting number of floats allocated	Security
	Cash flow
Individual cashier code and separate till	Security
	Individual control and monitoring
Recording of all cash received	To check actual cash received
	Security
	Aid cash flow
Efficient processing of foreign currency and administrative charge	Prevent losing out financially
Other controls	
Credit check	Highlight peculiar spending patterns or possible bad debts
Impose credit limit	Ensure pay bill in regular amounts
Computer controls	For access and security

CHECK-OUT

Follow a standard procedure	Ensures all aspects covered
Agree the bill with customer	Overcome complaints
	Avoid future problems
Check breakfasts and telephone charges have been posted	Prevent loss of revenue
Set a procedure for dealing with each type of payment method	Aid staff
	Prevent fraud
	Prevent loss

COMMUNICATIONS

Ensure messages are relayed accurately and quickly	Avoid guest frustration and complaints
	Part of image
Ensure speedy system of posting telephone charges	Prevent loss of revenue
Provide information service	Part of image possibly sales producing

SECURITY

Safe custody of customers' valuables, with standard procedure	Customer comfort
	Prevent frustration
	Reduce liability
Staff aware to report suspicious events	Safety
Constant staffing in front hall	Safety
Security of main doors at night	Safety

6.4.1   Personnel control

The size, type, grading and scope of the operation will greatly affect the organisational structure of the Front Office, the number of personnel employed and the variety of grades of personnel to be employed.

In a small, privately owned resort hotel, a 'multi-skilled' receptionist may be employed who covers the whole range of activities. In a large city centre, four or five star hotel, different grades of personnel may well be responsible for the different Front Office functions – with a number of each grade employed, such as advance reservation clerks, receptionists, book-keepers (bill-clerks), cashiers, information clerks, telephonists.

By using simple recording techniques and analysing the customer's behaviour pattern it is possible to determine the mean number of transactions carried out over a period, their nature, also the time periods where peaks and troughs occur daily, weekly and possibly seasonally. This should influence not only numbers and grades of personnel but also hours of work and scheduling arrangements. Occupancy forecasts will also affect staffing levels.

Shift hours will be influenced by the type of operation and pattern of business which in turn will influence the hours of cover to be provided by the Front Office. A busy metropolitan or an airport hotel will require a 24 hour, three shift coverage, whereas, a small resort hotel, where guests stay for one or two weeks at a time may only require a minimal coverage midweek, but a 9.00 am to 9.00 pm coverage at the weekends.

In most commercial hotels a two shift system operates, eg 7.00 am to 3.30 pm, 3.00 pm to 11.30 pm (an overlap occurring to enable communication to occur at changeover time). For security, safety and emergency reasons, it may be necessary to employ a Night Porter and some hotels still employ night auditors to post accommodation charges, carry out a business analysis and produce the required management information. In large Front Office organisations, a Head of Section may be required to supervise and control each function, ie Head Receptionist, Head Book-keeper, Head Cashier, Head Hall Porter. It is essential in any Front Office to have a designated shift leader on duty, particularly when Heads of Section are off duty or where the size of operation does not warrant such grades.

6.4.2   Control of physical resources

Physical Front Office resources which have to be managed include Front Office equipment and Front Office accommodation.

The range of equipment required, its design and suitability for purpose in relation to the systems to be used is just as important to the Front Office as it is elsewhere. Front Office equipment should be selected and purchased following the procedures suggested in Chapter 5. The following Front Office equipment may be required.

- telephone network
- fax machine
- filing cabinets, trays, index files
- accounting machine, bill trays, tills
- computer, printers, VDUs, keyboards
- credit card terminal and credit card machines
- photocopier
- racking and charting system
- safe, safe deposit boxes
- stamps – hotel, date and time
- staplers and punches
- calculators
- key depositry
- mail/key racks
- typewriter/word processor
- electronic key encoding machines.

Maintenance arrangements will have to be made for mechanical, electronic and computerised equipment. With rapid advancements in technology, the useful life-span of the complex computerised equipment may be limited, with obsolescence becoming an in-built feature. Thus creating the need for an effective replacement cycle to operate and flexibility in design and layout of the Front Office. Careful selection and siting of all the equipment is necessary to aid efficiency of workflow, movement and motion economy.

Front Office stationery will also be required, which is appropriately designed to satisfy functional, and marketing requirements. 'Customised' or standard items of stationery may be purchased. In a large concern where corporate image is considered important, design decisions may be imposed from head office.

6.4.3 The design and layout of the Front Office

The planning and design elements discussed in Chapter 2 are obviously applicable to the design of the Front Office area. Although the psychological aspects of design, such as the ambience created and the initial impact of the total design scheme of this area on the arriving customer, are very important design issues, the practicalities of designing for functional efficiency are also important. Some design features relating to siting and security control have been highlighted already. The size and layout of the Front Office will be influenced by the number of customers and their activities and the Front Office activities which have to be undertaken, the systems devised, the flow of data, the number of transactions to be carried out, the amount of tour and conference business, the required equipment and the number and grades of personnel required to work at a particular time. Conversely, the space available is a constraint when redesigning the layout, an opportunity often created by the decision to install a computer.

6.5   MARKETING AND SELLING THE PRODUCT

There is a need to promote or market any type of accommodation product, whether it is marketing a contract cleaning service to a potential client; engendering a sense of well-being and comfort through the efficient provision of a clean environment to a patient or ward sister in a hospital or selling space to generate revenue. Even in 'non-profit' making operations, generating income may be a managerial task and will be discussed later in this chapter. In an hotel operation, the aim is continually to increase revenue and subsequently profit, by attracting new business and increasing in-house sales. This involves marketing, promotional and selling activities.

6.5.1   Marketing and promotion

Marketing

Marketing is a creative process of satisfying customer needs profitably and effectively. It is about getting the right product to the right customers at the right time at a price they are willing to pay.

Marketing is a management process involving analysis, planning, implementation and control and should manifest itself in carefully formulated programmes to achieve desired responses, based on advanced planning, not random actions. It seeks a response from a targeted market rather than a general one by formatting a sufficiently attractive product appropriate to that targeted market. It thus helps an operation survive and prosper through serving its targeted market more effectively. It is about designing the product to suit the needs and requirements of the target markets rather than imposing its own ideas which may not match those of the markets.

Any operation must identify its particular marketing problems and requirements by undertaking a marketing audit. This will involve defining the operations mission; its position in the market place; its self-image and the image it portrays to others; the resources available; its management and organisation; the market size and trends; competitors and strategies or tactics with regard to products, finances, etc that it needs to develop.

It will also involve undertaking market research (both primary and secondary) to establish the needs of its existing and potential customers and consider environmental issues and the competition.

A Marketing audit, together with a SWOT analysis, will form the basis of the marketing plans devised.

● **SWOT Analysis**

A SWOT analysis is a valuable business analysis technique which can be used to build up a picture of the reality of the business and identify strengths, weaknesses, opportunities and threats to the accommodation product.

The accommodation product will possess features which distinguish it from its competitors and are the basis of its appeal, ie its strengths. In the case of the accommodation product this could include the age and design of the building; its style and décor, the facilities and services offered or the friendliness and helpfulness of the staff. The strengths should be listed and described, and their value and appeal to the customers evaluated. The product may possess some unique features, which in marketing terms can be described as a USP, ie a *unique selling proposition*. These form the basis of powerful advertising.

It is also necessary to list and describe all the things which may be seen by the customers, not necessarily by management, as weaknesses, for instance no car parking, 'seedy' public rooms, no leisure facilities or insufficient or unfriendly staff. The best way to find out what customers perceive as strengths or weaknesses is to ask them.

The information acquired thus far, together with knowledge of the operation, its objectives, markets and competitors for instance, can then be used to determine the opportunities available for developing or improving the product. These may include redecorating the public rooms, training staff, introducing a customer-care policy or converting low or non-revenue generating space into leisure facilities.

It is also worthwhile trying to identify factors which may adversely affect business and are thus perceived as threats, such as the construction of a by-pass, retirement of key personnel or new competition.

SWOT analysis can be simple or complex depending on the needs of the operation but continuous reappraisal of the business should become standard procedure thus enabling the operation to be pro-active. (See Figure 6.7).

● **Market segmentation**

It is worth segmenting the market into different sections or categories by, for instance, customer type (male, female, businessmen), geographical area (Yorkshire, France) or business type (eg leisure, transient, corporate) in order to target more effectively.

Figure 6.7 *Product analysis room chart*

Room no.	Room size	No. of beds	Possibility of altering bed configuration	Décor	Convenience			Good features	Poor features	Room rate
					Private bath/ shower	View	Near lift stairs			

- **Marketing mix strategy**

A marketing mix strategy must be developed and adapted to the target market. The marketing mix involves the particular controllable marketing variables which the operation uses to achieve its objectives in the target market. These include the four P's:

1 *Product* – existing, new, quality, features, options, services
2 *Price* – rackrate, discounts, credit terms
3 *Place* – locations, timing
4 *Promotion* – advertising, sales promotion, selling, publicity.

The market mix selected must support and reinforce the chosen competitive position of the operation, whilst the chosen competitive position dictates the elements of the marketing mix.

Promotion

Promotion is about converting needs to wants. Promotional activities should:

- *attract* attention of potential customers
- *arouse* interest in the product
- *create* desire for the benefits
- *prompt* action to achieve sales.

Promotion obviously needs to be planned, using a mixture of techniques such as *personal* public relations, familiarisation trips (fam. trips), telephone selling; *non-personal* press and the media, brochures, advertising, direct mail, giveaways. The mixture selected is known as the *Promotion Mix* and may well vary from one target to another. Promotional literature needs to reflect the image of the operation and the product, indicate the benefits of the product to the potential customer and use copy and imagery that is understandable to the reader.

6.5.2   Selling the product

Everyone concerned in an operation from the commissionaire to the manager is a salesperson, responsible for selling the product (LAVENSON, 1974[2]). They 'sell' to customers in every word and action, and the relationship created between personnel and customer creates a unique opportunity for increasing sales. The behaviour of personnel and their attitudes to customers is an integral part of the service package. Of course the attitude and approach of personnel could also have a negative affect on sales.

The attitude towards selling has had to change. An operation cannot afford to sit back and wait for business to 'come by' or customers to 'ask' for anything. They must adopt a positive sales orientation. Selling is about analysing the needs of customers, converting them to wants and providing the services and facilities to fulfil these wants.

Everyone in the hotel should be concerned with caring for the customer (see Section 6.6). The relationship developed by personnel may or may not impress the customer, may or may not encourage the customer to sample the facilities and services available, may or may not encourage the customer to return or recommend the hotel to other potential customers.

At a basic level 'selling' is concerned with welcoming the customer; making the customer feel comfortable, relaxed and at ease; with 'serving' the customer and with providing benefits to the customer for which they are no doubt paying. 'Selling' should also be about making each customer feel as if they are **the** most important customer in the hotel.

Certain characteristics, some of which have already been discussed in Chapter 2, associated with selling space or accommodation must be understood, particularly those which impose constraints. These include such facts as:

- Hotel accommodation is a saleable commodity which provides a greater contribution to fixed costs, and subsequently profits, than any other sales outlet or product element in the hotel. This is because the marginal costs, ie the cost of the items that are used by the guest whilst staying, are comparatively low.

  In this context accommodation not only includes residential accommodation, ie bedrooms, but a much wider range of spaces such as conferences, meeting, function and banqueting accommodation.

- Accommodation, unlike food and liquor, is limited by time and quantity. Accommodation is, therefore, a perishable product. If a room is not sold on a particular night, then that revenue is lost for ever, hence the limitation of time.

  Also the quantity of rooms is static and cannot fluctuate to meet demand, although there is some flexibility, albeit limited, with regard to the number of beds which can be provided.

- The accommodation product contains some intangible elements, making it difficult to describe for selling purposes.
- Unlike many products on sale, accommodation cannot be sampled or tried out before purchase. Although if customers have stayed before they will have previously sampled and will have a particular impression in mind when repurchasing. On some occasions it may be possible to view the accommodation prior to purchase, but even then the potential customer will not really know what it is like until it has to be paid for.
- It is highly improbable for a hotel to achieve and maintain a 100% occupancy over even a short period of time. The popular concept

that a 100% occupancy, meaning that every room is occupied by someone, is really far from a state of 100% occupancy. It is only if someone is sleeping in every bed in the hotel, with two people in every double bed, that a true 100% occupancy will actually be achieved. In reality how often does this happen?

- Rooms income for any hotel comprises the highest percentage in the total profitability of the hotel. No hotel gets the absolute maximum from its rooms income, even when it is running at a so-called 100% occupancy. There is always room for improving income from room sales. There are many factors which influence the amount of income received from rooms, such as special rates, discounts, and 'single' rates for double rooms, all of which should be controlled. In fact the selling price is subject to more fluctuations and variations over a period of time than any other product element.

In many hotels in the past, the analysis of sales, usually in financial terms (for accounting purposes) may have taken place, but the information was not necessarily used effectively and promptly as a basis for increasing sales through the introduction of a positive sales policy.

'Positive' selling of the hotel and its facilities, if carried out at all, was more often than not the responsibility of a separate Sales and Marketing Department and, to some extent, the Banqueting Manager. Sales and selling has not always been considered a fundamental responsibility of all Front Office personnel. If a hotel is to remain competitive and retain, if not increase, its level of revenue, the sales function must be recognised as an integral part of the Front Office operation.

6.5.2.1 Sales orientation

A sales orientation or awareness should be an integral part of the operation's culture, particularly where there is a continuous need to increase occupancy and revenue levels.

It should be possible to monitor and analyse sales levels at any point in time and compare the present position with historical data. Areas for investigation can then be identified, appropriate action taken and future targets set (see also *Yield management* Section 6.8.3).

The following checklist could be used to enable the above analysis to be conducted:

- list all the sales outlets or product elements within the hotel, ie all facilities and services which are revenue producing, including any facilities which are leased or franchised to independent operators, eg shops, hairdressing
- from Front Office accounting sale summaries and statistical documentation, identify the level of sales both in terms of income and

usage/occupancy for all sales outlets over a period of time. Comparisons with the previous period and like period last year, may highlight trends and potential problem areas

- determine in percentage terms the contribution which each sales outlet makes to the overall profitability of the hotel, eg 70% profit from accommodation sales
- determine the potential revenue for each sales outlet over a period, together with the optimum usage/occupancy, to achieve this revenue
- compare actual and potential sales figures in order to highlight problems and decide where further investigation is necessary, asking such questions as:
  — why are sales so low?
  — why are customers using or not using the facilities?
  — where do customers go to use this type of facility if they are not using it here?
  Determine where extra sales effort is required and set future sales targets
- compare, if possible, with competitors in the locality or similar types of operations through the Inter-Hotel Comparison system.

From the information collated it is possible that some of the following problems have been detected:

- insufficient knowledge about the hotel and its facilities and services
- little emphasis on the sales function by Front Office personnel
- lack of training in sales and selling techniques
- lack of feedback on sales performance
- no incentive or motivation to sell or increase sales
- insufficient or lack of monitoring of sales
- lack of realisation of the overall impact on profitability which a positive sales policy may have
- lack of emphasis on sales opportunities which occur during the guest cycle
- lack of realisation of the proportion of sales that each outlet contributes to the overall profitability of the operation
- lack of social skills.

It is essential to:

- conduct a full product analysis
- identify all sales opportunities within the guest cycle
- train staff and give feedback regularly
- frequently and effectively monitor achievement.

6.5.2.2 Product analysis Three distinct procedures are involved in analysing the product:

- conducting a product analysis
- sampling the product
- evaluating customer satisfaction

● *Conducting a product analysis*
Conducting a product analysis involves a systematic approach to collecting pertinent information such as that outlined in the *Product Analysis Checklist* Figure 6.8. This product analysis checklist is not only useful when defining and describing the product, but can be subsequently developed for use when evaluating the quality standards and efficiency of the product and identifying strengths and weaknesses which may need to be improved.

When conducting a product analysis it is usual to compare the product with the competition and the customers' expectations and satisfaction.

● *Sampling the product*
To really know the product package on offer it is very beneficial to put oneself in the customers' shoes and sample the product as a customer would sample it. This is a unique opportunity to perceive the product objectively from the customers' viewpoint. Although it is easier for supervisory and managerial personnel to sample for themselves, it may be beneficial for new room attendants or receptionists, for example, to stay overnight or at least have a comprehensive tour of the whole operation. This exercise also aids evaluation of quality standards, service provision and staff attitudes. It may incur some expense, but the benefits must be weighed against the cost involved.

Guest tests or surveys are useful to evaluate the system, either done personally or by 'employing' colleagues or even a regular well-known customer. Phoning for accommodation or to arrange a conference meeting, or asking a specific question about services or facilities, will enable the answers and impressions given to be evaluated.

● *Customer satisfaction*
It is a good idea to use a checklist as an aid to questioning customers in order to determine customer satisfaction. The one provided in the HCTB's (now the HCTC) publication *Marketing for Independent Hoteliers*[3] is suggested as a guide. A summary of such information should be recorded as soon as possible after the 'interview' as the memory is fickle (Figure 6.9). If a couple of such interviews are conducted every day, a valuable database is soon built up.

Product knowledge is necessary for a number of reasons including:

● to enable more effective management of the product
● to enable the product to be advertised, promoted and 'sold' more effectively
● to describe the product effectively to the customer, either verbally over the telephone, using the right descriptive words to convey an accurate mental picture or in writing in brochures and promotional literature

Figure 6.8 *Product analysis checklist*

The operation	What is the name of the operation? What is the star rating? What types of customer are catered for? What is the total number of rooms? What are the variety of room types? What are the benefits over the competition?
Location	Where is it precisely? What are the directions by any means of transport? What are the car parking arrangements? On what type of site is it located (garden/concrete)? How much land does it possess?
Premises	How old is the building? Was it purpose built? In what style was it constructed (Victorian/chalet)? What is its image? How many floors/storeys? What size is it?
Accommodation Residential, ie bedrooms	How many of each room type? Where are they? What are they like? What facilities do they have? How adaptable is the space?
Non-residential	What types? Where are they?
1 Public areas	What are they like? How adaptable are they?
2 Conference, Meeting rooms, etc	Number of areas Variety of areas Seating capacities in various formats Style and design Facilities and services Adaptability

Facilities and Services
eg Food and Beverage
  Entertainment
  Sports
  Health and Beauty
  Shops
  Utilities
  Valet
  Portering
  Medical
  Transport
	As above
	  + Opening times
	    Types of services
	    Costs

Pricing structure	Tariff types Rack rates Price variations and discounts Market segments What customer receives for price Extra charges for items Price discretion at certain times
Organisation and Policies Organisation Policies	 Form of ownership Structure of company Hierarchy Duty personnel Health and Safety Liability Security Credit checking Credit sales Trading day Checkout times
Competition	Local operations Similar facilities Where are they located? How much do they charge?

Figure 6.9 *Product analysis checklist*

We are trying to improve our services to our guests and would be grateful for your help by answering these questions. Your name will not be recorded with the answers.

1 Is this your first visit to this hotel?   Yes/No
  When before?
  Do you notice any changes?
2 What made you choose this hotel this time?
3 Where did you find out about it?
4 Is it up to your expectations?
5 When you choose an hotel what are the things most important to you?
6 What do you feel about:
  — the bedrooms (eg bath facilities, the size, the décor and furnishings)?
  — facilities in the hotel (swimming pool, lounges, bars, games, dancing, etc)?
  — food (standard, quality, type, choice, the restaurant, breakfast)?
  — the service and staff (availability, attitude)?
7 How would you describe the people staying here?
8 Are you relaxed here?
9 What else would you like to see available?
10 Is this hotel expensive, reasonable, cheap?
11 Finally, would you tell me where you have come from and what is your occupation.

                                                          Thank you

  Questions would be varied to suit the manager's interests, but these questions would provide a good basis for understanding the guests and their wishes.

- to evaluate the quality standards of the product being promoted
- to compare the product with that of the competitors
- to identify strengths and weaknesses which can be either maximised, removed or improved
- to determine if the product is right for the target market(s)
- to monitor performance in terms of volume of sales and determine the viability of the whole and its parts
- to assess and monitor its contribution to the total product
- to analyse the cost of provision
- to enable more effective staff briefing.

Obviously any manager responsible for managing a product must have product knowledge. Many personnel are involved in the provision and care and maintenance of the accommodation product, some of them having direct contact with the customer and they must have a knowledge of the package and its attributes too. Customers are likely to ask questions about the product, such as:

'How do I get to your hotel? – I shall travel by car.'
'How long does the laundry service take?'
'What is the difference between your £150 suite and your £200 suite?'

Being able to answer such questions quickly and correctly and, at the same time, convey a caring and helpful attitude is part of the service package and will obviously have an impact on the customer's contact experience.

Product knowledge may be imparted to personnel through briefing sessions, conducted tours, sampling and documentation, to use as an *aide-mémoire.*

Sampling may be too expensive if too many staff are involved, but parts of the product may be sampled such as watching the in-room video. In fact, making a video of the product may not only be useful as a way of introducing personnel to the product but also a useful sales and marketing aid.

Quizzes (see Figure 6.10 for an example of a quiz sheet) and competitions are a good way of keeping staff up to date and on their toes and are useful as a means of refreshing memory. 'Room Inventories', brochures and photographs are useful *aide-mémoires.* Staff must be updated when any changes in the product occur.

6.5.2.3 Sales opportunities
If effective selling is to take place, all sales opportunities within the Guest Cycle must be identified, such as:

- *Advance reservations*
  A great opportunity may occur to convert an enquiry into a sale if the potential customer is undecided. The selling of the accommodation package over the telephone is extremely difficult, and training in telephone and selling techniques is recommended to allow

Figure 6.10 *Product knowledge quiz*

1 How many rooms have you got in your hotel?
2 Where are they situated?
3 How big are they?
4 What style are they decorated in?
5 What facilities do you offer in your rooms?
6 How many restaurants do you have?
7 How much does a three-course meal with wine cost?
8 What type of food is served in the restaurant?
9 Do you serve food anywhere else in the hotel?
10 How many bars do you have? What are they called?
11 What are the opening and closing times of your bars and restaurant?
12 What special promotions are being offered in the bars/restaurant now or in the future?
13 What banqueting facilities do you offer?
14 What other services are offered in the hotel?
15 What are your room rates?
16 What special packages do you offer at weekends?
17 How would you direct a guest to your hotel – by car? by public transport?
18 How would you direct a guest to your car park?
19 What other hotels do you have?
20 Where are they?
21 What are they like? (modern, traditional?)
22 Where do you find out about their rates?
23 What type of entertainment is there in the area?
24 What places of interest are there in the area?
25 What speciality restaurants are in the area?
26 Where are the nearest churches and their times of service?
27 Where are the bookshops, department stores, leisure facilities?
28 Which day is half-day closing (if any)?
29 Where is the nearest Tourist Information Office?

You can probably think of plenty more questions. Your answers should form an information folder so that you have the answers at your fingertips should you forget.

personnel to capitalise on this opportunity. The voice can be regarded as a sales tool and the way in which the telephone is answered, and the telephone manner, can make or break a sale. Personnel must be able to visualise accurately the room they are selling and use the right descriptive words to convey a mental picture to the potential customer.

● *Check-in*
After the customer has registered, the facilities and services which the hotel has to offer, which may otherwise go unused, must be promoted. The receptionist has to use some discretion. If the customer arrives late, he may wish room service or a snack in the coffee shop. Even simple questions such as: 'May I book dinner in the restaurant for you, Mr Jones?', may result in increased dinner sales.

- *En route to the bedroom*

  There are a number of opportunities which can be exploited en route to the room. Details of sales outlets, facilities and services can be advertised in the lift, particularly special promotions and activities.

  The porter can mention particular items which may be of interest, like saunas, hairdressing, entertainment, whilst conducting the customer to the room.

- *In-room*

  Directories of services may be placed in rooms and an in-room video can be used to publicise facilities, services and events.

- *Check-out*

  Opportunities even occur at check-out to encourage the customer to return in the future or promote other hotels in the group. Reply-paid reservation postcards or the reservations 'hotline' telephone number may be issued to aid future bookings. Some hotels offer incentives such as discounts or the use of services free of charge, to encourage return or usage of other hotels in the group. Even asking the customer if they have enjoyed their stay, and if they have any complaints or comments, may help to re-establish goodwill before departure, and encourage the customer to consider future patronage.

  To make the most of these opportunities, personnel must have time to give undivided attention to customers. Thus satisfactory staffing levels are essential.

6.5.2.4   Staff training and feedback   If Front Office personnel are expected to promote and increase sales, they need to understand the reasons for the enforcement of the sales policy; know the product and where the sales opportunities occur in the guest cycle. Some training in communication skills and possibly another language and in sales and marketing, particularly sales techniques, must take place. Some of the following tips on selling could be included, such as:

- do not quote minimum rates unless asked. Offer a range of rates, starting at the highest and selling down, clearly indicating the advantages of one room over another. It is harder to 'sell up' than down. Let the customer select the room rate required
- sell the room, not the rate. Describe the accommodation clearly in an endeavour to convey the right 'mental' picture to the potential customer. This is particularly important:

  — when selling over the telephone. The reservation clerk is selling an intangible product which cannot be seen or sampled prior to purchase
  — when trying to convey to the potential customer what they will receive for the price quoted. The potential customer may well

have stayed in another hotel last night and paid the same rate
and will therefore visualise similar standards

- attempt to sell the room to fit the potential customer. Questions
give clues. Do not undersell, many people may take higher priced
accommodation when they learn of special features and facilities
- if necessary, show several room types. This could promote goodwill
and is a public relations exercise
- the voice is an important sales tool especially when selling over the
telephone. Undivided attention should be given to the caller and
the call should not be treated lightly, even if the reservation clerk
is busy.

When personnel are involved in a positive drive to increase sales
for instance, they will soon lose motivation if they do not know what
results, if any, their extra effort is producing. Therefore regular feedback of results is imperative, particularly as the personnel will be
under additional pressure to achieve their targets.

Incentive schemes may be introduced to encourage personnel to
increase sales, stimulate interest and increase motivation. These
incentives may include for instance:

- an Occupancy Bonus based on room or sleeper occupancy over a
period, eg nightly, or weekly
- a commission or flat rate for each sale made, eg an extra room;
meal, etc
- a competition, eg 'Receptionist of the Month' to see which member
of staff has achieved the most sales over a period of time
- badges awarded for most sales.

6.5.2.5 Monitoring system
A frequent and effective system of
monitoring sales must be incorporated as part of the sales policy, not
only to assess the current situation but also as a control measure.

This monitoring system should allow sales performance to be
analysed over a set period of time, in both financial and occupancy
terms, in order to make valid comparisons with previous performance
last week, last month, this month, last year, etc.

If performance is to be monitored and measured as suggested, then,
ideally, realistic sales targets can be set, which must be conveyed to
the personnel involved, together with actual achievements.

6.6 CUSTOMER CARE

Customer care is an important part of the 'product' and can be an
effective market and promotional tool that can help an operation
increase its profits, but only if it works and is not allowed to lapse.
According to BROWN (1989)[4] many operations who are good at

customer care take it for granted and do not perceive it as something to make a fuss about.

Customer care is basically an attitude of mind, which stems from senior management and percolates throughout the operation, involving a focusing on the customer as the most important person in the operation, rather than an intrusion which sometimes appears to be the case. It must be understood by everyone in the operation and it will only work if all personnel are enthusiastic and committed to it and all pull in the same direction.

In a service industry, particularly a profit-making industry, it is essential to attract and retain custom.

It is five times cheaper to keep an existing customer than attract new ones, therefore an operation needs to encourage repeat business or develop a good reputation. When a good service experience is enjoyed and customer care works, customers tell other people and profits, growth and sales are likely to occur. Genuine customer care encourages loyalty but when a bad service experience occurs, customers may not only never return but will also tell ten times as many people. The bottom line is that in a competitive market, the operation will only get business if the customer chooses to give it.

Customer satisfaction is becoming essential for an operation to gain a competitive advantage in the market place. In the first place the product must be right in terms of standard of accommodation, availability, price and administration, otherwise there will never be any customers to care for, and customer care becomes meaningless. Customer care is about the interaction between individuals in the operation and the customers and adds value to the product. A customer oriented approach, therefore, should be a normal part of the job, particularly for those involved in the customer interface.

The customers' first impressions of the operation will have a great impact on the relationship which they subsequently develop with staff. Staff should realise that each customer is an individual with an individual name and should use it at every opportunity. Staff *are* the organisation to the customer.

BA who adopted a PPF (Putting People First) (HELPBY, 1990)[5] strategy, suggest that the way personnel are managed strongly influences how staff react with customers and customers can see what sort of management style an operation has by the service they receive from its employees. (This is known as a *Transparent Organisation*.) Company philosophy is reflected in personnel's attitude, happiness, enthusiasm for the job, pride in themselves and their work, appearance, product knowledge and professionalism. Enthusiasm is catching and bringing a smile to a customer's face can only be done by another smiling face. One hotel has even put a mirror in reception, so that as staff look at themselves they will smile. Staff need to be attentive, good listeners and observers and ask the right questions to ascertain customers' needs and requirements, to be helpful in any way possible, at any time, and provide relevant information without intruding or interfering. Attention to detail is important as 'little things' make a qualitative difference.

New customers will have a service expectation and, in fact, some will have higher expectations than others. If they have a bad experience they are likely to think that is the norm and will not necessarily be impressed with anything else. It is useful to think about what you would expect as a customer if you were in their shoes. Sampling the package as suggested in Section 6.5.2.1, will allow personnel to compare expectations with reality.

Research shows that for customers to experience satisfaction on a continual basis, the total package must be considered. Firstly the *tangible* or *procedural dimensions*, such as efficiency, receiving correct documentation, speed of service, the quality standard of the physical elements of the product, customer feedback and communication systems. Secondly the *intangible* or *convivial dimensions* such as staff attitudes, attentiveness, body language, tone of voice, friendliness, solving problems, enthusiasm and so on. All these should be incorporated into the product (see Chapter 1) and customer-care strategy, which must be supported by training and feedback in terms of results.

6.6.1 Customer characteristics

Management can never know enough about their customers. The following questions will give some insight into the characteristics which may be useful when considering ways of improving customer care and increasing occupancy revenue and thus sales levels:

- what type of occupants are attracted to the enterprise? (socio-economic group, sex, occupation, income level)
- from where do they originate? (country, county, area of origin or company/organisation and its location)
- from what source is business generated? (travel agents, tour operators, central reservation or agency, business house and companies, organisations, individuals)
- how long in advance do they reserve? (what is the 'lead' time?)
- what proportion of potential occupants cancel or do not show?
- why do they stay?
- how long do occupants stay? (what is the mean average length of stay per month or how many guests stay 1,2,3,4 or 5 nights, etc, in a month)
- when do they come? (weekend, weekdays, spring, summer, etc)
- how much do occupants spend on average? (Generally or per type of guest, eg tours versus individuals, or per nationalities – Japanese versus Americans)
- what method of payment do occupants use? (foreign currency,

Figure 6.11 *Age Profile over a defined period*

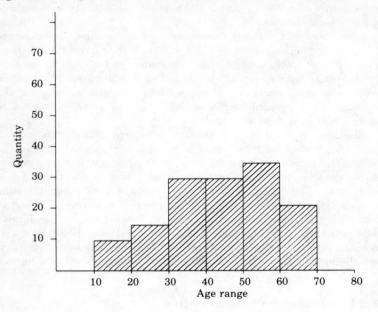

travellers' cheques, cheques or Euro-cheques, credit card, cash, transfer to ledger)
● how many bad debts are incurred? (this is usually expressed as a percentage of turnover)
● are the occupants satisfied? what do they like, dislike, complain about?

Much of this information can be extracted from existing records, if they are so designed, and is often summarised on a quarterly, six monthly or annual basis. More frequent summaries are often less meaningful. Graphic compilation, such as histograms or pie charts, may well aid interpretation of this type of data. See Figures 6.11 and 6.12.

6.6.2   Customer feedback

Satisfied customers tell their friends and return again. It is impossible to quantify the numbers of customers who do not complain but who just do not return a second time because they were dissatisfied. At least if customers complain, the operation has a chance to make

Figure 6.12 *Breakdown of Market Segments by Country of Origin*

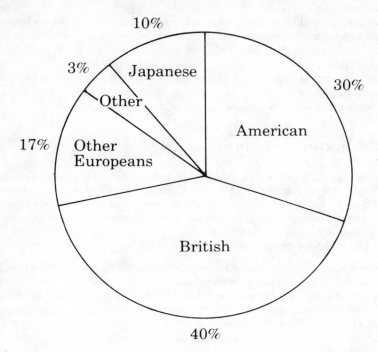

amends to that customer and retrieve goodwill, and identify the problem and take appropriate action.

It is essential, therefore, to have an organised complaint reporting and recording system. Customers should be encouraged to complete a customer satisfaction questionnaire, which may be placed in bedrooms, bars or restaurants or given to customers on departure. Unfortunately it is the avid complainer who tends to complete the questionnaire. A number of customers will also complain verbally to personnel and these complaints need to be recorded. A frequent analysis of complaints should occur and appropriate departmental heads should be informed and comment on actions taken. Complaints, particularly recurring complaints, should, of course, be investigated. Personnel need to be trained in complaint handling techniques.

Compliments should also be recorded, with frequent feedback to those concerned.

6.6.3 Guest history

Guest history records are a useful means of providing continuity in the treatment of regular customers. Thus a record containing dates of stays, rooms used or preferred, total bills and likes and dislikes, particularly in terms of food, drinks, types of pillows, duvet or traditional bedding, etc, provides a useful database. Most software packages include a guest history facility, which can be expensive to maintain manually, and which will allow a customer to be identified as a 'returner' on reservation. Subsequently the customer can be greeted appropriately on registration. Some operations even have a separate, more informal registration area for regular customers, which also assures a speedier check-in.

6.7   PRODUCT IMPROVEMENT

It is essential not to become complacent about the product being offered and to monitor continuously levels of performance, as described in Section 6.8.1, and carry out a 'product audit' at intervals. This type of analysis would include reviewing the product, the market, the marketing mix and the competition.

The **product review** would involve establishing:

- how each product relates to other products in the range, in terms of production, marketing synergy and customer utility. For instance, comparing the food and beverage product with accommodation or conferences, functions and mini-break packages, or even single versus double room sales
- how each product is meeting its sales targets. This may include analysing:

  — the sales volume of the product elements, eg single, twin rooms or shirt service, dry cleaning service
  — sales by market segment, eg conference, function, European, airlines
  — sales through the sales and marketing office, reception, booking agencies, central reservations, travel agents
  — sales of different package mixes by the above channels of distribution
  — average size of order eg no. of rooms, beds or revenue produced

- how vulnerable each product element is to technological obsolescence, product substitution or loss of customer appeal, eg leisure facilities
- the profitability of each product element in terms of targets set, average room rates achieved, customer spends, average occupancy, contribution to net profit, break-even points, etc
- the expected life cycle of the product or product elements, such as leisure facilities and their profit cycle. See Figure 6.13.

It would also involve analysing the demand for the product in relation to its availability and capacity, analysing its production

Figure 6.13 *Product life cycle*

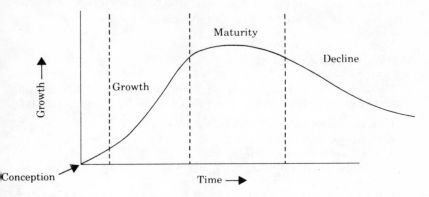

capacity and availability, and also estimating the cost of lost business opportunities.

It is then possible to undertake a value analysis to consider cost reductions by changing processes, reducing resources required, increasing standardisation and analysing purchasing decisions, thus also attempting to improve profitability.

A marketing analysis would involve reviewing the segmentation policy to establish if all the targeted market segments are sufficiently large, accessible, available, and find the product appealing. It would also involve quantifying the resources being used to achieve the desired targets per market segment and rating the customers' opinions of the product, particularly in relation to competitors.

Finally the marketing and promotion effort and competitive strategies need to be analysed in terms of prices, sales and promotion activities and channels of distribution. For instance:

- are the prices too high or low for the customer?
- is the price compatible with the desired quality standard?
- is the price consistent with the other elements of the marketing mix?
- are discounts and price variations in line with competitors?
- are the sales and promotion tactics appropriate and effective?
- is the advertising and promotion budget and expenditure appropriate overall *and* per market segment or different media?
- how does the promotion mix compare in terms of quality, cost, receptivity, coverage, creativity?
- are the sales channels serviced appropriately in terms of:

  — detailed product description in brochures, mailing shots, etc?
  — information update re changes in products and prices?

- does the operation employ sales and marketing staff who are trained, motivated, and monitored?

- is the operations product range comprehensive, versatile and of a good quality to attract the most influential or lucrative market segments and does it allow for selling economies?

6.7.1   Product deletion

The analysis undertaken might suggest that a certain product element should be deleted from the range. This may be for such reasons as:

- an unsatisfactory contribution to net profits
- decline in demand
- new superior competitive products
- incompatibility with the customer's image of the operation, or other product elements in the range
- incompatibility with production or marketing economies of scale.

However, there may be counter arguments for retaining that product element if:

- it completes a range which is more attractive to customers and sales and marketing agencies and gives a competitive edge, eg leisure facilities
- it was released ahead of the development of the market and finds a suitable niche in the short term, eg the introduction of fax facilities, before most hotels installed them for customer use
- the operation is bound to continue until a contract expires, eg with a travel operator.

If the retention of a product element is justified, attempts should be made to reduce the cost of provision. (See Chapter 7, *Productivity*.)

6.8   MAXIMISING POTENTIAL

To survive and succeed an operation needs to be constantly reviewing its performance to determine where and how it can improve and develop (as suggested in the sales and product improvement sections). It goes beyond just making the best use of resources available (see Chapter 7, *Productivity*) and is concerned with maximising its potential, for instance being *proactive* – anticipating the market; *opportunistic* – being ready to respond to every opportunity presented; *capitalising* on its resources, particularly its strengths (see *SWOT analysis* Section 6.5.1). This is often referred to as 'maximising potential' and obviously infers that maximum potential is articulated in some way for all involved in sales and marketing to be well aware.

However, it is essential to evaluate carefully the cost and resource implications of each proposed maximisation scheme.

Where accommodation is revenue producing, the aim must be to achieve capacity occupancy with maximum revenue, ie the best possible return or 'yield' from the space available.

If possible, it is a good idea to think about accommodation in terms of space, ie 200m², of meeting room with partition walls or three interlinking spaces with private sanitary facilities and pantry rather than a two-bedroomed suite. Thinking in terms of room types might be constraining, for instance if a customer wants an interview room for three hours and the receptionist only has a twin room with an overnight rack rate to sell, then revenue could be lost.

Capacity occupancy, as stated earlier, can only be achieved when someone is sleeping in every bed. Maximum revenue can only be achieved when all customers pay full rack rate. Even if true 100% occupancy can be achieved on occasions, it is very difficult to achieve maximum revenue as well, as room rates are subject to discounting for a number of reasons (see Section 6.8.2). To maximise revenue the right mix of business has to be achieved every day, with the right balance between the various market segments and the best achievable revenue. This is yield management. (See Section 6.8.3.)

6.8.1 Performance analysis

If personnel are to be focussed on maximising potential, it is essential to:

- determine the potential maximum occupancy and revenue for the operation
- calculate existing levels of occupancy and revenue being achieved
- monitor achievements and identify peaks and troughs in business
- compare actual against potential, targets and previous periods
- set future targets.

6.8.1.2 Occupancy Essential basic data must be identified to ensure occupancy levels can be calculated and monitored. This includes:

- the total number of rooms available
- the breakdown of room types and number of each type
- the configuration of each room, ie number and types of beds and design, eg fitted furniture or free standing
- the number of foldaway beds that can be accommodated if necessary.

From this information the maximum capacity, with and without foldaway beds, can be calculated. The information required to calculate the occupancy levels being achieved is generated daily through the normal Front Office reception and accounting activities. Various occupancy statistics, such as those presented in Figure 6.14, may be calculated either by the night auditor or the audit or management information facility of the Front Office software

Figure 6.14 Occupancy statistics

Type	Calculation	Uses	Limitations
Room occupancy	$\dfrac{\text{Number of rooms sold}}{\text{Total number of rooms}} \times \dfrac{100}{1}$	Indicates % of rooms sold	Does not reflect number of occupants Does not reflect rooms unavailable, for whatever reason
Available room occupancy	$\dfrac{\text{Number of rooms sold}}{\text{Number of rooms available for letting}} \times \dfrac{100}{1}$	Reflects number of rooms not available for letting, out of order, refurbishing, etc	Still does not reflect number of occupants
Bed occupancy	$\dfrac{\text{Number of beds sold}}{\text{Total possible beds}} \times \dfrac{100}{1}$	Indicates number of beds occupied rather than rooms	Does not reflect number of occupants if double beds are available Does not reflect rooms unavailable
Sleeper occupancy	$\dfrac{\text{Number of sleepers}}{\text{Total possible sleepers}} \times \dfrac{100}{1}$	Indicates number of occupants Can compare room v sleeper occupancy	Does not reflect rooms unavailable
Double occupancy	$\dfrac{\text{Number of doubles let as doubles}}{\text{Total number of doubles}} \times \dfrac{100}{1}$	Includes also number of twins let as twins Reflects number of doubles sold as singles Reflects skill of reservation clerk to 'fill' doubles or twins	
Income occupancy	$\dfrac{\text{Actual accommodation income}}{\text{Number of rooms sold}}$	Reflects discounts, complimentaries Reflects strategy of doubles sold to single occupants Indicates the percentage of potential income lost on a particular night	

package. All these occupancy statistics are of value, but taken in isolation do not necessarily reflect an accurate picture. The statistics produced can be summarised on a weekly, monthly, quarterly or annual basis as a continuing basis for monitoring performance and comparing with past achievements.

Over a period of time fluctuations in occupancy levels can be plotted reflecting peaks and troughs in business, and recurring trends can be identified – such as high occupancy from transient business October to April, medium occupancy from leisure business April to August; which room types are most popular; are double rooms let to single occupants? are a high proportion of rooms always out of order? and which market segments occupy which room types at what time of the year? The reasons for these occurances can be analysed if necessary.

Future occupancy levels can be forecast. Forecasting involves extrapolation of information from past records, such as daily management reports and reservation records to analyse average performance trends, ie rises and falls in performance, seasonal patterns and any random fluctuations. It also involves predicting future needs, bearing in mind such aspects as the introduction of new product elements, including those of the competition, sales promotions, changes in customer requirements and in the economy, using market research/intelligence and economic life-cycle predictions. The two aspects can then be reconciled to produce the target or budget figures and policies from which courses of action can be constructed.

It is also useful to monitor lost business opportunities by analysing why reservation offers and requests are rejected. Is it:

- rate resistance – are the prices too high for the targeted market or the wrong market targeted
- poor selling – where reservations, conference and banqueting and sales and marketing are not working as an integrated team or the switchboard takes too long to answer the telephone
- a period of high demand where rooms are not available or where low rated high volume business, eg tours and series booked well in advance, has displaced high rated lower volume business which occurs near the period in question.

It is thus imperative to forecast periods of high and low demand and consider ways in which occupancy levels can be increased. An increase in occupancy levels should also increase sales in the other sales outlets if they are effectively promoted. Thus a relationship between accommodation sales and other sales outlets exists.

However, an increase in occupancy does not necessarily increase the average room rate particularly if low rated business is accepted.

6.8.1.2 Revenue It is not sufficient to aim for purely capacity occupancy, attempts must also be made to maximise revenue. This means, again, that it is essential to calculate the maximum potential revenue, that is capacity occupancy at full rack rate. Even then extra revenue can be attained from the use of foldaway beds and from a room being sold twice in one day, as a dressing room for instance. This information will help management to realise the extent of the potential revenue which could be achieved and thus how much revenue is being lost to the operation. It is also useful to know such facts and figures as:

- the potential revenue at full rack rate with only single room occupancy
- the occupancy percentage required to break even, ie cover variable and fixed costs.

Some idea of the number of complimentary rooms allocated and the amount of discounted business in terms of what type of business, how much discount, how much revenue is lost by discounting and when it tends to occur, may help to decide on the measures to be taken to maximise revenue.

It is relatively easy to ascertain on a daily basis the actual revenue achieved from the daily trading accounts. This figure will reflect price variations such as discounts, special terms and complimentary accommodation. It can be correlated with occupancy levels and used to monitor performance in financial terms and highlight variances when compared with previous figures. This can then be analysed to discover the reasons for fluctuation, bearing in mind any price increases which have occurred.

The average room rate is often used to measure financial performance:

$$\text{Average room rate} = \frac{\text{accommodation income}}{\text{no. of rooms sold}} = \text{£}$$

This statistic provides a useful measure of the standard of room sales. An increase in the average room rate achieved reflects maximisation of double occupancy or proportionally higher number of more expensive rooms sold whereas a decrease reflects selling rooms at less than rack rate or single occupancy. A calculation of standard deviation will indicate whether proportionally more rooms at the top (or bottom) end of the scale have been sold or whether most were sold around the average room rate. It is usually possible in most operations to increase the average room rate.

It is also useful to calculate the potential average room rate, ie the average rate that would be achieved if all the occupied rooms were sold at full rack rate and no discounting had occurred. The actual average room rate can then be compared to the potential. The **rate spread** is the difference between the potential average room rates at double occupancy and single occupancy, thus denoting the maximum and minimum potential average room rate.

The average sleeper rate can also be calculated.

LOVELOCK (1984)[6] suggests the idea of an Asset Revenue Generating Efficiency Index (ARGE) to measure the extent to which an operation's assets are achieving their full revenue generating potential. This is based on the assumption that a hotel cannot achieve 100% occupancy at full rack rate and, therefore, occupancy will fluctuate and discounts will be offered. It is, therefore, possible to establish what is a reasonable level of potential revenue for a combination of different levels of occupancy at different rates. For instance: in a 300 bedded hotel with a rack rate of £60, the potential total revenue is £18,000 per night. If 120 rooms are occupied at a rack rate of £60 and 60 rooms are occupied at 40% discount, ie £36, then the occupancy rate is 60% and the average room rate is £52.

The average unit price efficiency rate, being the average room rate as a percentage of the rack rate, ie £52 as a percentage of £60 is 86.7%.

The asset revenue generating efficiency index (ARGE) is the average unit price efficiency rate (ie 86.7% in this example) multiplied by the occupancy rate (60%)

$$\text{ie } \mathbf{0.867 \times 0.6 = 0.5202 = 52\%}$$

Therefore, the operation is operating at 52% of its full potential (LOVELOCK, 1984).[6]

6.8.2 Pricing

As the price level will affect the volume of sales and revenue and consequently profitability, it is essential that the price level is correct. The price level must not be so high as to dissuade custom or so low that it fails to cover operational costs. At the same time it must be competitive. Pricing policy is so critical and complex that it is rarely up to the Unit Manager, let alone the Accommodation or Front Office Manager to decide on room rates (unless it is a privately owned enterprise).

It is useful to understand the nature of a room charge. The room price charged effectively constitutes a hire or rental charge which has to cover the cost of items used by the customer, such as stationery, giveaways, beverages, cleaning (labour and agents), soap, toiletries and bed linen. This is the marginal cost (defined as the cost of producing another unit) or the operational cost which is negligible in comparison to the rack rate charged but which does not include those costs involved in providing accommodation, whether or not it is sold, such as rent and rates, cleaning and heating of public areas, telephone and TV rental costs.

The gap between the marginal (or operational) cost and the selling price, which is often referred to as the price discretion, gives rise to the possibility of varying the price between covering marginal costs and the stated selling price, hence the practice of discounting room rates to attract more business.

Discounting can be defined as the practice of charging a rate less than the quoted rack rate to customers who generate a large amount of revenue through frequent usage or conference groups or travel agents/tour operators who reserve large blocks of rooms for a period of time (LANE and HARTESVELT, 1983).[7]

Discounting for volume business may be advantageous in terms of economies of sales as it involves one sales and marketing transaction for a number of sales. This practice may improve sales revenue but have a detrimental effect on profitability. It prevents the operation achieving its potential room rate. Discounting should be perceived as a 'cost of doing business' and the impact of, and necessity for discounting should always be carefully evaluated. A discounting grid can be prepared to evaluate the impact on revenue of different pricing decisions. The grid will show the equivalent occupancy that must be achieved in order to maintain a certain room revenue level as the amount of discounting is increased or decreased.

Equivalent Occupancy

$$= \text{Current Occupancy} \times \frac{\text{Rack Rate} - \text{Marginal Cost}}{\text{Rack rate} \times (1 - \text{discount \%}) - \text{Marginal Cost}}$$

The following simple example is based on the concept suggested by LANE and HARTESVELT.[7] (1983).

The hotel in question has a rack rate of £50 and the marginal cost is £3.50. The equivalent occupancy to be achieved at 5%, 10%, 15% and 20% discounts is calculated for occupancy levels of 80%, 75%, 70%, 65%, 60% respectively. (See Figure 6.15.)

The first example is shown below:

$$\text{Equivalent occupancy} = 80\% \times \frac{50 - 3.50}{50 \times (1 - .05) - 3.50}$$

$$= 80\% \times \frac{46.5}{44}$$

$$= 84.55.$$

The room rate is subject to more variations and fluctuations in price than any other sales item. The price charged may vary for the following reasons:

- the room type, whether single, twin, etc. The greater the number of room types, the greater the number of different room rates
- the convenience of the room, that is its size, décor, view, facilities and services
- the number of occupants in a room. A twin room sold to a single occupant will be sold at less than normal rack rate, whereas if a foldaway bed is put up a higher room rate will be charged
- the market segment or type of customer:

— a businessman not paying his own account is not as sensitive to the price charged
— high prices attract a certain segment of the population who prefer to use the most expensive hotel
— a business executive may be willing to pay more for a little extra service
— regular customers may receive discounts
— celebrities may be offered complimentary accommodation for the publicity
— the guest attending a function, wedding, dinner dance may be offered a discounted room rate

- discounts for bulk reservations, conferences and tours
- complimentary accommodation for promotional reasons; as prizes; for visiting personnel.

Figure 6.15 *Hollin Hotel discounting grid*

Current occupancy level	New occupancy level required to maintain profitability if rack rates are discounted by:			
	5% ($\times$ .05)	10% ($\times$ .10)	15% ($\times$.15)	20% ($\times$ .20)
80%	84.55	89.64	95.38	101.92
75%	79.26	84.04	89.42	95.55
70%	73.98	78.43	83.46	89.18
65%	68.69	72.83	77.5	82.81
60%	63.41	67.23	71.54	76.44
55%				
50%				
45%				
40%				

Fluctuations in price may occur:

- at certain times of the year. This usually relates to supply and demand, lower rates being charged in the low season
- at certain times of the week. Midweek may be very busy and businessmen will pay rack rate, but a lower price may be charged at the weekend to encourage occupancy
- special events and promotions, eg Christmas or New Year events
- to undercut competition
- after a certain time in the evening, prices of vacant rooms may be lowered in an attempt to encourage extra sales.

The nature of the room price also means that an extra room sale contributes more to profits than an extra sale from any other sales outlet, where the marginal cost tends to be a much larger percentage of the selling price, eg a meal. Although the higher the discount the lower the contribution to profits, prices may be adjusted according to occupancy trends, for instance, prices may be lowered at periods of low occupancy in an attempt to attract more business and the established rack rate charged at periods of higher demand. A lowering of room rates does not automatically lead to an increase in room sales, owing to a phenomenon known as *elasticity of demand*. Where price changes do not proportionally effect changes in the quantity of rooms demanded, there is an inelastic demand which tends to be the case in the hotel industry. According to KASAVANNA (1978)[1]:

> '*research (viz a viz the hotel industry) has illustrated that there is only an indirect relationship between price and demand, and that within certain percent changes in price, demand may be totally unaffected.*'

The optimal room price, according to KASAVANNA (1978)[1] must reflect all the internal and external factors listed below.

- **Internal considerations**

  — A reasonable rate of return, over and above the standard rate of interest, for taking the risks of going into business
  — The proportion of services which incur costs but do not receive direct revenue to be covered in part by room revenue, eg floral services
  — Overheads (cost centres) which are apportioned to the rooms department
  — Fluctuations and variations in room rates according to the market segment, eg commercial rates, complimentary rates, family rates, weekend rates, etc.

- **External considerations**

  — Competitive factors – the intensity of competition, the type of competition, the market share (of rooms sold) and whether a price leader exists
  — Elasticity of demand (defined as the change in room price as related to changes in the number of rooms sold).

- **Other factors** include:

  — Location within the market area. The geographical location will influence the demand for rooms and, therefore, the price that can be charged
  — Location and convenience (ie size, décor, what it contains) of a room within the hotel in terms of views and proximity to other facilities, will influence the specific price to be charged for that room
  — Charge per room or per occupant.

Belief that pricing must be dynamic and responsive to market forces (a belief shared by STEADMAN and KASAVANNA (1988)[8] and the

Figure 6.16 *Three factors to be reconciled*

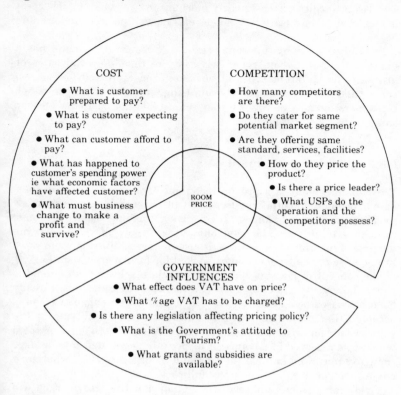

COST
- What is customer prepared to pay?
- What is customer expecting to pay?
- What can customer afford to pay?
- What has happened to customer's spending power ie what economic factors have affected customer?
- What must business change to make a profit and survive?

COMPETITION
- How many competitors are there?
- Do they cater for same potential market segment?
- Are they offering same standard, services, facilities?
- How do they price the product?
- Is there a price leader?
- What USPs do the operation and the competitors possess?

ROOM PRICE

GOVERNMENT INFLUENCES
- What effect does VAT have on price?
- What %age VAT has to be charged?
- Is there any legislation affecting pricing policy?
- What is the Government's attitude to Tourism?
- What grants and subsidies are available?

HCTC)[9] has led to the development of pricing philosophies rather than a strict adherence to mathematical models.

These mathematical models, all of which are explained in hotel accounting text books, include the following:

- cost plus pricing
- rate of return/Hubbart room formula
- marginal or contribution pricing
- break-even analysis
- rule of thumb (1:1000).

One of the problems associated with using mathematical models is that the price calculated is an average one which has to be charged over a period of time rather than an actual price to be quoted.

Market forces pricing, basically involves reconciling the three factors identified in Figure 6.16.

Consideration must also be given to the tarrif type, ie whether full board, half board, bed and breakfast, American plan or modified

American plan and to whether the room rate is inclusive of certain services or facilities such as early morning tea, or whether the guest is expected to pay for every single extra, such as iron and ironing board.

In reality, so many different prices may result if the hotel has a great variation of room types, a variety of tariffs, special rates or discounts for different types of business, and high and low season rates, that it becomes extremely confusing for Front Office personnel. Customers too may be upset if they realise another customer has the same room type at a lower price.

6.8.3 Yield management

Yield management is a proven technique for maximising revenues, having been used in other industries, particularly the airline companies, to measure market forces. It involves applying basic economic principles to pricing and controlling the supply of rooms for the purpose of maximising revenues. It also involves adjusting room rates in response to the level of rooms booked for future arrival dates.

The concept of lowering prices to stimulate sales when demand is poor, and raising prices in response to excess demand, has already been discussed (see Section 6.8.3). It has also been suggested and is accepted that customers will pay different rates for staying in the same room, for instance the conference delegate will have a room which was reserved in advance at a specially negotiated rate, a large company may well be able to command a corporate rate, whereas a chance customer will have to pay full rack rate.

Yield management embraces the notion that the rate charged will depend primarily on specific market demand for a particular date. Thus yield management is different from traditional pricing practices because of the frequency and scope of the decision-making process and it challenges, according to RELIHAN III (1989),[10] such notions as prices correlating to physical room type and seasonality. Yield management is, therefore, about bringing price into alignment with actual market forces by striking a balance between supply and demand through constant adjustments to price.

It is necessary, therefore, to understand customers' purchase behaviour, compare current demand with forecasts of future occupancy and identify sales opportunities.

Obviously yield management relies on accurate demand forecasts for particular dates not seasons, which must incorporate a system of continuous updating. It is useful to compare the booking level for a particular day with a desired or ideal level, which has been derived from an analysis of the operations booking history, including business available but rejected for that date. This level can be defined as the **threshold value**. If strong demand results in the booking level for a particular day crossing the threshold, then an opportunity is created to offer rooms at a higher rate. If demand is weak, then the system identifies the need to stimulate demand by offering discounts.

In practical terms it is necessary to anticipate late demand and hold an appropriate number of rooms to be offered at the higher rate which these customers are willing to pay. This is particularly so where an operation has a leisure market, which tends to plan in advance and book early, and where price may well be the most important factor in the decision-making process, and a business market, which tends to book just prior to a trip and is willing to pay more.

If on a date of high demand an operation has filled up in advance with lower rated business, the difference between the higher rate at which custom could have been charged, and the lower rate at which rooms were actually reserved, is lost or **spilled**. (RELIHAN III (1989)).[10] Therefore, the **displacement** of future, high rated transient business by lower rated business must be a carefully considered and controlled decision. This is one of yield management's primary functions. It is worth noting that a proportion of the displaced custom may have booked into a competitor's operation.

It can now be seen that yield management encompasses two basic strategies:

- when demand is high the emphasis must be on receiving the highest rate possible for a room, ie maximising revenue
- when demand is low, and/or late booking demand is unlikely, the emphasis must be on maximising room sales, ie offering rooms at discount to stimulate, eg leisure custom, to avoid the waste of room nights.

Planning is obviously an integral part of yield management and it is important to plan carefully for the future, reconsidering all past decisions and commitments rather than continuing to do things that have always been done, such as committing a series of rooms to aircrew or tours, because that has always been the case. It is particularly necessary to analyse the most desirable mix of market segments to maximise yield.

To take advantage, therefore, of this technique, the appropriate policies and procedures must be in place, strategies and tactics developed to respond to varying demand conditions, personnel trained and possibly incentives offered to sales staff to increase revenue. It has been suggested (DILLON, 1991)[11] that as many as three meetings a week are required in order to monitor 30, 60 and 90 days in advance, respectively. As usual the system itself must be monitored and evaluated to provide feedback on the effectiveness, in terms of increased sales revenue and the tactics used, the performance of individuals, and to motivate and inform personnel of their achievements.

This technique is rather more sophisticated than the explanation belies, and technology is being developed to enhance its value and usage. This technique could also find application in other operations such as increasing conference revenue in educational establishments or bed occupancy in hospitals.

The yield statistic is closely related to occupancy percentages and average room rates but is a more flexible and consistent way to judge a hotel's performance. The yield statistic is: 'a straight forward measure of the effectiveness of practices and policies applied to generating revenue from room sales.' (ORKIN, 1988.)[12]

$$\text{Yield} = \frac{\text{Revenue Realised}}{\text{Revenue Potential}}$$

Revenue potential is, of course, the revenue expected from 100% occupancy at full rack rate (including double occupancy rooms) whilst revenue realised is the actual revenue received. For instance:

$$\frac{\text{Revenue Realised} = 150 \text{ beds @ £60 average room rate} = £9,000}{\text{Revenue Potential} = 200 \text{ beds @ £100 rack rate} = £20,000}$$

$$\text{Yield} = 45\%.$$

6.8.4 Ways of improving performance and maximising potential

To achieve full potential is an aim rather than an ultimate reality but the following courses of action may be considered:

- avoid, if possible, letting twins and doubles to single occupants at a single rate, it may be possible to attract a different market
- is it possible to sell a double or twin at full rack rate even if to a single occupant?
- offer a special deal for business travellers to bring their spouses to fill twin or double rooms
- is it really necessary to sell rooms at discounted or special rates especially in periods of high demand. Would the market pay the full rack rate?
- change the bed configuration if necessary. For instance, if twins have to be sold to single occupants, substitute the twin beds for a double. Flexibility remains, the room can still be sold to two people but could be sold as a 'luxury' single at a slightly higher room rate, than an ordinary single
- charge a higher room rate for rooms with a view, better facilities, better furnishings or more space
- review the market mix – is high volume, low rated business, displacing high rated? Impose booking constraints as appropriate
- consider promoting minimum stay packages. For instance, over Bank Holidays it may be possible to sell three nights instead of two

- provide a few extras at negligible cost and sell at a higher rate as a speciality package or to a particular market. For instance, provide bathrobe, perfumes and toiletries, hair dryer, curling tongs, iron and ironing board, sewing kit, fruit and cheese basket, floral arrangement to the woman business executive. A portering service or an in-room evening meal service may provide 'value-added'.

- rigidly control 'complimentary' accommodation, only consider this for potentially very lucrative future business, eg for a conference executive

- allow Front Office personnel discretion to negotiate room prices at particular times, eg after a certain time in the evening. It may be better to sell a room at a discount than not sell it at all, and the customer may well spend in the bar and restaurant also

- negotiate a credit card guarantee service with the credit card companies to encourage customers actually to arrive and the company to honour payment regardless of arrival

- scrutinise correspondence or fax messages where information, such as job title or professional qualifications of the signatory, the company's letter head or indeed the content of the letter, may give 'leads' for potential sources of future business, and follow up

- consider setting up a referral system, particularly in a group or syndicate operation, to pass reservations on to other establishments. The system is reciprocal, reservations will also be passed on to your business. This may be computerised and is more effective if dealt with, when the guest checks-in rather than at check-out

- offer future accommodation when turning down reservation requests due to lack of room availability. Presumably the potential customer was interested in staying at your establishment, and may be persuaded to alter dates required

- identify how much business is lost through personnel's ineptitude, ie at answering the phone, making a favourable impression with the potential customer, making it easy for the potential customer to talk to or meet the right people quickly, realising the enormity of the potential future business. Carry out 'guest tests' or surveys as suggested earlier

- consider a concerted sales effort (see Section 6.5.2) to attract new business, eg advertising locally, mailing shots or telephone calls to local business and organisations, conference packages in bedrooms – a business executive might just be looking for a venue for a company or professional organisations function or conference

- in periods of high demand

  — restrict or close availability of low-rate categories and packages to transients
  — require minimum length stays
  — commit rooms to those groups willing to pay higher rates

- in low demand periods

— provide reservation agents with special promotional rates to offer transients who balk at standard rates

— solicit group business from organisations and market segments that are rate sensitive

— offer limited availability low-cost packages to the local market

- organise special promotions, events and activities aimed at very specialised markets and offer 'one-off' events. The following list includes actual events offered by a number of hotels:

  nationality functions
  'space invaders' weekend
  photography, cookery, interior design schools – using key personnel or local experts
  sporting packages and competitions
  keep-fit and leisure clubs
  'Green' conferences

- organise special deals or packages relating to local events and activities, eg races, cricket, shows and fairs, nature spots
- offer mini-breaks and/or mini-weekend packages
- employ a selection of Front Office personnel who speak a range of languages to correlate with the various nationalities who visit. Arrange speciality 'English' or 'Olde Englishe' events for their benefit
- ensure that personnel are aware of ethnic cultures and values, if overseas markets are targeted. If possible accommodate particular customs, eg the Japanese approach to bathing. This may have an impact on the design of spaces
- chase up 'no-shows' to retrieve lost revenue
- control overbooking if necessary and, therefore, the cost of booking-out customers.

This list is by no means comprehensive and some of these suggestions may be of absolutely no use in particular operations, thus emphasising that extensive knowledge of the operation, the service package and the market is essential.

6.9   CONFERENCES

6.9.1   Selling conference space

There is no doubt that conference business is very lucrative, in fact research in 1991 suggested that the conference trade in British universities was worth £65 million. Attracting a conference market, if facilities permit, may be one way of maximising potential and filling troughs in business. Universities and colleges with residential accommodation which is only occupied for about two-thirds of the year, cannot afford to sit back and lose a considerable amount of potential revenue which could be used to improve standards and the facilities available to students.

BERKMAN et al (1978)[13] suggests the need for a formalised business plan in order to sell conference space and subsequently service a conference. This would initially involve a product analysis to define the conference package, its attributes and particularly its strengths. This would also involve an analysis of major competitors including an analysis of the operation's competitive situation as far as location and accessibility by air, car, train, etc, and outside attractions are concerned. Only then can the operation's strengths and weaknesses and ability to satisfy the varying needs of conference buyers be assessed (see Section 6.5.1).

In order to improve yield and maximise potential it is essential to identify specific needs for income improvement in terms of increasing occupancy, particularly where deep troughs in business are occurring, double occupancy, income from existing occupancy, sales of banquets and functions, and food and beverage sales. It should then be possible to identify the conference markets which best satisfy the operation's revenue needs.

Creating buyer awareness by means of advertising, using the most appropriate media; publicity through featured articles and press releases of prestigious conferences or speakers; public relations through relationships with customers, suppliers and sales promotions; literature such as brochures or conference packs and events, eg familiarisation visits, mini-breaks for conference buyers, must all be considered.

It is essential to maintain a good information system incorporating all enquiries, negotiations with potential customers and all communication and agreements with actual customers. Potential 'leads' should be also documented.

Enquiry and reservation procedures must be designed for dealing with conference customers separately from normal day-to-day business, mainly as more time is required to sort out all arrangements, and larger numbers of customers are involved. The selling process occurs as soon as the potential customer contacts the operation and a good impression must once again be created.

Correspondence must be dealt with quickly and the telephonist or reservations clerk geared to realise the potential importance (in terms of revenue) of the call and direct it speedily to someone who can help. The potential customer is not impressed when told 'the conference officer is out or off-duty, ring back tomorrow'. The initial enquiry and reservation stages should be made as easy as possible for the potential customer. Conference business should be perceived as a whole culture, running through the operation. Unfortunately, this is not always the case. A total package incorporating liaison between all the departments involved, ie Front Office, Sales and Marketing, Banqueting and Conference and Food and Beverage, must be promoted to the potential

Figure 6.17 *Conference organiser's checklist*

Client organisation details	Client's name
	Address
	Telephone number
	Fax number
General conference details	Dates – including degree of flexibility in the selection of data
	Function type
	Length of stay
	Arrival and departure times
	Conference programme — number of sessions session titles starting and finishing times break times
	Non-delegates programme
	Children's programme
Delegate details	Minimum and maximum number
	Nationalities
	Language difficulties
	Number of residents/non-residents
	Age range
	Sex
	Marital status
	Number of non-delegates, eg spouse and children
	Any handicapped/disabled
	Any special diets
Guest speakers	How many?
	Who?
	Any special arrangements, eg security
	Number of nights staying
	Arrival and departure times
	Room type
	Any extra facilities/services
Accommodation	
Conference	Number and types of conference rooms
	Size of rooms
	Layout style
	Demonstration/exhibition areas
	Storage of equipment and audio-visual aids
	Specialised equipment requiring special installation – by whom, when will it arrive?
	Conference equipment – flip charts, lectern, OHP, microphone, simultaneous translation, audio-visual equipment
Residential	Room types/price range
	Number of rooms
	Number per room/room sharing
	Provision of any extras
Reception	Client organisation reception area — where? — how much space?

Administrative	Client organisation office area
	Secretarial/duplicating service
	Communication/computing
Social/Leisure/ Entertainment activities	What?
	When?
	Numbers
Catering arrangements	Meals on arrival/departure days
	Break times
	Meal times
	Menu types/price range
	Service style
	Special diets
	Childrens meals
	Bar facilities – when
	Official functions — sherry reception
	— menu/price
	— service style
	— seating plan
	— menu/place name printing
	— flowers
	— microphones
	— guest speaker
	— toast master
	— dance band/disco
Miscellaneous	Flowers
	Newspapers
	Laundry services
	Baby-minding
	Transport

customer, otherwise business may be lost. Often the potential customer experiences difficulties in arranging to see all the key personnel involved at one meeting.

6.9.2   Establishing customer needs

By far the best way of finding out what the potential customer requires and explaining or selling the conference package is a face to face interview incorporating a tour of the premises and facilities. This involves, in the first place, identifying and inviting the decision-maker(s). Many potential customers may have never organised a conference or function before and many others may wish to devote their energies to organising the programme, the reception and involvement of delegates and the needs of their guest speakers rather than the practicalities of the arrangements.

It is not the customer's representative who will be criticised in the first place by delegates but the operation if the physical details are not satisfactory. Therefore, it is beneficial to both parties if Accommodation Managers use their expertise to ask the right questions and make suggestions. As with normal reservations, a standard checklist may be used to record all the relevant details, but it will be a more complex document, see Figure 6.17. Generally speaking, the arrangements discussed will fall under the following headings: general details; sleeping accommodation; food and beverage arrangements; conference programme; social programme and leisure facilities; reception and registration arrangements.

Room availability must be checked at this point and thus liaison with advanced reservation personnel and knowledge of business trends are essential. Prices can then be negotiated. The opportunity can be taken to present the particular benefits of the conference package which will suit the needs and requirements of that particular customer including value received for money spent, before the potential customer goes back to their committee for deliberation or confirmation. The operation's representative may actually present the conference package to the customer's committee. The operation may well wish to research the credit worthiness of the potential customer organisation, particularly where a potentially large income is concerned. Management may encourage the potential customer not only to visit and inspect the accommodation but also to stay over and sample the product first hand and try out all the facilities. Once an agreement has been reached, a formal contract may in fact be drawn up and signed by both parties, incorporating the important details, the procedure for cancellation, deadline for numbers, damage to property and payment arrangements.

Organising a conference involves not only identifying in great detail the potential customers' needs and requirements to ensure their ultimate satisfaction but also planning, preparing and directing the conference activities at the time, besides dealing with the accounting and follow-up procedures. The conference cycle of activities is highlighted in Figure 6.18.

6.9.3 Managing the conference

6.9.3.1 Planning and preparation
The planning and preparation of a conference is a classic application of project management.

The comprehensiveness of the briefing details and the efficiency of the communication system set up will affect the planning and preparation stages and the quality of the conference package experienced. From the information gained at the briefing stage, supplemented through liaison with the customer, it is possible to plot the time scale (the lead time tends to be long – one hotel is known to reserve conference space ten years in advance) and decide when various activities must occur and which departments are involved.

Network analysis techniques, specifically critical path analysis, to identify stages, their sequence and the time of the critical path and a

Figure 6.18 *The conference cycle*

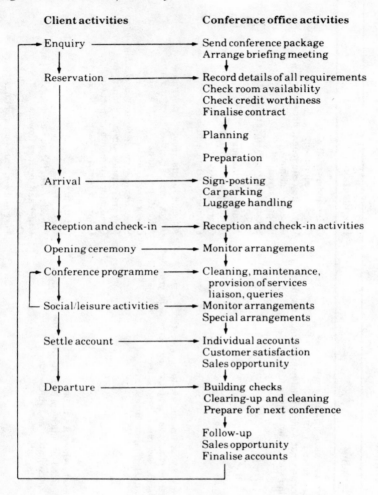

Client activities	Conference office activities
Enquiry	Send conference package Arrange briefing meeting
Reservation	Record details of all requirements Check room availability Check credit worthiness Finalise contract
	Planning
	Preparation
Arrival	Sign-posting Car parking Luggage handling
Reception and check-in	Reception and check-in activities
Opening ceremony	Monitor arrangements
Conference programme	Cleaning, maintenance, provision of services liaison, queries
Social/leisure activities	Monitor arrangements Special arrangements
Settle account	Individual accounts Customer satisfaction Sales opportunity
Departure	Building checks Clearing-up and cleaning Prepare for next conference
	Follow-up Sales opportunity Finalise accounts

checklist system are useful aids to planning and control. Figure 6.19 shows the decisions and activities to be considered at the planning and preparation stages. Attention to detail during these stages can make a great deal of difference to the quality of the conference experience. Liaison must be maintained with the customer and it is beneficial if a specific individual in the conference office is designated as liaison officer for that customer throughout the entire planning, preparation and execution of the conference. Customer interface is enhanced if a relationship is built up with a defined individual from

Figure 6.19 Planning and preparation checklist

	Planning	Preparation
Conference	Decide which facilities/room to use Plan room layouts Decide what audio/visual equipment is required Plan staffing arrangements	Order audio/visual aids Check all equipment Install any equipment necessary Assemble displays Prepare layout Set up with requirements – water, chalk, felt-tip pens, etc Arrange technicians Arrange secretarial and duplicating services Clean all areas Provide sufficient ashtrays or 'no smoking' signs
Residential accommodation	Decide which rooms are to be allocated Decide what facilities/provisions have to be provided Decide how much linen is required Plan staffing arrangements	Allocate specific rooms to delegates Check linen, allocate, make up rooms Allocate provisions Check fire notices Prepare sanitary areas, provide cleaning agents Prepare pantries, provide utensils and beverages Conduct maintenance inspection Clean all rooms
Reception area	Decide where it will be Decide how much space is required for the client organisation and the venue Plan layout	Set up area Clean area Provide room list and all delegates packs Order and arrange flowers Organise registration and key allocation Post function name on meetings board

Public and leisure areas	Decide which areas will be used Plan times of usage Plan layouts	Clean areas Prepare and layout area Order and arrange flowers
Catering	Plan meal and break times Decide which restaurants/dining rooms required Plan menus and types of service Plan room layouts Plan bar times and location Plan formal conference function Estimate cutlery, glassware, crockery, linen requirements Plan staffing arrangements Book band/disco	Order food and liquor stocks Print menus, name cards, table plans Check cutlery, glassware, crockery, linen stocks Procure licences Clean rooms Prepare layouts, set up
Staffing	Estimate all staffing requirements Plan staff schedules and rotas	Brief staff Train staff if necessary
Miscellaneous	Decide on portering arrangements Plan sign-posting Plan security arrangements	

the operation. However, where conferences are booked years in advance, it is probable that the individuals involved in the initial negotiation will have moved on and others taken their place. It is essential, therefore, that all details are well documented and filed for easy retrieval at a predetermined time in advance of the conference, so that communication links can be re-established. It is important where conferences are booked a long time in advance that a contractual document is agreed and signed. This should highlight the financial liabilities involved if the customer went down or something untoward occurred and the event had to be terminated, particularly if the operation had made a heavy capital commitment already. To assure a successful conference it is important to establish (or re-establish) the responsibilities of both parties and ensure that all terminology is mutually understood. Frequent liaison between the conference office and all relevant departmental heads is also essential.

The activities involved in the preparation stage particularly will differ from an hotel to an educational establishment.

In a university, conference delegates will obviously use student accommodation and provisions, such as soap and towels, coat hangers, beverages, which are not allocated to students, will have to be provided for conference delegates.

Students will have to be notified to clear their rooms, so provision for storing student belongings may be required; delegates name cards may be stuck on doors and room lists displayed in prominent places. Unlicensed premises will have to obtain licences, decide where the bar facilities will be sited, and what security arrangements are required. Many educational premises do not have a physical reception desk, so one may have to be organised.

Some educational establishments actually possess special conference stocks of those items either which they do not generally provide for students or of a higher quality than those they do provide. These stocks may include bed linen, towels, soaps, cutlery, crockery, glassware and table linen.

6.9.3.2 The conference Once everything is prepared, a final inspection should occur to ensure that the standards are being achieved, nothing has been overlooked and the existing condition of the premises noted in case of accidents and vandalism occurring during the conference.

Figure 6.20 shows the activities which occur during the conference.

Liaison with the customer representative must still be maintained throughout the duration of the conference and an effective quality assurance and monitoring system established to ensure all arrangements proceed smoothly, according to plan, and quality standards are achieved.

At the end of the conference, customer satisfaction may be investigated to ascertain delegates views, preferences and perceived

Figure 6.20 *Flow chart to show delegate and conference activities throughout duration of conference*

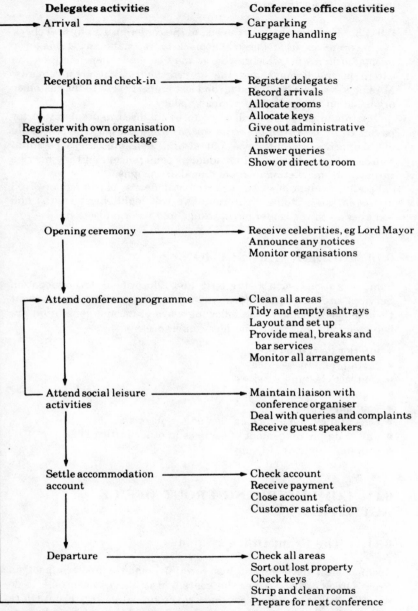

Delegates activities	Conference office activities
Arrival	Car parking
	Luggage handling
Reception and check-in	Register delegates
	Record arrivals
	Allocate rooms
	Allocate keys
Register with own organisation	Give out administrative
Receive conference package	information
	Answer queries
	Show or direct to room
Opening ceremony	Receive celebrities, eg Lord Mayor
	Announce any notices
	Monitor organisations
Attend conference programme	Clean all areas
	Tidy and empty ashtrays
	Layout and set up
	Provide meal, breaks and bar services
	Monitor all arrangements
Attend social leisure activities	Maintain liaison with conference organiser
	Deal with queries and complaints
	Receive guest speakers
Settle accommodation account	Check account
	Receive payment
	Close account
	Customer satisfaction
Departure	Check all areas
	Sort out lost property
	Check keys
	Strip and clean rooms
	Prepare for next conference

The accounting arrangements will vary – sometimes delegates will pay individually for accommodation prior to arrival or on departure, sometimes delegates pay for accommodation with their conference fee and their Conference Organiser then pays all accommodation costs.

strengths and weaknesses of the conference package, in order to effect improvement for the next time.

6.9.3.3   Follow-up   At the end of the conference a physical check of the premises used may take place to estimate any damage or misplaced items for which a charge may be made, depending on the extent of the damage and the agreed contractual arrangements. Missing keys must be chased up and lost property sent to the customer organisation, depending on company policy.

Outstanding accounts will have to be finalised and submitted for payment. An opportunity occurs to encourage not only the rebooking of this particular conference, but also all delegates are a potential source of future business, individual or conference, and they may be targeted for marketing or promotional campaigns.

Finally, evaluation with departmental heads, personnel involved and even the customer representative will highlight strengths and weaknesses in the conference package and its organisation.

6.10   INCOME GENERATION

Some operations, such as the NHS and Educational Accommodation Services, are having to find ways to generate income to supplement their budgets. Some of the following ways of income generation are being employed in reality besides conferences:

- interior design services
- curtain making services
- contract cleaning services
- laundry services
- equipment hire
- consultancy and advice on cleaning problems
- day to day management of services in other institutions
- seminars and training days.

6.11   COMPUTERISING FRONT OFFICE ACTIVITIES

6.11.1   The Front Office system

Technological development has certainly made a great impact on Front Office activities over the years and is likely to continue to do so in the future. Software packages cover virtually every Front Office function from reservations, registrations, room allocation, guest history, billing and accounting to producing management information. Room management systems such as room status, message waiting, early morning calls, baby listening, fire detection, security systems and electronic keys, drinks dispensers, in-room video, teletext, telephone logging and energy control systems can all be networked. The BRAVO reservation system now provides UK hotels with access to reservation systems at 150,000 travel agents worldwide; 7,500 of them in the UK. BRAVO provides national telephone centres, where customers can freephone in the UK, Europe and the USA to make credit card bookings.

To be of value the computerised system must be a cost effective and viable proposition. Although the cost of computer systems is decreasing, they can still be expensive to purchase. Selection of hardware and software, installation, staff/computer interface and training must be given consideration. A feasibility study to consider anticipated functions, siting, installation, staffing and customer implications, breakdown, security and control aspects, should be undertaken to decide whether or not a system would be advantageous and financially viable.

If the costs outweigh the advantages, as may still be the case, in a very small operation, it is unwise to proceed. Generally speaking, a computerised system is required in order to:

- improve the provision of information for decision making
- improve customer service by providing more accurate information, more quickly
- improve control of operations.

It also releases personnel from undertaking repetitive clerical tasks so they can give more time to productive tasks such as selling, public relations or investigating 'abnormalities'.

Once a decision has been made to purchase a computerised system, great care must be taken to define exactly what it is that the computer is required to do, and purchase the most suitable system for the particular operation. It is unwise to purchase rashly and realise too late that the system does not really carry out the functions required or produce the data in the formats needed by the operation. When identifying the requirements of the software package, consider the type of operation, its market segments, existing systems and procedures, general occupancy trends and levels of business and areas of improvement. The guest cycle can be used as a guide to estimate the type and number of transactions over a period and the specific inputs and outputs which the system must handle for each Front Office function or stage in the process, and the storage capacity required. It is possible, for instance, to estimate how many advance reservations are taken over a period of time, and specify the mean length of 'lead' time between reservation and arrival as a means of estimating the disc storage capacity for the advanced reservation function. An attempt has been made in Figure 6.21 to identify the features to be considered

Figure 6.21 *Specification for a computerised Front Office System*

ADVANCE RESERVATIONS

- Allow room availability check

  — by date of arrival
  — by room type
  — by price range
  — for period of intended stay   } on the screen and as a printout

- Input potential guests reservation data

  — what data, what order
  — store until date of arrival
  — file trace — by date of arrival
        — surname
        — first three letters of surname
        — surname and initials   } and printout
  — transfer to registration sections of system
  — printout as registration card
  — store for lead time
  — update room availability
  — record as confirmed/unconfirmed
  — allow cancellation but transfer to cancellation file and printout
  — amend details
  — record deposits
  — printout letters of confirmation/alternatives/regret

- Printout arrivals and departure lists
- Produce occupancy forecasts by market segment – on screen and as printout
- Produce room type/density chart type summary – per day; week; month; period
- Allowing overbooking facility – by how many; limit who; alter for different periods/days

RECEPTION AND CHECK-IN

- Retrieve A & D lists by confirmed/unconfirmed
- Retrieve alphabetical guest list for defined day
- Printout registration forms
- Allow arrivals to be registered and thus open account
- Allocate room numbers on registration/prior to registration as required
- What rooms/room types available and suggested in priority order for allocation
- Produce room status for day/week and with guest details as required

  — total
  — for floor/area
  — for room types
  — by market segments
  — for individual tours/conferences   } on screen and as a printout

- Allow amend/complete registration details
- Allow room changes to occur
- Record booking-out details with required information such as alphabetical list; where, etc

- Store registration details for defined period
- Retrieve registration details after 12 months and delete

ACCOUNTING

- Open account as guest registers/transfers deposit and code for rack rate
- Allow posting — from point of sale (POS)?
  - by room and/or batch of item/sales outlet
  - automatically do accommodation posting or allow one press
  - automatically update subtotal

- Compile non-resident bills
- Check credit levels, eg above a level – on screen and as printout
- Produce breakdown of bills by method of payment including ledger bills and with totals per method of payment
- Produce draft bill – screen and printout
- Allow two bills per room, eg company and individual expenses or two different people
- Allow transfer of one or more bills to one room number for payment
- Total final bill; record payment or transfer to ledger
- Automatically calculate VAT and service charge
- Calculate foreign exchange and change rates
- Record departures
- Produce departures list
- Produce debtors list and who paid/unpaid
- Telephone logging — transfer to bill/itemise calls
  - produce telephone bill
- Allow alterations/allowances to bills
- Update guest history.

MANAGEMENT INFORMATION AND STATISTICS

- Produce management report re sales summary of each POS/Operating Dept; summary of total revenue for each POS/Operating Dept, segregation of VAT, VPOs, allowances   daily weekly monthly

- Statistics — room occupancy   per
  - available room occupancy   market
  - bed occupancy   segment
  - sleeper occupancy   or as
  - double occupancy   required
  - income occupancy/income per room
  - average room rate
  - average guest spend
  - yield

- Compile guest histories as defined eg as number of return visits, by spending level, by market segment
- Compile black list.

---

at each stage in the Front Office process. This could well form the basis of a software specification or evaluation checklist.

MITCHELL (1986)[14] also suggests defining the key performance standards which the system must satisfy in terms of the speed of response required at critical points in the system, such as rooms available, the production of the registration details or the bill, and even to specify the maximum delay acceptable. This would also include defining the numbers of personnel using the system at the same time; terminals required with special features such as number of printers required; security of information links with other systems, maximum acceptable down time; training requirements of users, expandability and any other special requirements peculiar to the specific operation.

Obviously, hardware requirements also have to be defined not only in terms of the number of printers required but also the networking system, point of sales terminals, number of VDUs required and the features they must possess, and the number of Central processing units and their capacities.

It is necessary to shop around and evaluate the systems available on the market through demonstrations and visits to existing installations. The checklist given in Figure 6.21 would also be useful as an evaluation checklist. Suppliers proposals, including the specification of their system, prices offered, delivery and installation arrangements would then be considered.

Before a final selection decision can be made, the operation must weigh up the following criteria:

- does the system meet the operation's requirements?
- what level and quality of support is given, ie training, maintenance, breakdown?
- what is the reputation of the suppliers and the system?
- what is the financial stability of the supplier?
- what is the suppliers planned software development programme?
- what hardware must be used/is required?
- what are the initial costs and annual operating costs?

6.11.2   Installation

Once a system has been purchased, it is useful for it to be available, somewhere in the building for a period of time before installation in the Front Office. This will enable training and allow staff, particularly those who are anxious about computers, to become familiar with the system. It is sensible to actually install the computer in the Front Office (having already decided where it will be sited and made any physical alterations) at the quietest time of the week to minimise inconvenience to personnel and customers. In a commercial hotel with a high occupancy during the week, the most convenient time for installation is at the weekend. If physical installation for instance took place during Friday night, relevant data could be fed into the system during the weekend and the system could probably be operational after balancing at the end of the first shift on Monday morning.

Personnel must be sufficiently well trained to ensure that once the system 'goes live' they can operate effectively and confidently.

6.11.3 Staff training

Training is essential to ensure a smooth changeover from the previous system to the computerised system. Training must commence well in advance of installation so that staff have time to overcome their feelings of insecurity, and doubt in their own ability to cope – very frequent problems of which management must be aware.

Once the initial barrier is overcome, staff must not only be 'taught' how to operate the system but also be given time to build up confidence, so that when the system is physically sited in the front office and 'goes live', operation is second nature.

It is useful to identify which groups of personnel require training, what knowledge and skills each group requires and thus the duration of their training. One hotel chain identified the following groups of personnel and placed them in the indicated priority order for training purposes:

Group 1 Front Office Manager, Head Receptionist and Cashier
Group 2 General Manager, Assistant and Duty Manager
Group 3 Controller, Night Auditor, Control/Accounts Clerk
Group 4 Front Office Personnel
Group 5 Housekeeping Personnel
Group 6 Other sales outlets personnel
Group 7 Porter

Training should also allow staff to discuss potential changes in their grading, scheduling arrangements and daily routines.

The installation of a computer may require personnel to subsequently cover the whole range of Front Office activities so becoming 'multi-functional' as opposed to retaining traditional grades with specified responsibilities, eg book-keeper. Their daily routines will certainly change. Personnel will have more time, due to speedier processing of data and management information and statistics being produced by the system, which may be used to improve the quality of the customer interface and increase their sales effort. However, personnel must be aware that this will be the case and thus be trained to cope with changing responsibilities.

6.11.4 Control

Control measures must be implemented to ensure efficiency, security and continuous operation is maintained. The following control measures may be considered:

- **For efficiency**
  - On-going training, supervision and monitoring
  - Prohibition of eating or drinking in the area whilst using the system
  - Storage of discs in encased filing trays
  - Correct care of floppy discs, eg not put on window sills or radiators to be affected by heat; coffee cups, etc, not be stood on them
  - Duplicate copies of vital information on disc
  - Regular printouts of vital information, particularly audit trails
  - Regular data validation checks in programmes to ensure right data is fed in and rubbish is rejected
  - Precautions to be taken to prevent static occurring in the area.

- **For security**

  - All personnel to be issued with a password control code for access into the system
  - Access limited to only that part of the programme which personnel need access to carry out their duties
  - All confidential information and vital financial data on disc to be stored securely
  - Duplicate copies of vital information kept off site in case of fire or other emergencies
  - Vital discs kept in fire proof storage cabinets (which also prevent discs melting in the case of fire)
  - No personnel to have access to the operating or set-up system
  - Management audit trail for checking and control purposes.

- **For maintaining continuous operation**

  - Planned preventative maintenance of system
  - Effective 24 hour call-out in case of breakdown
  - 24 hour contact in case of problems
  - Duplicate VDUs or printers in case of failure
  - 'Duplex' system, ie two processing units – in case of failure
  - Regular printouts particularly audit trail at least at the end of each shift, so that in case of a breakdown, it is only necessary to back-track to the last printout to commence manual system.

References

1 KASAVANNA, M L, *Hotel Information Systems: A Contemporary Approach to Front Office Procedures*, Van Norstan Reinhold 1978
2 LAVENSON, I, 'Think Strawberries', paper delivered to American Medical Association, New York, 7 February 1974
3 HCITB, *Marketing for Independent Hoteliers*
4 BROWN, A, *Customer Care Management*, Heineman Professional Publishing 1989

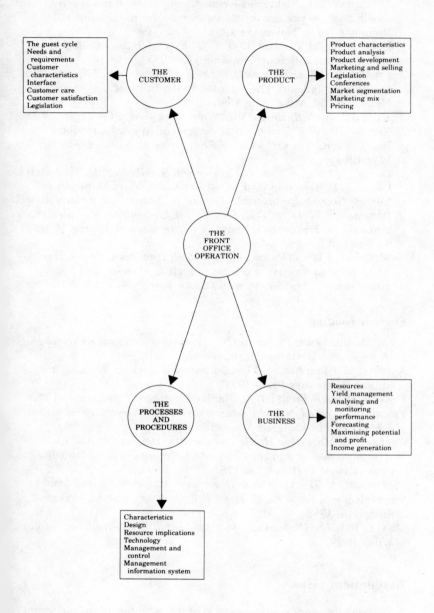

Concept Map summarising the Front Office Dimension.

5 HELPBY, M, 'Ace Services' *Caterer and Hotelkeeper*, 23 August 1990
6 LOVELOCK, C H, 'Strategies for managing demand in capacity constrained service organisations' *Service Industries Journal* Volume 4 No. 3, November 1984
7 LANE, H E and VAN HARTESVELT, M, *Essentials of Hospitality Administration*, Renton Publishing Co 1983
8 STEADMAN, C E and KASAVANNA, M L, *Management of Front Office Operations*, 2nd edn, The Educational Institute of the American Hotel & Motel Association 1988
9 HCITB, *Small Business Aid*, 'What price should I charge?' 1979
10 RELIHAN III, W J, 'The Yield Management Approach to Hotel – Room Pricing, *Cornell Hotel & Restaurant Association Quarterly*, May 1989
11 DILLON, E, 'In the Balance', *Caterer and Hotelkeeper*, 18 April 1991
12 ORKIN, E B, 'Boosting your bottom line with Yield Management, *Cornell Hotel & Restaurant Association Quarterly*, February 1988
13 BERKMAN, F W, DORF, D C, OAKES, L R, *Convention Management .and Service*, Educational Institute of American Hotel and Motel Association 1978
14 MITCHELL, I D and PHIPPS, D K, 'Hotech Handbook No 1 – How to buy a hotel and catering computer system', *Caterer and Hotelkeeper* in association with Oxford Poly 1986

Further reading

ABBOT, P and LEWRY, S, *Front Office Procedures, Social Skills and Management,* Butterworth Heinemann 1991
ASTROFF, M T and ABBEY, J R, *Convention Sales and Services*, 3rd edition, Waterbury Press 1991
BRAHAM, B, *Hotel Front Office*, Stanley Thornes (Publishers) Ltd 1990
FENTON, L, FOWLER, N and PARKINSON, G, *Hotel Accounts and their Audit*, Inst of Chartered Accountants 1989
GREENE, M, *Marketing Hotels into the 90's*, Heinemann 1983
KOTAS, R, *Accounting in the Hotel and Catering Industry* 4th edition, International Textbook Co. 1981
THUNHURST, A, *Front of House Operations*, Caterbase, Macmillan
WHITE, P B and BECKLEY, H, *Hotel Reception*, 5th edition, Hodder & Stoughton 1988
MARTIN, R J, *The Professional Management of Hotel Operations*, John Wiley 1986

Assignment tasks

1 Using the *Guest Cycle Concept,* plot the activities of the customer in a private hospital and a hall of residence and compare the operations activities and consequently the structure of the interface.

2 Visit a hotel, conducting a survey of the systems and procedures used for reservations, reception, room allocation, room status, billing and accounting, credit checking, communication and information functions. Comment on the strengths and weaknesses of each.

3 Collect two or three brochures from various hotels and using the Product Analysis Sheet (Figure 6.8) evaluate and compare the product offered. Compare tariffs and then compare with other types of operations such as private hospital or old people's home.

4 Develop a customer care programme for a particular operation.

5 Compare the philosophies, systems and procedures used to promote and manage conferences in at least two of the following:

— an hotel
— a conference centre
— an educational establishment.

6 Find out about two Front Office computer systems on the market and either visit an installed customer to evaluate or if you have the opportunity, operate a system and evaluate it.

7

Quality and Productivity

Objectives

- To emphasise the key role of staff and good staff management in achieving controlled quality standards and productivity levels.
- To give a clear indication as to the concept of quality and the application of this to the field of accommodation.
- To demonstrate the different means of defining standards of quality, with respect to accommodation and where these different methods are appropriate.
- To illustrate the means of quality control appropriate to use in Accommodation Management.
- To investigate the relationship between quality standards and productivity.
- To show how productivity within the accommodation field can be measured and controlled.

If return custom is to be encouraged, reputation developed or, indeed, hazard-free accommodation provided for any need, the Accommodation Manager must develop systems which will provide consistency of the final product.

The product has been discussed in some length at the beginning of this book and it will be appreciated that the 'product experience' of any two customers will never be identical, because of the human element, ie the customer and the staff involved.

In order to achieve total quality management, all aspects of the product need to be considered, these include:

- **the building and its design** If an analysis of customer requirements is made at the design stage of a building, quality considerations can be incorporated into the total features of the building. For example:
  - building materials which require little maintenance
  - surfaces and furnishings can be selected which are durable and easy to maintain
  - standardisation of rooms can be achieved (some hotel groups operate a policy of 'no surprises', ie standardisation within a hotel group is almost total). Of course not all accommodation outlets aim for such standardisation, although there can be no doubt of the benefits of simplification

— room layout can be planned with quality assurance in mind.

- **the human resource**   With standardisation of the physical elements of the product, staff can be selected purposefully and trained in standard procedures, good morale can be managed and a well motivated, effective workforce maintained
- **equipment and materials**   With a knowledge of tasks to be completed, staffing implications and standards required, specifications can be devised for equipment and materials and an effective material management system devised
- **the Front Office functions**   Good customer interface techniques will vastly affect the customers perception of quality
- **the accommodation services**   If the specific needs of particular customers are identified, the product package produced will be more likely to meet customer needs and will be perceived as a 'quality' product.

It will be seen that the above headings, the building, the human resource, materials management, Front Office functions and accommodation services, comprise the previous chapter headings and, to a large extent, the good practices advocated in these chapters incorporate quality assurance considerations.

In this chapter the accommodation services functions will be used as a basis for examples, but Total Quality Management will also be discussed in more general terms appertaining to the overall management of accommodation.

7.1   QUALITY MANAGEMENT

Individual customers will have individual needs and the product production process will require a certain degree of flexibility. The application of continuous production techniques, used in manufacturing industries to ensure product conformity are not entirely appropriate. Nevertheless, certain elements of these techniques, such as:

- product design
- standardisation – of raw materials (eg cleaning agents and equipment, surfaces, furniture, etc), and methods
- systematic production planning
- simplification of processes and products
- matching the capacity of different equipment and processes
- monitoring and quality controls
- the development of 'feedback mechanisms'

can all be effectively applied.

BS 5750 has served to highlight means by which total quality management can be achieved (see Appendix 6).

In addition, limiting the customer/staff interface to certain 'front of house' personnel can also assist product conformity. Selection, training and supervision of these staff can focus on the 'customer encounter' and in this way aim to control it.

7.1.1.   The concept of quality

Quality is not an absolute term as are, for instance, temperature, costs or quantities, and this is a critical aspect to grasp. A product may be of a high standard or a low standard, yet still be a 'quality' product. It is the consumer's perception of whether or not a product or service fulfils a need, which is important.

A small sparsely furnished guest room, with shared bathroom facilities is a quality product if it is perceived by the customers as consistently fulfilling their needs for clean and comfortable overnight accommodation. The room does not need to have silk fabric wall-coverings, state-of-the-art telecommunication systems and onyx fittings in an en suite jacuzzi and bathroom, to be of quality. Indeed, such a room as this would not be a quality product if, for example, on occasions the fittings were not clean or failed to function correctly.

The two rooms are of different standards, not qualities and would appeal to different customers, aiming to fulfil that particular customer's needs. This is an important aspect to grasp with respect to BS 5750 (see Appendix 6). The standard seeks to achieve conformity of quality, not to improve the standard. Factors which will affect the customer's perception of quality include:

* price
* function (does it meet requirements/fitness for purpose)
* reliability
* prestige.

To produce a successful product, the Accommodation Manager will understand the particular market segment being targeted by that particular establishment. An assessment will be made of the specific requirements of those customers with respect to the accommodation services and these requirements will be translated into a standard.

7.1.2   Why quality management?

The costs of poor quality in the accommodation industry can be measured in terms of:

* wasted work (involving both labour and material costs)
* reworking
* reinspecting
* lost custom

- liability claims
- complaints handling
- staff demotivation

Taguchi methods of Quality Management[1] are concerned with all such losses related to poor quality.

Quality controls, ie costs of monitoring work, can be expensive in themselves. Company slogans such as 'Right first time' and 'Zero defects' indicate the emphasis of some institutions on proactive, or preventative measures, rather than reactive measures associated with poor quality.

Conversely, quality management techniques have their own cost implications, eg

- management time in product design, process development and in devising specifications for equipment and materials to be used
- training
- management time in devising documentation and procedures
- the monitoring process and equipment.

7.2   SETTING THE STANDARD

Four stages can be identified in the process of setting standards, within the Accommodation sectors.

7.2.1   Establishing the standard

To establish a standard, company policy with respect to quality must be clear, eg 'nil defects' or a certain percentage of complaints per customers served, are two possible approaches.

Having identified the market segment targeted and the aims and objectives or *terms of reference* of that particular accommodation department, the customer requirements must be identified.

Physical requirements may include, for example:

- comfortable bed
- clean linen
- clean floor covering, comfortable to bare feet
- adequate, clean storage space for clothes
- comfortable temperature
- variable, controllable lighting
- thermostatically controlled shower
- clean wash basin and bath with hot and cold water, etc.

Intangible elements may include, for example:

- privacy
- security

- courtesy
- a feeling of self-importance.

Physical requirements must not only be provided but must also function in the correct manner, and intangible or implicit elements, such as courtesy, must be perceived by the customer.

7.2.2   The work load

In the life of a building, its use may change and certainly the customer requirements will. The implications of current customer requirements must be translated in terms of the 'Work Load' of the department, ie changing of bed linen, suction cleaning of floors, cleaning of sanitary fittings, etc.

7.2.3   Methods, times and frequencies

Standard methods, times and frequencies of tasks in specified areas must be determined. If:

- the method of performing a cleaning task
- the frequency of completing the task
- time allowed for completion
- the equipment and materials to be used

are defined and quality assurance techniques applied to ensure their availability and standard (see Chapter 5), then the outcome is largely, though not completely, controlled and the standard is so set. (See *Work Specification and Work Schedules*, Chapter 3.)

7.2.4   Staffing

Finally, and most importantly, in setting standards, staffing decisions must be made in terms of numbers, hours of coverage, organisation and selection criteria. (For further details, see Chapter 4).

7.3   DEFINING THE STANDARD

It is often stated that to set a standard the requirements should be **explicit** and **measurable**. This is more easily achieved in the case of physical requirements. In the case of intangible elements it becomes more difficult. In addition, terms such as *'clean'* linen, *'clean'* floor covering or *'clean'* sanitary fittings, are open to different interpretations. The difficulties in defining 'what is clean' or 'how clean is clean' are not new ones.

7.3.1 Qualitative and quantitative standards

Sometimes standards are defined in qualitative terms, for example:

'table cloths are neatly folded'
'floors are bright and attractive'
'each customer receives a friendly welcome'.

Such definitions are obviously open to different interpretations. Very often it is possible to define elements quantitatively;

by product eg in hospitals, a maximum bacterial count may be defined for a given surface;
'floors are free from visible soilage'
by process eg 'table cloths are screen folded'
'floors are spray cleaned, weekly'
'each customer is greeted with eye contact, a smile and the appropriate salutation, dependent on the time of day'.

7.3.2 Definition in terms of product

In some cases it is possible to describe explicitly the outcome required at the end of a process. The standard in this case is defined in terms of the product. For example, 'When a bath has been cleaned there should be:

no hairs in the plug hole
no discernable grease line
no waterspots on the tap
no traces of cleaning agent
a dry internal surface
shiny taps
plug chain hung over tap
new soap in the soap tray
a clean bath mat over the side'.

Another example could be: 'When a guest first enters their room:

curtains will be drawn back
the room temperature will be 16°C, plus or minus 2°
all drawers and wardrobe space will be empty
television and radio sets will be switched off', etc.

7.3.3 Definition in terms of process

In some cases, as has been seen above, it may not be possible to define the standard in terms of the product, eg 'clean' 'attractive' floors. Such terms are neither explicit nor measurable but, if the process of

Figure 7.1 *The fluctuating level of soilage*

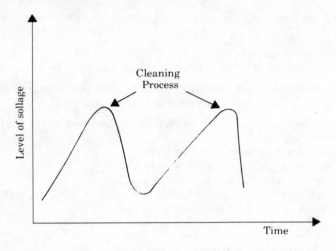

achieving the required standard of floor surface is defined, this is both explicit and measurable.

Another difficulty, with respect to tasks associated with Accommodation operations, is related to the nature of many of these tasks. The state of cleanliness of any item is dynamic. The product is 'perishable' or short lived. Immediately the cleaning process has been completed (or, in some cases, even before), the resoilage process commences. The floor in a busy casualty department within a hospital will become soiled more quickly than the floor in a vacant guest room in an hotel, though even here, with time, dust will start to settle, draughts will carry dust, and insects too may deliver their own soilage.

As the graph (Figure 7.1) shows, the standard of cleanliness of any item will be constantly fluctuating.

The degree of soilage between cleaning processes will depend on the use of the area and various environmental conditions. The degree of soilage after the cleaning process will, in addition, depend on the cleaning process itself.

In the case of the guest room it would be appropriate to define standards in terms of the product at the end of the cleaning process. In practical terms, the room is likely to be reoccupied before significant deterioration of standards occur.

In the case of the casualty department floor, however, the area is likely to be in constant use and significant resoilage may well occur before the cleaning process is complete. A more appropriate standard would be defined in terms of process, ie the method of cleaning and the products to be used, the time allocated for the task and the frequency of completion. Difficulties with definition by process, however, can be experienced at the monitoring phase (see below).

7.3.4 Further defining standards

For practical reasons it may be important that the standard is defined in more than one way to ensure that requirements are fully understood by staff. One such way of further illuminating the definition is if an explanation of the method of assessment is given. See Figure 7.2 for an example.

Figure 7.2 *How the method of assessment can be used to further illuminate the standard defined*

Item or surface	Standard required	Method of assessment
Floor covering	No stain, litter, spillages, dust, scuff marks	Visual check, mobile items moved
WC	No stain, soilage, dust or splash marks on the unit	Visual check inside and outside unit
etc . . .		

Quality standards must be constantly updated to keep in line with changing requirements and any changes in job breakdowns. Of course, quality standards and any amendments must be communicated to staff through training and supervision. In fact, if a participative management style is used, eg *Quality Circles*, (see Section 7.4.1) employees could well be involved in formulating quality standards.

As a large number of quality standards will be required to cover all aspects of the Accommodation services, it would be appropriate to retain them on computer if possible.

7.4 CONTROLLING THE STANDARD

In any service industry, and Acccommodation services are no exception, the key to the control of standards is the motivation of the staff involved.

The most effective equipment and agents may be provided; surfaces may be in excellent condition and easily maintained; staff may have been trained in the appropriate areas, but, without the necessary motivation, staff may not achieve the required standard.

Staff motivation may be achieved through appropriate selection and training, appraisal, reward systems, profit sharing and other means.

7.4.1   Quality circles

Quality circles is a concept, launched in Japan (as part of the Company-wide Quality Improvement, CQI, philosophy) by a Japanese professor, KAORU ISHIKAWA.[1] An explanation of the professor's theories and findings are shown in Appendix 7.

In essence, quality circles aim to increase quality awareness and responsibility amongst staff and supervisors, at the same time as enhancing their jobs. In this way motivation and quality improvements are linked. Quality is seen as the responsibility of all staff, not only those who perform a quality control or monitoring function, or senior staff who set quality policies.

Groups of workers are set up, on a voluntary basis, and, in an on-going process, these staff are trained in problem-solving skills. They meet on a regular basis and identify, for themselves, where quality improvements can be made and develop means of tackling these problems.

In the Accommodation sections it is not difficult to see how such techniques could be productive. Many staff in the course of their work will be aware of all sorts of difficulties which affect the standard of their work. Some of these would not have been identified by the Accommodation Manager.

Providing opportunities to deal with such problems would not only relieve frustrations and improve motivation, but also improve standards achieved.

In service industries it is impossible to monitor all work completed and, therefore, the standard achieved in many cases will be that set by the person completing the task. There are, however, means by which a certain amount of the work can be monitored and to some extent by increasing the rate of monitoring, standards can be improved.

7.4.2   Monitoring

Monitoring is a means of control. It may be applied to measure work quality and/or quantity by in-house staff or contractors.

7.4.2.1   Why monitor?   Monitoring identifies the standards of performance being achieved and compares these against those specified. It also identifies shortcomings in the work specification.

Monitoring is a continuous process. Its possible aims can be summarised as follows:

- to ensure and report that the service has been provided/received
- to detect unsatisfactory performance, incomplete work or work performed to a standard higher than the level set
- to support payments to be made and identify any needs for deductions from payments
- to identify problems, particularly recurring ones
- to enable the work specification to be amended where necessary, to achieve improvements in the service, reduce too high standards and, if possible, reduce costs.

Monitoring should not be seen as the only means of controlling quality. As has been shown above, staff motivation is a vital ingredient and it would be impractical to monitor every task completed in the accommodation sections. In the situation where staff are outside the control of the monitoring body, however, as in the case of contracted work, then monitoring will fulfil a well defined quality control function.

7.4.2.2 Designing a monitoring system

Designing a monitoring system involves making decisions about the following issues:

- what is the purpose of the monitoring process, how will results be used and by whom?
- what activities/areas/items have to be monitored?
- to what quality standards do they have to conform and how will they be measured?
- when will monitoring take place and how often?
- who will be involved in the monitoring process?
- how will results be documented and what reports are required?

7.4.2.3 Defining the scope of the monitoring system

The monitoring system starts with the determination of the 'basis' for monitoring, ie by product or process. (The relative merits of using 'product' or 'process' as the monitoring base are discussed later.) Within the product (this could be a physical area or a particular item), or the process (eg the method of cleaning a particular surface), the particular aspects, such as tasks, surfaces, equipment, subprocesses, etc, to be monitored, would be specified. For instance, in an hotel bedroom, with en suite bathroom (product/physical area), the aspects to be monitored would include:

- floor cleaning
- furniture cleaning
- bed making
- sanitary fitting cleaning.

These could then be further broken down, eg bidet, bath, basin, etc. There will also be a number of general aspects, such as hygiene, health, safety, security and equipment usage and maintenance which have to be monitored.

GRANT THORNTON (1987)[2] suggests that it is then useful to consider grading, ie monitoring aspects of physical location:

- the monitoring aspects could be graded according to their contribution to the quality service provision, ie primary aspects which are 'fundamental to the service and where failure would be regarded as serious breakdown to the service', with significant cost implications and secondary aspects which are not critical to service delivery or cost. Where cost and size of the total monitoring operation are issues, the secondary aspects might not be monitored or only very infrequently.
- the physical location may be graded according to the degree of risk or usage, so that a higher level of monitoring can be applied to a higher risk or usage area, eg in a **hospital**, *high risk clinical areas* such as operating theatres, *low risk clinical areas* such as patient areas, wards, and *non-clinical areas* such as residences, offices may be designated or in an **hotel**, *high and low usage areas*, eg main entrance versus *store areas* or *prestige areas* such as suites, restaurants versus staff canteen may be designated.

This classification may affect the frequency of monitoring.

7.4.3   Using quality standards

As one of the main aims of monitoring is to assess the standard of quality of service being provided, it is essential to have defined the standard of quality expected and how it is to be measured. This involves defining, by product or process, the specific quality standard for each aspect. In this way the precise method to be used to test the quality achieved, against the standard set, can be determined. It will be necessary to determine how the results of the tests will be analysed. These decisions will impinge on decisions relating to frequency of monitoring and who will be responsible for the processes involved.

GRANT THORNTON[2] promotes the concept of developing Quality Assessment Standards for each process or physical area. Two examples, one using a process and one using a physical area (or series of products) as the monitoring base are shown in Figures 7.3 and 7.4.

The standard defined will be based on 'normal' circumstances but sometimes unexpected or abnormal circumstances might have occurred, such as inclement weather or vandalism which could affect the method used and the result achieved in the case of monitoring by product. Monitoring must be adapted.

Figure 7.3 *Quality Assessment Standard – by physical area*

Location: Intensive Care Unit

Grade: High Risk

Servicing principles: The area will be cleaned in a manner which will facilitate the proper functioning of the unit.

Monitoring aspects	Standard required	Method of assessment	Responsibility for assessment
Floor covering	No stains, litter, dust, spillages or scuff marks	**Daily:** Visual check mobile items moved	Domestic Supervisor Theatre Sister
		Weekly: Bacterial count	Control of Infection Officer
Wall covering	No stains, spillages, smears or dust	**Daily:** Visual check, mobile items moved	Domestic Supervisor Theatre Sister
		Weekly: Bacterial count	Control of Infection Officer
etc . . .			

7.4.4   Hazard Analysis and Critical Control Point

The concept of HACCP was originally applied in the United States to develop a 'nil defects' programme in the production of food for astronauts. It started as a means of identifying and controlling stages in the food production process where the food might be most susceptible to bacterial contamination. The most susceptible stages being identified as the 'critical points'.

The process has since been used widely in industry and is seen as a preventative process of hazard control. Risks associated with different stages of production are estimated in a rational, logical manner. A given process is broken down into its constituent parts and areas identified where significant hazards could be introduced. The control of these hazards is then directed at the Critical Control Points, ie the points where it is essential to ensure that potential hazards do not become reality.

Figure 7.4 *Quality Assessment Standard – by process*

Process: Stripping, resealing and repolishing floors treated with water-based polish.

Servicing Principles: In the agreed time and using the standard procedure, the floor surface will be in a condition appropriate for its normal use.

Monitoring aspects	Standard required	Method of assessment and timing	Responsibility for assessment
Stripping of previous floor treatments	All visible traces of dirt and previous treatments removed without causing damage to surfaces being treated or in the vicinity	Visual check at commencement of products, equipment and methods. Visual check at completion of surface and surrounding area	Domestic Supervisor
Application of specified seal	Specified product is used effectively. The minimum number of coats being as specified; additional coats should be applied if needed to produce a smooth finish suitable for polish application	Visual check at completion of final coat	Domestic Supervisor
etc...			

Figure 7.5 *Hazards associated with infected linen and the critical control points*

Hazard	Critical control point
Contamination by the user	Stripping of beds
Delay in the laundering process (allowing micro-organisms to breed)	Collection of soiled items Reception and flow through laundry process
Laundry process	Temperature control and process selection
Tranportation and storage of clean items	Bagging of clean items Transport Linen stores

Such principles can effectively be applied to accommodation services, for example in linen and laundry systems, materials management, infection control and cleaning and maintenance.

To take linen as an example, infection hazards and their critical control points are shown in Figure 7.5.

7.5 MEASURING QUALITY

As has been shown, quality standards may be defined in terms of product or process, but wherever possible they should be defined explicitly and objectively, rather than subjectively.

In certain health care situations, for example, quantitative monitoring may include:

- bacterial counts taken in high risk areas or where clinical standards are required
- air counts taken to determine bacterial levels in the atmosphere
- swab tests taken on equipment, in cleaning water, toilets, dish washing water, etc to assess numbers and types of micro-organisms present
- a slit sampler can be used to evaluate the effect on air disturbance caused by using different equipment, eg suction cleaners, mops and brushes

A good deal of work on objective measurement techniques has been carried out by the British Carpet Technical Centre and Cleaning and Maintenance Research and Services Organisation (CAMRASO).

Techniques developed include:

- soil monitoring for measuring the cleanliness of hard floors and other smooth surfaces
- measuring gloss levels for hard floors and ceramic tiles
- soil recovery measurement to assess the amount of soilage removed from carpets
- colour measurement for assessing changes in carpets, upholstery and hard floors
- disclosing dye for assessing the cleaning efficiency on sanitary ware
- co-efficient of friction (or the measurement of slipperiness) of hard floors.

Some of these have been found of value in assessing cleaning standards.

As can be seen in Figures 7.3 and 7.4, whilst standards defined by product are appropriate for the monitoring base, standards defined by process may cause difficulties. If each stage of the process has to be monitored, as the example above, the monitoring process becomes time consuming. A process might nevertheless be selected as a monitoring base in the case of infrequent, costly operations perhaps performed by contractors, or as an appraisal tool for NVQ assessment or assessment of other staff.

Due to these difficulties with monitoring by process, subjective standards may be set in the Accommodation services area, particularly when monitoring contractors. For example, 'at the end of the process the floor is safe to use, looks attractive, with a good shine', etc; the absence of soilage can be defined quantitatively, but not the aesthetic qualities.

It can be seen, therefore, that in defining standards, the purpose and the use of the definition must be identified. The definition may be chosen as a control measure in its own right (eg process definition) or the definition may be used as a tool to assist a tight monitoring system (and some such definitions, for reasons shown above, may be subjective). Results from subjective measures will be variable, differing from one monitor to another, but are frequently unavoidable. The form of measurement adopted must be consistently repeatable by different monitors. It must be a valid measure of definable characteristics which is acceptable to both the service provider and the service users (particularly if the latter are involved in the monitoring process). To achieve best results, a combination of monitoring processes (production control sampling) and finished products (acceptance sampling) should be planned.

7.5.1 How will the standard be assessed?

As management will base their evaluation of performance and calculation for payment in some cases on the results of the assessment, it is essential that methods of assessment are carefully selected.

GRANT THORNTON[2] suggests a number of methods for assessing both laundry and cleaning services. These include:

- **For cleaning domestic services**
  — **Time based assessment** where the time value for each task is given a number of points dependent on the amount of time allocated and the importance of the task. If the task has not been adequately performed then the relative number of points are recorded as a penalty. The total number of penalty points achieved can be expressed as a percentage of the total available points for all tasks in that physical area. A specified number of areas will be sampled over a period of time, eg week or month. This information can then be used to produce a general statement of performance and/or calculate financial deductions from payments to contractors.
  — **Point scoring system** where each type of task will be allocated a number of points according to its importance, degree of risk and type of location. A failure limit is set for each area above which the overall standard will be considered unacceptable

(referred to by CAMRASO[3] as the acceptable fault level – AFL). The higher the degree of risk, the lower the acceptable fault level. The number and types of areas failing can be compared against the total number of areas and the contract price/budget. (This tends to be the most appropriate for cleaning/domestic services.)

— **Activity observation reporting** where observation of an actual process has to occur if the quality standard is defined by process. This may be appropriate for occasional tasks, but is time consuming and, in reality, the end result is probably checked rather than the process. It will include spot checks on the use and cleanliness of equipment and observance of safety, hygiene and waste disposal methods.

All these assessment procedures are complex and generate large amounts of information which has to be recorded, stored and retrieved as required, and ultimately disposed.

7.5.1.1 Statistical sampling

The above methods of assessment are based on visual inspection of products or processes undertaken to check the quality standards attained. These inspections must be conducted on a regular basis to be valid but are time consuming and it is rarely appropriate to inspect all products/areas or processes every time they are performed.

There are various sampling techniques which may be applied, whereby a limited number, rather than all tasks, are inspected.[4]

Simple random sampling, whereby tasks to be monitored are chosen entirely at random, like names out of a hat, is difficult to apply, simply because the 'random' process can so easily be biased.

Stratified sampling involves sampling 'one of each type', eg one sleeping area, one sanitary area, etc, and multi-stage sampling involves dividing the tasks into groups, eg bathrooms, public areas, etc, and then choosing a few of these at random to sample. These latter sampling techniques are probably the most appropriate for accommodation. Quota sampling, whereby a certain 'quota' of, say, sanitary areas, office areas or sleeping areas, are selected for sampling, is also used.

A number of computer software packages are available, such as COMOSYS (Computerised Monitoring System of International Hospital Group) which not only select the areas/activities to be monitored according to the parameters defined by the software user, but also record the outcome of the inspections undertaken. Adjustments can be made to ensure, for example, that higher graded areas, such as high risk, clinical areas are monitored more often.

One hospital monitoring system is based on selecting a quota of 15% of rooms in each area. There is a degree of selectivity as on ward areas, the sample must include at least one bedded room, the kitchen and one sanitary room. Two samples for each item/element on the checklist are checked, eg highdusting is checked in two places within the room, two items of furniture checked, and so on.

The frequency of performance of tasks as indicated in the work specification and the grading according to degree of risk, type of area or other defined priority, will determine the frequency of monitoring. Too frequent assessment will be time consuming and costly and there may well be no appreciable change in the observable results since the last time. The system must encompass the monitoring of periodic activities/tasks and the recording system must ensure that these are brought to the attention of the monitor so that they are not overlooked.

7.5.2   Who will monitor?

As can be seen from the sample Quality Assessment Standard outlined in Figures 7.3 and 7.4, a number of different people might be involved in monitoring. In fact, responsibility for each aspect to be monitored must be allocated to a particular person. Those involved in actual monitoring quality standards and performance could include service users or receivers such as the client (in a contract situation) or departmental heads; independent monitors employed to monitor a contract; the service provider such as the in-house Housekeeping or Maintenance Manager (and their supervisors) and technical specialists such as Microbioligists, Pest Control Officers, Fire Officers, Control of Infection Officers, Health and Safety Inspectors, and BS 5750 Inspectors. A balance between service users'/receivers' reports and actual sampling by monitors/supervisors has to be achieved.

Those involved must be fully conversant with the work specification, the terms and conditions of the contract (if this is applicable), the standards to be achieved and the assessment methods to be used. They must also be aware of how to record their results, collate and summarise the information produced, how it will be used and presented to management and how frequently.

Monitors must be professionally competent to make decisions which could cause variations to be made in the work specification or affect the payment to the service provider. Individuals will bring their own values, perceptions and bias into the process and steps must be taken to ensure that misconceptions do not occur and results are not distorted.

7.5.2.1   Checklists   It is usual to design checklists and/or report formats to be used by the various people involved in the monitoring process. A checklist is only useful if it is well designed, covers all essential aspects/items to be monitored, allows enough space for comment, is simple and easy to complete and encourages a systematic approach. It will focus attention and aid concentration. The format

should allow the time of the assessment to be recorded and by whom. In some instances it may be verified by another party, eg a ward sister or a departmental head. Work schedules will assist the monitor to know what activities/tasks are being undertaken, in which physical areas at which time.

In the housekeeping/cleaning context a checklist will be needed for each physical area or area type, showing the particular aspects/items to be assessed and how the results are to be measured. See Figure 7.6 as an example.

Attention to detail can make the difference between a high and a mediocre standard being attained. Inspection of less obvious places such as under doors, in corners, behind open doors, backs of wardrobe tops, under basins, behind toilet pedestals, should be made.

Figure 7.6 *Part of a checklist*

Location: Intensive care unit

Grade: High risk

Servicing Principles: the area will be cleaned in a manner which will facilitate the proper function of the room.

Monitoring aspect	Standard required	Accept/ reject	Failure points value
Floor covering	No stains, dust, scuff marks or spillages		10
Wall covering	No stains, spillages, dust or smears		5
Light fittings	Light shades free from stains, dust or smears		10
etc . . .			

NB   It is worth noting that checklists may be used to monitor cleaning standards, service standards and maintenance aspects. Although the Accommodation sections may not be responsible for completing maintenance, it is often considered to be a cost effective way of monitoring maintenance requirements in a running maintenance system, if regard is taken of maintenance needs as rooms are being checked.

7.5.3   Remedial action for unsatisfactory work

Good work and the attainment of the required standard should, of course, be given credit, and praise given when it is due. How often does this happen in reality? In fact the attainment of high standards on a regular basis could provide the basis for a reward scheme and hence provide an incentive for improvement. If performance and standards achieved are unsatisfactory then a feedback control system should ensure that the work can be rectified.

In the case of the checklist illustrated, total failure points values would be added and, depending on the policy within the particular establishment, above certain set figures, different actions might be taken, eg completely recleaning the area, item noted for remedial action in the next cleaning process, etc. In an in-house situation the person responsible for the unsatisfactory work should, ideally, be seen before going off duty and the deficiency rectified.

Repetitive failure points on certain items should trigger some investigation, eg is retraining of staff necessary? is equipment in need of servicing? is the area being used in a different manner? are disciplinary precedings appropriate?

In the contract situation, the contractor will be informed of the unsatisfactory results and given a period of time, as specified in the contract, to rectify the problem. Following this, a further inspection will be necessary. As stated previously, this could lead to financial penalties being inflicted on the contractor.

In monitoring contracts, and large in-house operations, the monitoring process can be complex and involve much data which can only really be economically and practically evaluated by computer. There are various software packages incorporating monitoring systems.

7.5.4 Documentation and reports

A number of documents, such as Quality Assessment Standards and Checklists, will have to be designed. Results will also need to be recorded and retained, either manually or by computer. Results obtained will have to be collated, summarised and analysed for presentation to management and possibly clients or users/receivers of the service at specified intervals. Management will decide what information they require, for what purposes, in what format, and how often it is required. Generally information will be required to:

- indicate that the service has been provided/received
- indicate the level of service provided
- support payments to be made to contractors and make deductions from payments if necessary
- identify recurring problems/difficulties
- enable the work specification to be amended where necessary, to achieve improvements in the service and/or reduce too high a standard being achieved and therefore reduce costs.

All decisions and changes must of course be documented.

It is of value to devise documentation of the monitoring procedures.

Figure 7.7 *The costs associated with quality*

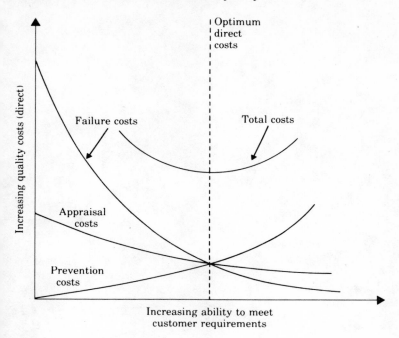

Such a document would enable continuity of the monitoring role, it could be updated when necessary, so providing a useful record for such purposes as the training of monitors.

The monitoring system needs to be cost effective and thus the control costs must themselves be monitored and measured against implications of not monitoring.

Figure 7.7 shows the cost associated with quality.

The graph shows that:

- costs associated with preventing poor quality increase with the product's ability to meet customer requirements
- total costs can be calculated and an optimum level assessed.

The monitoring process is complete and a summary of the elements to be considered is shown in Figure 7.8.

7.6   FROM STANDARD TO QUALITY

It has been shown how standards can be defined, set and monitored. To achieve a 'quality' product two conditions must be met:

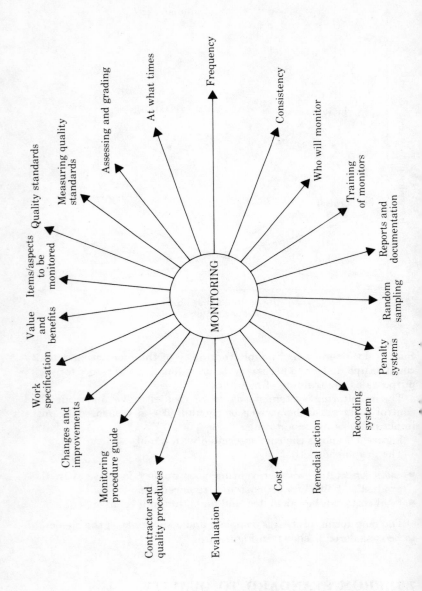

1 The customer must recognise the product as satisfying their needs.
2 The standard of the product, including the intangible service element must be consistent (eg the hotel customer must be afforded the same courtesy, time, assistance, etc, as they were last time, and this should be the same as other customers are enjoying).

The customers' perception of the product will be affected by functional aspects such as does the shower work? the reliability of the product, ie if a customer regularly stays in a particular hotel, can they always be confident that all the elements will always meet requirements? the price (and here the customer will have their own perception of what is 'value for money'); intangible elements, eg a feeling of importance, prestige, acceptability, trend setting, etc.

7.7 QUALITY VERSUS PRODUCTIVITY?

Must there be 'trade off' between quality and productivity? If output increases will this mean that quality standards must be allowed to fall, or, conversely, must lower productivity have to be accepted if consistent standards are to be achieved? In the next few sections it will be shown that the answer to both these questions is 'No'.

7.7.1 Definition

Productivity is defined as the relationship between input and output, ie $\dfrac{\text{Output}}{\text{Input}}$.

'Input' relates to costs associated with producing the product, eg equipment, materials, labour and building costs, and 'output' relates to the total produced. An increase in productivity can be achieved, therefore, by:

- reducing costs and maintaining output
- maintaining costs and increasing output
- increasing costs and output, but increasing output by a disproportionate amount.

Productivity improvement may be set at four levels within an organisation:

1 **corporate level**, where a change of policy is determined
2 **systems level**, ie organisational aspects may be reviewed, structures redefined, procedures simplified and more efficient use made of resources
3 **process level**, ie the process may be redesigned, new technology applied or new materials used

Figure 7.9 *How productivity may be increased*

Productivity increased by	Examples of application in Accommodation Management
New technology	Automatic spreader/feeder in the laundry, computerised accounting – costed from a terotechnological stance
Organisational management reviews	Numbers of management and supervisory grades, proportional to staffing grades
Management information	Budgeting information, staff appraisals, monitoring details, etc
Bonus schemes	eg for consistent quality
Training	For all grades. Job enrichment. Retraining
Operations research	To forecast demand and staffing implications
Job design	To reduce wasted time moving from one section of the building to another. Method improvement. Environmental conditions
Sequencing of tasks	Particularly important for individual projects eg conference planning
Equipment scheduling	To achieve optimum use of expensive equipment, eg water injection machines, whilst ensuring that staff do not have to wait for them

4 **workplace level**, ie where individual workers achieve higher efficiency.

7.8 HOW CAN PRODUCTIVITY BE INCREASED?

Many ways of improving productivity have been identified, and in Figure 7.9 some of these, are shown, with their applications to Accommodation Management.

Overall methods of improving productivity can be divided into:

Scientific, eg research activities to produce new materials or processes

Technical, ie using the results of scientific research and knowledge
Operational, ie procedures are developed to make the best use of scientific knowledge

Scientific and technical processes must be viewed as long term projects. The Accommodation Manager can apply operational processes for short term, quick returns.

7.8.1 Measuring productivity

Existing productivity must be evaluated and issues for subsequent investigation identified before improvements can be made. In some situations productivity can be measured in work study terms. For instance it is possible to measure the productivity of workers using the 'standard minute' as the basis for calculation.

$$\frac{\text{Output of work in standard minutes}}{\text{Input of labour time or machine time in clock minutes}}$$

In other situations, productivity may be relatively easy to calculate using the definition of productivity given earlier.

In a laundry, for instance, the amount of work produced in terms of weight of dirty linen processed or number of pieces of linen processed is divided by a period of time.

In a cleaning operation, the output of work per hour may be calculated, for example in terms of $\times 000$ m^2 floor covering to be cleaned per operative hour.

It is not easy, in all cases, to identify a unit of production by which to calculate the amount of work produced. For instance, in the front office, although it could be argued that here occupancy levels would be a yardstick. (See Chapter 6.)

Within the field of Accommodation Management, labour related measures of productivity are most appropriate as labour is the most significant cost.

Another measure of productivity appropriate for use in Accommodation Management is by Measured Added Value:

$$\text{Added value} = \pounds(\text{Sales--Costs}).$$

$$\text{The Added Value Index} = \frac{\text{Total employment cost}}{\text{Added value}}.$$

The difficulty here, however, would be in separating costs from different departments and evaluating their individual impact on the value added.

7.9 IMPLICATIONS OF LABOUR ON PRODUCTIVITY

The accommodation industry is labour intensive and the main costs related to production are staffing costs. These have been discussed in

Chapter 4. The manager must be aware of the true cost of labour and a regular operating statement will be invaluable providing it properly reflects the work of the accommodation sector. An operating statement which, for instance, includes the cost of kitchen porters, who undertake cleaning tasks but are not employed by the Domestic Manager, is not appropriate.

7.9.1   Assessing staffing levels and scheduling work

The calculation of staffing hours, grades required and the scheduling of work has been covered in Section 4.6. Employing excess staff will obviously reduce productivity, as will employing the wrong grades of staff or poor scheduling incorporating lengthy waiting times. Calculation of staffing needs must be an on-going process and work study techniques have been effectively applied in this area.

Having calculated total staffing requirements, the hours need to be broken down into schedules and with careful scheduling, waiting time can be reduced and more expensive pay rates minimised. Some aspects which may be considered include:

- employment of part-time staff to reduce employment costs and increase flexibility of workforce around peak times of demand
- schedule low priority, infrequent or periodic work to smooth demand in otherwise quiet periods
- pay overtime rate to full-time staff where just an odd hour is involved, instead of appointing another employee for a very short shift
- schedule annual leave of personnel to coincide with lower demand periods, or ensure, by scheduling, an even level of absence through annual leave
- employ temporary staff or contractors to cover for peak demand periods.

In these ways, not only are wage costs controlled, but the demand is also controlled.

7.9.1.1   Equipment scheduling   In order to utilise staff and equipment, particularly expensive 'capital' equipment, efficiently, equipment, as well as staff must be scheduled. This will help to reduce waiting time when equipment is being used elsewhere, being transported or receiving maintenance. It should also ensure that equipment is neither overloaded nor unproductive.

If a scrubbing machine is shared between two departments, for example, then floor maintenance must be scheduled at different times in the two departments. If two employees are to undertake all cleaning activities in one area together, with only one set of cleaning equipment, then a schedule must be devised whereby the two do not require the same equipment at the same time.

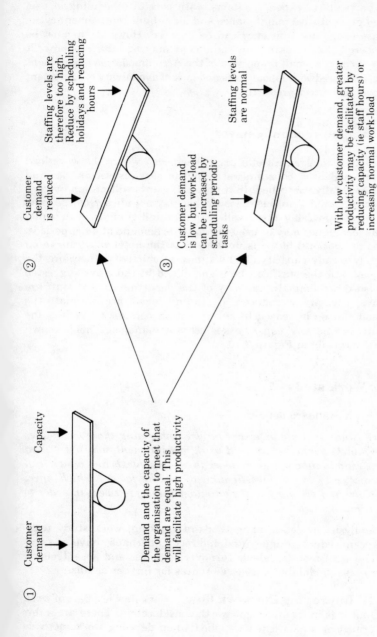

① Customer demand | Capacity

Demand and the capacity of the organisation to meet that demand are equal. This will facilitate high productivity

② Customer demand is reduced | Staffing levels are therefore too high. Reduce by scheduling holidays and reducing hours

③ Customer demand is low but work-load can be increased by scheduling periodic tasks | Staffing levels are normal

With low customer demand, greater productivity may be facilitated by reducing capacity (ie staff hours) or increasing normal work-load

Figure 7.10 The effect of capacity management on productivity

It may be cost effective to purchase minimum quantities of equipment, particularly expensive items; with careful scheduling of use, planned preventative maintenance and an in-built replacement cycle, optimum usage and efficiency can be ensured. However, it must be remembered that to skimp on equipment may be false economy. It represents only a small proportion of the Accommodation department budget, compared with labour costs and lack of availability of equipment will adversely affect productivity.

7.9.2   Capacity management

In any situation, greatest efficiency is achieved where the work load is maintained at a constant rate. In the services sector, demand cannot be totally controlled. In a hospital, wards will normally work to capacity, but, for various reasons, this may not always be the case. In an hotel inevitably there will be peaks and troughs in demand. Various techniques may be used to stimulate demand at quiet periods, such as promotions, but it is unlikely that the hotel will achieve an absolutely steady capacity. To maximise productivity, therefore the work load and the staff can be manipulated in the ways suggested above, so controlling the capacity of the department, ie if staff are on leave, capacity is reduced, if staffing levels are 'normal', the workload can be increased by incorporating periodic tasks into the schedule. In this way, capacity is effectively managed. This is shown diagrammatically in Figure 7.10.

7.9.3   Work study

The British Standard definition is:

> 'Work Study is a management service comprising those techniques particularly method study and work measurement, which are used in the examination of human work in all its contexts and which lead systematically to the investigation of all the factors which affect efficiency and economy of the situation being reviewed, in order to effect improvement'.

By analysis, in detail, of methods of working, work study techniques can reduce fatigue (and indirectly, perhaps, have positive effects on staff morale, labour turnover, sickness and absenteeism), and increase productivity. (See references for further details.)

7.9.3.1   Improving the work flow   Work flow is a part of work study, but it is in its own right worth consideration. There are a few basic principles which can be applied when devising work methods and processes. AXLER[5] suggests the following guidelines:

- keep work flowing in one direction in a short, straight line
- design the work area to be self sufficient, eg consider siting and design of utility areas within the work area, to avoid unproductive time spent in obtaining supplies and preparing for work. If there is no convenient utility area, provide the room attendant with a trolley
- plan the work system around the human element, ie consider the capabilities of personnel and speeds at which it is possible to work
- where appropriate, consider bulk processing. For example, it is more effective for the book-keeper to post a number of charges onto a number of guest accounts at one time, rather than post them haphazardly
- consider the team approach to scheduling where a high degree of skills and/or knowledge is required, eg floor maintenance; where an activity must be completed in a short time or where proportionally less energy is expended by a number of personnel undertaking an activity over a shorter period, compared to an individual undertaking the same activity over a longer period.
- assign unavoidable, nonproductive work to cheaper labour
- consider the layout or the venue of elements of the system to avoid criss-crossing, backtracking or unnecessary movement of personnel or work.
- build flexibility into the system, eg bed configurations can be changed to suit occupancy requirements.

7.9.3.2 Motion economy This aspect is again part of the work study technique and involves designing work and work methods which allow the employee to perform tasks in the shortest possible time with the greatest ease and satisfaction, expending as little energy as possible. *Kinetics*, an element of *ergonomics* (see Chapter 2) are involved in the process and, when the system has been designed, staff are trained, for example, in the correct ways of lifting, carrying and using equipment in order to reduce fatigue.

7.9.3.4 Ratio Delay In an existing operation, Ratio Delay, a form of Activity Sampling, is a useful technique which involves observing personnel, equipment and work at random and at regular intervals in order to study the relative activity of individual personnel and equipment.

The process identifies productive time, and time which is used up by delays. The ratio of the delay time to total working time can be calculated and the reasons for delays analysed.

Delays may include waiting for supplies or a piece of equipment, waiting for the completion of another operation by a different employee or waiting to gain access to an area.

Ratio Delay also reveals other unproductive time, eg collecting supplies, preparing for work, walking from one place to another,

Figure 7.11 *Graph of the learning curve*

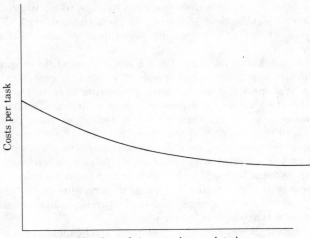

Number of times task completed

cleaning equipment after use, etc. In the case of a domestic assistant in a hospital, these delays may be, say, 1.5 hours in an eight hour work day. This can be translated into financial terms to realise the enormity of the problem. Planning work to reduce such idle time is another means of improving productivity.

7.9.3.5 Sequencing work   In programming work it will be found that some tasks have to be completed at certain times, eg in a hospital the service of hot beverages to patients; some must be completed at the same time as others, eg suction drying of a floor which is being stripped of its seal; some tasks must be completed before others can be started, eg mop sweeping or suction cleaning of floors prior to spray cleaning.

Network Analysis techniques, such as Critical Path Analysis, Programme Evaluation and Review Technique, can assist at the planning stages of scheduling tasks as well as at the control stage. Such techniques are particularly useful in planning large projects, eg the refurbishment of a hospital ward, or a floor of guest rooms in an hotel. Staff resources are high in such operations and, in addition, the operation must be completed in the shortest time to allow normal usage to resume.

By network analysis, the sequence of tasks is identified, highlighting which tasks are dependent on others and which are independent and can be completed in parallel with others. The 'critical path' can be identified, this being the sequence of tasks which take the longest time (see reference). In this way, waiting time can be reduced, labour costs minimised and the operation completed in the shortest possible time.

7.9.4 Motivation

Well-motivated staff are of critical importance with respect to productivity within a labour intensive industry.

Productivity is affected by lateness and absence as, usually, other personnel often have to cover key aspects of the missing operatives work and rescheduling must occur. In the calculation of labour hours, a percentage to cover absences, sickness and lateness, as well as annual leave of staff, may be included. Whilst annual leave can be accurately forecast, sickness, absence and lateness cannot. It is important that any allowances made are realistic as overstaffing will obviously reduce productivity.

7.9.4.1 Experience/learning curve
The cost, (in terms of time and materials) to complete a task drops in a regularly definable way, as the total quantity made by an individual increases. This is shown in Figure 7.11.

There are many 'doublings of production' achieved early on. As learners become more competent, they will complete tasks more quickly, with less waste in terms of any materials or other resources used and require less supervisory time, ie at less cost. As learners become more and more competent, so savings become more difficult to make. Times taken to complete tasks become more difficult to reduce further and similarly, wastage. The curve on the graph flattens out. So, in Accommodation Management, it can be seen that there are productivity advantages for maintaining a low labour turnover. Not only does high labour turnover incur replacement costs, retraining costs, etc, but also it takes time for new employees to achieve good productivity.

The experience curve has to be **managed**. It happens as a result of improvements in:

- labour efficiency
- training
- motivation
- work force stability
- work force organisation.

7.9.5 Employee performance

The performance of individuals can be rated by assessing the rate at which an employee works, relative to the observer's (usually a trained

Work Study Officer) concept of the standard performance rate. The standard performance is defined by British Standard as:

> '*the rate of output which qualified workers will naturally achieve, without overexertion, as an average over the working day or shift, provided they are motivated to apply themselves to their work. This performance is denoted as 100 on the standard rating and performance scales*'.

Employee performance will normally be improved by training and this aspect should be carefully planned with respect to all employees, not only new ones. Training should be on-going. Changes in equipment, materials or methods will necessitate training and, even without changes in the system, it may be found that staff will benefit from retraining.

7.10   EQUIPMENT AND AGENTS USAGE

The selection of appropriate equipment and agents can affect productivity by improving the speed and efficiency with which operations are completed. Inappropriate materials may cause work to have to be redone so increasing labour costs and, in addition, attention should be paid to equipment scheduling (see Chapter 5). The correct use of equipment and agents should be included in the training programme. This will prevent overloading, over use, damage to surface, equipment or staff, and reduce effort. Personnel should be trained to maintain equipment after use, eg cleaning, emptying and reporting any faults.

7.11   THE PHYSICAL ENVIRONMENT

An employee who is physically comfortable in the work environment will be more productive and maintain the pace for longer periods. Ergonomics, especially anthropometrics and applied physiology, are important aspects in this context (see Chapter 2). Temperature, acoustics, humidity, lighting and other factors will affect comfort, as will overalls worn, and dimensions of equipment or furniture used or worked with.

7.12   JUST IN TIME MANAGEMENT

J.I.T. is a Japanese management system which aims to integrate, to a very high degree production, sales and, in manufacturing situations, distribution. The system leads to a continuous flow in the work situation, as follows:

Materials	→	Work in progress	→	Finished product

Scheduling is tight and there is no 'slack' built into the system. Only materials which are required are ordered, no extra and no long lead times are allowed for. The system uses a *Kanban card*, relating to a particular order and customer. As the work flows through the system, it is accompanied by the Kanban.

The technique can be applied to the system of Accommodation Management in that demand must be forecast and staffing capacity, equipment and material requirements developed in line with requirements. Staff would only be employed when there was work for them and waiting time would be eliminated. This would require the strict scheduling of work, to respond to changes in, for instance, expected occupancy levels and careful monitoring of material requirements, as well as careful management and control of demand (and therefore the need for Accommodation Services).

7.13 TECHNICAL EFFICIENCY

Productivity relates to technical efficiency as stated earlier; it measures output from a given input level. It must be stressed that this is *not* the same as *economic efficiency*, where inputs and outputs are all priced.

A department could demonstrate *technical efficiency* by, for example, servicing more rooms, to the required standard, without increasing staffing costs. However, if these rooms were not required for letting, (perhaps they had been scheduled for redecorating) it would not represent *economic efficiency*.

There is no virtue in making goods efficiently if they are not sold!

References

[1] RYAN, N E, editor, *Taguchi Methods and QFD: Hows and Whys for Management*, ASI Press 1988
[2] THORNTON, GRANT, *Management and Monitoring of Contracts for Domestic, Catering and Laundry Services, A Practical Guide and Handbook*, Nuffield Provincial Hospitals Trust 1987
[3] British Carpet Technical Centre and Cleaning and Maintenance and Services Organisation publications (BCTC CAMRASO)
[4] MORRIS, CLARE, *Quantitative Approaches in Business Studies*, 2nd edition, Pitman 1989
[5] AXLER, BRUCE H, Management of Hospitality Operations, Bobbs-Merrill 1976

Concept Map summarising Quality and Productivity.

Further reading

HCIMA. *Technical Brief Quality Systems Guidelines*, HCIMA 1991

Assignment tasks

1 Explain the different methods of defining standards and identify the use and limitations of each.
2 Discuss the role of Accommodation staff with respect to quality assurance and productivity.
3 In an establishment of your choice, taking just one room as an example, devise a monitoring system, for the accommodation services.
4 Show how capacity management techniques could be applied by the Domestic Services Manager in a city hospital to control productivity.
5 Describe the merits of statistical sampling in quality assurance and show how this approach might be applied when monitoring a cleaning contract in a leisure centre.
6 In an establishment of your choice, compare how standards of quality might be set and defined for the purposes of:

- supervisory training
- a cleaning contract to be put out to tender.

Sample of Health and Safety Policy and Fire Policy

Sample: *Accommodation Department Health and Safety Policy*

The promotion of Health and Safety measures is to be regarded as a joint management and employee objective. The manager places great importance on the safety, and well being of employees together with other building users. Employees together with management will assist in deciding the necessary precautions to be taken. To ensure effort, management and employee representatives, together with safety officers will inspect all working areas and equipment every few months and recommendations to improve standards of health and safety will be progressed.

The general identified potential hazards and the proposals to minimise risks are given below.

1 Equipment is seen as a potential hazard where it is used incorrectly, inappropriately or in a badly maintained condition.
 Proposed controls of these risks are:
 (a) Equipment will be selected with due care to be used for identified tasks in specific situations.
 (b) Provision will be made for appropriate accessories including attachments or warning notices to indicate work in progress.
 (c) Equipment users will be given training and retraining where necessary in the safe use and care of equipment. Employees will not use equipment for which they have not received training.
 (d) Adequate supervision will be provided for equipment usage.
 (e) Scheduling of work will make adequate allowance for tasks to be completed safely.
 (f) Regular preventative maintenance will be practised and procedures developed for dealing with defective equipment.
 (g) Suitable storage conditions will be provided for all equipment.

2 Surfaces could represent slip, trip, fire, noise, infection or other hazards where they are defective, inappropriate or otherwise unsafe.
 Proposed controls of these risks are:
 (a) Selection of surfaces including floors, walls, furniture and sanitary fittings will be performed with due care.

(b) Appropriate planned preventative cleaning and maintenance routines will be applied.

(c) Adequate systems of inspection, hazard spotting and reporting will be devised.

(d) Design and layout of the interior will, wherever possible, make for safe conditions. Where hazards are unavoidable, suitable warnings will be used.

3 Chemicals represent a potential hazard, possibly causing adverse effects on users, on the building users and on surfaces through chemical reactions, odours and other means. Some may represent a fire risk or be a poison risk.

Proposed control of these risks are by the following:

(a) Careful selection of the chemicals which will be appropriate to specific surfaces in specific situations.

(b) Provision of appropriate protective clothing, eg rubber gloves and overalls.

(c) Provision of adequate training in the use and storage of chemicals.

(d) Provision of adequate supervision of use.

(e) Provision of warning notices or instruction information on usage, dilutions, etc, will be made.

(f) Appropriate equipment will be provided for use with chemicals.

(g) Provision will be made for appropriate storage facilities and stores control systems to monitor and control usage and availability of chemicals.

(h) Chemicals will be issued to authorised users only.

4 The general physical and psychological environment may represent health and safety risks through various ergonomic defects, eg temperature levels, privacy requirements, security needs and job satisfaction.

Proposed controls of these potential threats are:

(a) The monitoring and control of the environment to ensure healthy and comfortable conditions.

(b) The development of an efficient and sensitive personnel function which will provide staff welfare.

(c) The use of a well-staffed occupational health department.

(d) The efficient operation of safety representatives.

Sample: *Fire Policy*

Probably the greatest risk threatening any property owner is that of fire. Fire safety is regarded with great importance as it can threaten lives and livelihoods of all building users. Maximum co-operation of staff is sought to minimise the risks of fire by ensuring safe working practices are followed and any hazards reported with urgency.

The potential hazards and proposals made to minimise the risks are as follows:

1 The building itself is identified as the first risk. This includes the main structure, internal design and layout and all furniture, fittings and furnishings. Many of these components may be flammable, some may hamper fire detection, safety of escape or effectiveness of fire fighting.

Controls of these risks are:

(a) The building, its components and uses are scrutinised by the Fire Authority before the issue of the Fire Certificate. Any faults found by the Fire Authority are dealt with urgently to comply with requirements and recommendations.

(b) Selection procedures for any new items incorporate consideration of fire hazards.

(c) Smoke and fire detectors, smoke doors, alarms, alternative escape routes, exit signs, emergency lighting and extinguishers are fitted and maintained in line with recommendations.

2 Absence of appropriate procedures to deal with fire prevention, detection, alarm and escape would constitute fire hazards.

Procedures devised include the following:

(a) Daily inspection checks are implemented to identify any fire hazards and problems so identified are dealt with urgently.

(b) Stores areas are included in the regular inspection and items in storage are stored in line with requirements and recommendations.

(c) Procedures to follow, on the detection of fire and on hearing the alarm raised, are included in all staff's training and communicated to other building users on the approved fire notices.

(d) When normal procedures become temporarily inappropriate due to building work or other reasons, alternative procedures are devised and communicated to those concerned.

(e) Security procedures will be maintained to reduce the risk of arsonists, terrorists or the like gaining access to the building and a bomb threat procedure will be devised and implemented.

3 All building users represent a fire risk when unsafe practices occur. To minimise this risk:

(a) Regular staff training and retraining incorporate procedures to be followed to: promote fire prevention; deal with the detection of a fire hazard; deal with the detection of a fire; effect the safest means of escape for themselves and other building users in the case of fire; operate fire extinguishers where appropriate.

(b) Procedures to follow when a fire is detected or the alarm raised are communicated to other building users on approved notices posted as is required and recommended.

4 Items in short or longer term storage represent a fire risk,

particularly during the periods where personnel are not in their immediate vicinity to identify hazards.

To minimise this risk:

(a) Highly flammable items will not be stored in the long term and when short term storage is necessitated, such items will be stored in separate fire proof confines as recommended by the Fire Authority.

(b) Flammable items will receive strict stock control, minimum quantities will be kept and recommendations of the Fire Authority will be sought and followed.

(c) No smoking will occur in any stores areas.

(d) All items of stock and the physical stores areas themselves will be monitored and controlled with fire risks in mind.

Energy conservation

The standard system of hotel accounting does not provide for the reallocation or recharging of the costs of 'service departments' (including heat, light and power) to operated departments, eg rooms department. In the Health Service, each unit, eg a hospital, has an energy budget but separate departments within that hospital do not. Thus, in the past, probably the only information available on energy consumption in buildings was in the annual accounts. Even then, annual variations in building energy costs were generally apportioned to changes in energy prices and analyses of energy utilisation were rarely pursued. Gradually, the realisation of a predicted 'world energy crisis' is dawning. National government and EEC pressures are evolving.

At present some 30% of the total UK prime energy consumption is used in buildings (more than that used by industry for production purposes). In order to control this predicted world energy crisis, many would argue that a corporate responsibility must be fostered, mainly through a massive educational programme. Reduction in the use of heat, light and power can be encouraged by reduced fuel bills, but the savings must go further. Economic use of all things (from the use of disposables to the use of wall coverings) must be strived for and energy reclamation must be developed, eg recycling waste, if significant world energy conservation is to be achieved.

Tackling the problem on a much smaller scale, that is within a single building, the Accommodation Manager must be aware of the energy consumption of the department and probably the process towards conservation should follow a similar pattern. Reducing fuel bills in public buildings is, however, inevitably more difficult than cutting fuel bills in a private residence. The commitment and the direct financial incentives of most building users is lacking. Educating users in energy awareness must be the key. Setting up training sessions for staff is one way, but the education of customers is not so easy.

One way of ensuring more economic use of energy is to create an environment where excessive uses are neither desired by users nor, in any case, easily achieved and such an environment is best developed in the design and planning stages of a new building. The Department of Health recently opened a low energy hospital and the project received sponsorship from the EEC. Much was learned from the project though some features incorporated would not be recommended for future buildings. One aim was to achieve a 50% reduction of energy usage over comparable establishments – a significant financial reward over the life of a hospital.

A list of some design and construction features is given below, together with their implications:

1 Siting of the building
Exposed sites with high windspeeds give reduced U values and increased ventilation rates. Elevated sites are cooler. Polluted sites, eg noise or air require mechanical ventilation.

2 Volume, shape and layout of the building envelope
Smaller volumes give better energy economy. Smaller surface areas reduce heat loss. Open planned buildings require additional heating. Orientation of windows affects solar gain.

3 Construction
Structural insulation (wall and roof). Double glazing and reduced window sizes.

4 Heating systems
Heat sources should be centrally located for insulation. Zoned heating, thermostatically controlled is recommended. Fuel selection is vital, boilers easily converted to all alternative fuels may be cost effective. Exhaust heat may be reclaimed. Heat pumps are advocated. Waste incineration might be one heat source.

5 Fittings
Internal surfaces should reduce heat losses. Lighting systems should be cost effective, eg high efficiency lighting. Humidifiers may be needed where windows are reduced.

Monitoring usage in certain areas may be an incentive. Tight environmental monitoring and control can be achieved through computerisation.

Providing a low energy building is by no means the total solution. Such a building encourages economic use of energy and probably focuses attention of users on energy conservation but control must be on going. The employment of energy managers has been seen by some establishments as a means of ensuring a constant awareness of energy usage. One of the first tasks of an energy manager may well be to establish regular audits, whereby usage of power in different sections is monitored and analysed. Downward trends can be encouraged and upward trends quickly identified and faults hopefully rectified.

The Energy Efficiency Office has developed Energy Monitoring and Targeting (M & T) programmes which are management approaches to energy control.

Training staff in awareness of energy use may be a significant means of encouraging the development of processes which require less energy. Equipment and materials may be selected with energy conservation in mind, and suitable maintenance programmes developed to ensure that all items work at their optimum efficiency. To encourage the best use of energy, emphasis must be placed on the control and usage, rather than on the monitoring of wastage.

An example of a training plan for a session on cleaning sanitary areas

TITLE	**Cleaning sanitary areas** Part 6 – Toilet cleaning
GROUP DETAILS	Number – 2 Background – 1 previously employed as a maid – 1 returning to work after a period at home
VENUE	Floor 6 – Section 2
DATE	10.10.93
TIME	10.30 am
TRAINER/SPEAKER	Floor Housekeeper
PREPARATION	Collect 3 sets of supplies: • toilet brush and holder • bucket and red cloth • neutral detergent Check area to be used for demonstration and practice
TEACHING AIDS	Toilet charts Supplies as above Mirror Job breakdown (see Figure 3.11, p. 104–5)
PREREQUISITES	Trainees must have completed Cleaning Sanitary areas Parts 1 to 5.
AIMS	To develop an awareness of the importance of achieving high standards of hygiene and cleaning the toilet effectively.

OBJECTIVES

At the end of the session the trainee will be able to:
- understand the need for hygienic practices when cleaning toilets
- understand the concept of colour-coding
- clean a toilet using the prescribed method, to the expected standard
- know the standard of appearance required

PLAN

Time	No.	Heading	Notes	Chart
10.30	1	INTRODUCTION	General remarks, eg reintroduce self if necessary, welcome back after break Outline plan of action – ie format, timing, objectives, etc	
10.35	2	HOW DOES A TOILET WORK?	Ask if either can explain Explain using Chart 1	CHART I
10.40	3	WHY IS IT NECESSARY TO CLEAN A TOILET CORRECTLY	Ask if either can explain If yes – then summarise If no – then outline points 1 2 3	
	4	WHAT PARTS OF THE TOILET NEED SPECIAL ATTENTION TO PREVENT ACCUMULATION OF GERMS?	Ask Explain using Chart 2	CHART II
	5	HOW WOULD YOU CLEAN A TOILET?	Ask trainee 2. Remember this is a regular task at home Listen and comment especially if correct.	
	6	HOW TO CLEAN THE TOILET	The reason for this method Demonstrate the method Using the Job Breakdown for guidance Break the task down into logical steps Demonstrate each stage Point out hygiene and safety factors	

PLAN Continued

7	PRACTISE		Stress need for colour-coded cloth and bucket
			Stress appearance required
			Ask trainee how method differs from method used in last job. Point out reasons for differences and for differences in Trainee 2's method
			Allow each to clean 2 or 3 toilets
			Ask questions
			Reinstruct as necessary
			Praise as necessary
			Do mirror check to show how monitor cleanliness
8	RECAP	Why important to clean Method	Ask questions related to stages, hygiene, safety, colour-coding
9	CONCLUDE	Standards Mirror test Time Fault reporting	

NCVQ Levels 1 to 5 Definitions

Level 1 Competence in the performance of routine work activities and/or achievement of a broad foundation of work competence as a basis for progression

Level 2 Competence in a broader range of work activities involving greater individual responsibility.

Level 3 Competence in skilled activities which are complex and non-routine, including supervisory activities.

Level 4 Competence in the performance of complex, technical and specialised activities, including supervision and management.

Level 5 Competence in the pursuit of a senior occupation or profession including the ability to apply a significant range of fundamental principles and techniques. Also, extensive knowledge and understanding of the field and appropriate managerial capability.

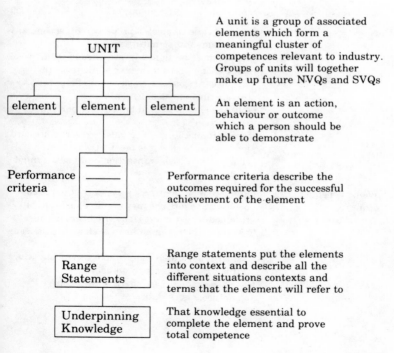

A unit is a group of associated elements which form a meaningful cluster of competences relevant to industry. Groups of units will together make up future NVQs and SVQs

An element is an action, behaviour or outcome which a person should be able to demonstrate

Performance criteria describe the outcomes required for the successful achievement of the element

Range statements put the elements into context and describe all the different situations contexts and terms that the element will refer to

That knowledge essential to complete the element and prove total competence

Control measures to adopt for each possible method of payment

Method of payment	Control measures
Cash	Record amount received in payment of account in Cash Received Book
	Total cash received book daily to tally with amount in till
	Record payment on tab ledger/against cash key on electronic machine/against cash code on computer
	Receipt guests account to denote payment
	Allocate an individual till to all cashiers on duty at one time
	Sign cash floats in and out
Cheques	Check cheque completed properly – date; company name; amount; signature
	Cheque must be signed in presence of cashier
	Check cheque card as means of identification
	Cheque card guarantees payment of a cheque to a certain amount, usually £50
	Only one cheque should be used for one transaction
	If more than £50, cashier must write cheque card number on back – this means transaction is charged as a cash transaction and guest cannot stop it later
Travellers cheques (sterling)	Often proof of identity, eg passport is required before travellers cheques are accepted – to be retained whilst guest signs travellers cheques
	Travellers cheque must have been signed on issue from bank
	Cashier must watch guest make second signature – if not guest must sign on back
	Check two signatures, check with passport signature, check date

Foreign currency	If going to accept foreign currency, have a well-organised system
	Know which currencies will and will not be accepted
	Foreign currency legally may only be accepted in payment of account – a foreign exchange should not be set up
	Check exchange rates daily if not more often
	Charge a realistic commission to cover administrative charges and unexpected fluctuations in exchange rate
	Monitor carefully as easier to defraud establishment than with other methods of payment
Credit cards (a) Visa/Access	Check individual credit limit if account is over £100
	Complete a sales voucher and credit card imprint
	Guest must sign
	Check validity of credit card – date of expiry, signature against signature on sales voucher
	Give copy to guest and retain copies – one to go to credit card company for payment
(b) Switch	Swipe card
	Retain whilst guest signs
	Check signature
	Give copy to guest and retain copy
(c) Travel/ Entertainment Credit Cards, eg American Express	As Visa/Access
	Establishment must pay a commission to company for franchise
Travel agents' vouchers	Check details – company, amount, signature, etc
	Guest must sign – check signature
	Retain copy for submission to travel agents with commission
Transfer to Outstanding Accounts Ledger	Ensure guest checks and signs account
	Send copy to control/accounts office
	Record form of payment appropriately in accounting system – must be segregated from other forms of payment
	Only creditworthy customers with satisfactory references will be offered this facility
	Require authorised users and credit limits if allow companies/business houses this facility

BS 5750: 1987 – An overview

What is BS 5750?
BS 5750 is the British version of the International Standard ISO 9000: 1987. The standard specifies guidelines for assuring that quality management operate effectively and consistently, it comprises three parts:
Part 1 (ISO 9001) covers design/development, production, installation, servicing, inspection and testing
Part 2 (ISO 9002) covers production and installation
Part 3 (ISO 9003) covers final inspection and testing.

Part 1 gives the most comprehensive cover, *Parts 2* and *3* being shortened versions of this.

The standard
The standard covers quality management systems, and organisations may apply for registration to this standard. Registration is a measure of the organisation's capability to work to a consistent standard, defined by that organisation. Registration and the use of the BS 5750 mark does not imply a high quality product.

The standard is predominantly applied to manufacturing systems but is suitable for any process which has a definable and measurable outcome.

How is registration achieved?
Registration is achieved by application to one of the accredited Certification Bodies. When an approach is first made, the Certification Body will usually have a preregistration meeting with the applicant with a view to defining:

- the most appropriate parts of the standard to apply ie *Parts 1, 2 or 3*
- the scope of the organisation's activities for which the standard will apply (most do not register all their activities)
- any other standard which need to be considered, relating to product quality, calibration, etc.

The assessment team will then make their inspection which will consist of 'snapshot' checks of relevant areas and processes. One of the main objectives will be to follow a particular item, document or process through a number of stages to ensure the 'system' works.

Why do organisations seek registration?
Registration will help organisations to achieve a competitive edge
and, in addition, cost advantages are often achieved.

What does the standard cover?
For BS 5750 Part 1, the main areas covered are as follows:

1 Management responsibility for:
    a Quality Policy
    Organisation
    Management reviews
2 The Quality system, eg included in a Quality Manual
3 The contract review
4 Design and development planning of the product
5 Document control, ie document approval and issue and document
   changes and modifications
6 Purchasing
7 Purchaser supplied products
8 Product identification and traceability
9 Process control
10 Inspection and testing (including inspection records)
11 Inspection measuring and test equipment
12 Inspection and test status
13 Control of non-conforming products
14 Corrective action
15 Handling, storage package and delivery
16 Quality records
17 Internal audits
18 Training
19 Servicing
20 Statistical techniques

Appendix 7
Quality circles

In studying quality, the Japanese professor, KAORU ISHIKAWA noticed that:

(a) many, apparently trivial, problems in industry were not tackled by managers who 'had more important things to do'
(b) most smaller problems were 'operator solvable' and were not even identified by managers
(c) labour alienation was a problem, as scientific management concepts separated the management and planning of work from the process itself, so deskilling the work.

Professor ISHIKAWA aimed to retain the economic advantages of scientific management structures but bring back craftsmanship to the job itself and develop the role of the supervisor. He suggested that teams of workers from the same department could be trained in problem solving and be regularly given time to: identify opportunities for improvement, make recommendations and, where possible, implement these.

In this way, he suggested that staff and supervisory roles would be enhanced and a spirit of company mindedness would be nurtured.

Index